Responding to Adolescent Needs

Responding to Adolescent Needs

Edited by

Max Sugar, M.D.
Department of Psychiatry
Louisiana State University Medical Center
New Orleans, Louisiana

SP

SP MEDICAL & SCIENTIFIC BOOKS

New York • London

18909

SPECTRUM PUBLICATIONS, INC.
175-20 Wexford Terrace, Jamaica, N.Y. 11432

Library of Congress Cataloging in Publication Data

Main entry under title:

Responding to adolescent needs.

  Includes index.
  1. Social work with youth—Addresses, essays, lectures. 2. Social work with youth—United States —Addresses, essays, lectures. 3. Adolescence— Addresses, essays, lectures. I. Sugar, Max. II. Title. [DNLM: 1. Adolescence. 2. Adolescent psychology. 3. Adolescent psychiatry. WS462.3 R434] HV1421.R47   362.7   79-26297 ISBN 0-89335-101-6

Printed in the United States of America

To
My brother Sam, and
his eternal optimism

Acknowledgments

I wish to acknowledge a debt of learning to my many mentors, who will not be named since they number not only my formal teachers but also the adolescents whom I have had the pleasure of treating as well as others whose troubled experiences are familiar to me.

Special thanks are reserved for my wife, Barbara, for her limitless support of this endeavor and assistance in the editorial task, and my secretary, Mrs. Marion Stafford, for her fortitude and expert checking on details as well as typing.

Contributors

IRVING H BERKOVITZ, M.D.
Southern California Psychoanalytic
Institute/Society
and
Associate Clinical Professor of
Psychiatry
University of California at Los Angeles
and
Senior Psychiatric Consultant for
Schools
Los Angeles County Department of
Health, Mental Health
Los Angeles, California

PEG A. BORTNER, PH.D.
Assistant Professor, Center for
Criminal Justice
Arizona State University
Tempe, Arizona

ROBERT T. BROWN, M.D.
Assistant Professor of Pediatrics
Associate Director, Division of
Adolescent Medicine
Assistant Director, Interdisciplinary
Training Program for Adolescent
Health Care
The University of Alabama in
Birmingham Medical Center
Birmingham, Alabama

DAVID H. CISCEL, PH.D.
Associate Professor of Economics
Memphis State University
Memphis, Tennessee

THOMAS W. COLLINS, PH.D.
Associate Professor and Chairman
Department of Anthropology
Memphis State University
Memphis, Tennessee

WILLIAM A. DANIEL, JR., M.D.
Professor of Pediatrics
Chief, Division of Adolescent Medicine
Director, Children and Youth Project
Director, Interdisciplinary Training
Program for Adolescent Health Care
The University of Alabama in
Birmingham Medical Center
Birmingham, Alabama

SOL GOTHARD, M.S.W., J.D.
Judge of the Juvenile Court
Parish of Jefferson
and
Adjunct Professor
Tulane University School of Social
Work
New Orleans, Louisiana

JOHN W. C. JOHNSTONE, PH.D.
Professor of Scoiology
University of Illinois at Chicago Circle
and
Visiting Scholar
Institute for Juvenile Research
Chicago, Illinois

NANCY J. JOHNSTONE, M.S.W.
Executive Director
Youth Guidance
Chicago, Illinois

MICHAEL KALOGERAKIS, M.D.
Clinical Professor of Psychiatry
New York University School of
Medicine

RICHARD C. MAROHN, M.D.
Director, Adolescent and Forensic
Services
Illinois State Psychiatric Institute
and
Associate Professor
Department of Psychiatry
University of Illinois
Chicago, Illinois

DEREK MILLER, M.D.
Professor of Psychiatry
Northwestern Medical School
and
Chief of the Adolescent Program
Northwestern Memorial Hospital
Chicago, Illinois

GEORGE W. NOBLIT, PH.D.
Senior Fellow
Desegregation Studies Staff of the
Educational Policy and Organization
Division
National Institute of Education,
Washington, D.C.
and
Associate Professor
Department of Sociology
Memphis State University
Memphis, Tennessee

WILLIAM RITTENBERG, J.D.
Attorney-at-Law
New Orleans, Louisiana

DAVID E. SCHARFF, M.D.
Director, Sex Therapy and Education
Programs
Preterm Center for Reproductive
Health
and
Washington School of Psychiatry
and
Assistant Clinical Professor of
Psychiatry
Children's Hospital National Medical
Center and the George Washington
University
Washington, D.C.

RALPH SLOVENKO, LLB., PH.D.
Professor of Law and Psychiatry
Wayne State University School of Law
Detroit, Michigan

MAX SUGAR, M.D.
Professor of Clinical Psychiatry
Louisiana State University Medical
Center
New Orleans, Louisiana

Foreword

Therapeutic work with adolescents is difficult, irrespective of the method of intervention chosen. This is due to our inability to distinguish serious psychopathology from mild identity crises. An adolescent, in the midst of severe emotional turmoil, is not merely having growing pains. Those of us in the helping professions do not serve those adolescents who seek our counsel when we tell them not to worry about their problems because they are just a part of normal development. Clinicians should be able to correctly diagnose the symptoms, feelings, behaviors, and social phenomena that adolescents present to them. With a more exact diagnosis, we can help more adolescents solve their problems and reach adulthood feeling hope rather than despair.

We have learned from the results of empirical research that most adolescents grow up with relatively little internal and/or external turmoil. The majority of teenagers grow up to become normal, well-functioning, relatively happy and productive individuals. In recent study, it was found that:

1. Relatively healthy, i.e. non-symptomatic adolescents, have a better self-image than symptomatic adolescents, psychiatrically disturbed adolescents, or delinquent adolescents.

2. Younger adolescents present themselves as having a poorer self-image than do older adolescents.

3. The adolescents' self-image correlated significantly and positively with other measures of personality assessment (including clinical interviews).

4. In countries other than the U.S. (i.e. Australia, India, Israel, and Ireland), adolescent males view themselves as being healthier than adolescent females. In the U.S., the adolescent female describes herself as having higher moral values than her male counterpart. On the other hand, the males say that they are more in control of their impulses and are happier than their female peers.

5. The American teenager sees himself/herself as considerably happier and better able to cope with his/her life than teenagers in other cultures.*

Every stage of the human life cycle has its critical periods, which need to be understood, coped with, and lived through. Most parents expect their children to become rebellious, moody, semi-delinquent, impossible to un-

---

* Offer, D., Ostrov, E., and Howard, K.I. *The Self-Image of Adolescents,* New York: Basic Books, Inc., 1980.

derstand, sexually overactive, failures in school, etc., when they become adolescents. It would help if the newer generation of adolescents was assured that most of them will grow up to become healthy, mature individuals. Such anticipatory guidance combats the self-fulfilling prophecies, described above.

But, what happens to the significant minority (approximately 25 percent) who have serious problems and need intervention? Adolescent problems can generally be classified as (1) psychological and/or psychiatric—for which they need psychotherapeutic help; (2) educational—for which they need counseling; (3) physical—for which they need medical care; and (4) social—for which they need legal, economic, or social help.

In 1976, over 20 million adolescents in the U.S. were counted, so we can assume that about five million teenagers were in need of some kind of helpful intervention. Although much has been written about the psychology of and the traditional psychotherapeutic work with adolescents, a practical book containing some practical solutions hs been lacking. The literature has only sparingly examined the realistic preparation that adolescents receive before entering the labor market.

Dr. Max Sugar has made a significant contribution to the literature by bringing together experts who have made meaningful observations on neglected aspects of adolescent development. Whether the subject is *Female Adolescent Development* or *Family and Group Psychotherapy with Adolescents,* we have come to expect from him exceptionally well-organized books which discuss the subject matter expertly.

This book is no exception. It deals with the more common adolescent problem areas, such as suicide, teenage pregnancy, and drug abuse. The discussions are fresh, data-based, and make practical recommendations.

In addition to discussing the more common problems, this book deals with issues which rarely are discussed with such compassion. These include legal rights of adolescents, special problems of minority students, physical problems of teenagers, how schools affect adolescent development, and adjustment problems involved in entering the labor market.

It is a book full of facts and figures, which presents unique suggestions to the professional working with adolescents. This book takes us one step further in understanding the young; an essential step if we are to alleviate adolescent suffering.

Daniel Offer, M.D.
Chairman, Department of Psychiatry
Michael Reese Hospital and Medical Center
Professor of Psychiatry
University of Chicago

Preface

The adolescent needs to have propitious arrangements to be able to attain what Freud cogently saw as the goal of emotional health for adults: the ability to work and love. This volume reviews how well the current environment meets these needs and, if not, what the barriers might be to attaining them.

Beyond healthy genes, a benevolent preadolescent development, and successful forebears who are emotionally, and physically healthy, the adolescent needs the optimal opportunity from the environment for suitable development to adulthood. Although reports of our successes and contributions have been well proclaimed and much vaunted by all disciplines, there have been grave doubts accumulating about how many slips there are 'twixt the lip and the cup.

The peer group and disturbed family relationships, including the state *in loco parentis*, are considered for their effect on adolescents. How well schools meet the educational needs of the adolescent—especially if one is a minority group member—is questioned. The legal issues of the adolescent's right to treatment and the controversy about the adolescent who is unable to manage for himself are examined, as are physicians' responses to adolescents' physical and emotional health needs. Two topics discussed—sexual exploitation of teenagers and some issues about teenage motherhood—have received recent national attention. Work is a relatively neglected area in the literature, and this section focuses on the transition from school with its attendant separation anxieties, as well as problems of minorities in vocational pursuits.

Throughout the book self-scrutiny is applied to the present, while the future is looked to for improvement by changing course to help the adolescent navigate past the shoals to a successful voyage in life. Hopefully, these remarks may serve as guides and stimuli for improved responses in the areas highlighted as well as those omitted.

Contents

Responding to Adolescent Needs

PART I
The Family

1

Family Maladaptation Reflected in Drug Abuse and Delinquency

DEREK MILLER

Whether or not the nuclear family can survive as the primary child-bearing unit of mankind depends on the strength of relationships within it as against the stress or support the family receives from society at large (Miller, 1970). This question is of prime importance, particularly as it relates to the area of adolescent development.

Most simply, adequate emotional development in adolescence requires meaningful emotional relationships for the child with parents, peers, extra-parental adults and social systems (Miller, 1969). If one or another of these first three is defective, then undue stress is placed on the relationships with the others. If, in addition, the social system is under stress and disintegrating, then a greater stress is thrown on the family and child-rearing experiences.

Ideally, these systems are consonant in the implicit and explicit communications that are offered to the child. In other words, what is said and what is done are not dissonant with each other. For example:

A mother told her 14-year-old son that she did not wish him to smoke marijuana. While cleaning his room, she noticed a "bong" on his

Note: This chapter was modified from "Adolescent Maladaptation: A Psychiatrist Examines Drug Abuse and Delinquency in the Family," Unit II, Report 2, *The American Family,* Philadelphia, Smith, and French Laboratories, 1978 Copyright © 1978 Smithkline Corp.

dresser. She asked him what it was and he told her; he also denied that he "smoked." She accepted his story, although, retrospectively, recognized that he was uncomfortable speaking to her. She did not remove the appliance.

Clearly, what has been said here is not consonant with what is being done. The action gives permission, but the words negate it. To further illustrate: usually small children are spanked for hitting a sibling; or their parents yell at them "don't shout." Actions in these situations implicitly invite behavior, but tell the child to be bigger and better at it (Miller, 1978). Because overt explicit messages in family and social systems change with the growth of the child, over time they may be less consistent than those which are covert and implicit. If a child's need for environmental consistency to avoid anxiety is excessive, because of genetic or nurturing vulnerability, the implicit rather than the explicit message is likely to be obeyed. For example, the more vulnerable the child is to persecutory anxiety—a side effect of excessive feelings of helplessness—the more likely he will internalize the consistent implicit message from the environment rather than the less consistent explicit one. Alternately, the youngster may feel he has gained permission for the act because whatever has been done has not regularly been explicitly negated. Typically, an adolescent may deal with conflict about antisocial behavior by stating that "you never told me not to."

SOCIETY AND THE FAMILY

Each individual seeks to keep anxiety to an optimal minimum. Within the nuclear family this is done by individual members occupying predictable roles and offering each other mutual support. Stress is constantly put on the family by the society at large, however, and the family is required to occupy the same role in relationship to society as it does to individuals within it. The family influences society and the society influences the family; similarly, parents may influence their children and vice versa. Adolescent children may be delegates from the society to the family; they may also act for the family and perform actions in society which individual family members would like, but dare not do (Stierlin, 1975). Marijuana smoking demonstrates these issues:

A decade or more ago most middle class families would have regarded intoxication in their children as deplorable. Most school systems could not have tolerated adolescents "drunk" in the classroom. The use of non-prescription drugs such as Visine to clear conjunctival injection does not adequately hide the fact that an individual adolescent is stoned. However, most adults choose not to notice that such young people are high. Even if they do, they often do not express concern providing that it does not happen too often. What is too often, of course, varies from individual to individual.

Society at large has impinged on families because many parents have become convinced by campaigns for legalization that the drug must be harmless. The provisos in these campaigns are ignored by adolescents who then reinforce the message to individual family units that the drug really must be all right because so many distinguished people want to see it legalized. The failure of the authority structures of the society, such as schools, to act when adolescents are "high" in their systems, and the provision of cigarette smoking areas wherein marijuana is almost always abused, reinforce this message. Adolescents assume that if adults know of an action, and do nothing, then they must approve. Young people appear to have persuaded their parents and other adults that a "natural high" is acceptable. This attitude has permeated society, been reinforced by it, and then has been carried back into the family by the young.

The issue is that marijuana (like alcohol) has become a prime drug of dependence among the young. It affects motivation and short-term memory, and it offers a false magical solution to emotional difficulties. Thus, it encourages young people not to seek genuine environmental mastery. All difficulties are ignored and socially acceptable regression provides a pseudo-solution.

Due to the increasing tolerance for this drug of abuse, those families which negate its use are forced to adopt extreme positions to justify their attitudes. They may imply that the drug is dangerous as a chemical hallucinogen, or that its use will inevitably lead to heroin addiction. By this attitude, they ignore the danger of the drug itself which to many adolescents offers a falsely seductive solution to the problems of growth.

AGGRESSIVE AND REGRESSIVE BEHAVIOR

The production of socially and psychologically unacceptable aggressive behavior (delinquency) and regressive behavior (drug abuse) in children and adolescents depends upon the interactive processes in the family and the dynamics of the personality. It also is a function of: the interaction between the child and society in its larger and smaller social systems; the genetic vulnerability of the individual to stress; particular varieties of neuroendocrine disturbance; and the effects of nurturing experience in childhood and adolescence. All these are significant in the etiology of both types of pathological behavior.

The issue of interfamilial relationships is, therefore, only one of the determinants of these behavioral disorders and it is simplistic to look at causation as being only due to family pathology. An attempt to assist young people abandon these types of behavioral problems, which impede normal personality development, cannot be made unless *all* the roots of the difficulty have been considered and a decision made as to which is most significant.

Treatment is applied optimally to those areas of conflict in which maximum positive impact may be expected; it is as inadequate to offer only family treatment to an adolescent who is genetically depressed, as it would be to offer only medication to a child whose parents were provoking antisocial behavior.

Once a disturbance has occurred—even though the ultimate solution to the difficulty may be in offering anything from sophisticated psycho-pharmacology to a variety of psychotherapies—feedbacks of disturbance have been created within the personality of the child and in the inter-relationships within the family. The child gains instinctual satisfaction from problem behavior and is, therefore, reluctant to abandon it; the parents may have the gratification of keeping a dependent child capable of only pseudo-maturity.

FAMILY TYPES

With all this it is equally important to understand family dynamics in adolescence as it is to comprehend the significance of personality development. Just as adolescent communication techniques differ within social class and to some extent ethnic groups, so there is a variation in the way families function.

Essentially within the tribal society, or its modern equivalent which is needed for adequate personality development, the way of life of families differs markedly. Insofar as overt attitudes are concerned, families' styles can be broadly conceptualized as belonging to two main types. Families which control impulsive behavior could be designated as *controlling families;* those in which more impulsive behavior, both regressive and aggressive, is tolerated could be known as *impulsive families.* These represent extremes. For controlling families to be adequate vehicles for mutual living and the personality growth of all their members, some impulsive and regressive behavior must be permitted. On the other hand, impulsive families need a variety of controlling techniques. Nevertheless, these designations clarify typical types of interaction. Insofar as pathological aggressive or regressive behavior is concerned, their significance for individual maladjustment to some extent differs depending on the type of family from which the youngster comes.

For example, predatorily aggressive behavior is the equivalent in modern society of hunting behavior in animals. Young people, however, may be taught to be predators to out-groups rather than the animal kingdom. In adolescents who come from family and social systems which teach this, such behavior, even though antisocial, is not necessarily indicative of personal pathology. When adolescents who come from family systems which do not teach this type of behavior act in this aggressive way, it is always related to emotional difficulties. Families teach their children techniques of relating to and handling objects in the world. The adolescent who shows predatory techniques which are consonant with family styles may, however, also have a variety of psychological disturbances. This is most clearly seen with violent behavior which on the one hand may be predatory, and on the other, affective, and related to rage responses. The latter represents psychopathology; the former does not. The learned "hunting behavior" which may be looked upon by the society as large as antisocial is not easily susceptible to change.

Controlling Families

In Western society, controlling families generally are members of the middle class or have that orientation. The child is taught by the family to mediate conflicts through words and to talk himself—or herself—out of difficulties (Goode, 1969). Such families generally value the toleration of psychic pain and frustration without an immediate recourse to magical solutions. This may be their explicit attitude, but if such families handle headaches with an immediate wish to take analgesics, anxiety with the use of mild tranquilizers, sleeplessness with sedatives, and ritualized drinks to deal with the tensions of the day, their implicit message may be that psychic pain is not to be tolerated. The use of medication to deal with minor pain and tension, in a family setting which overtly values its toleration, is not uncommonly found when the adolescent offspring of such families abuse drugs.

This type of family is sometimes overly rigid in its demands on the children. This may mean that the necessary expression of the parents' and the child's instinctual life is frustrated. Toleration of extramarital sexuality is not the norm for this group, despite the current beliefs of the news media, but this need not inhibit the expression of loving sexuality. When it does, an adolescent's sexual acting out may be used by the family to meet instinctual needs.

> A 14-year-old girl who lived in the suburbs of a large city was seen in consultation. She constantly ran away from her parents to the inner city. The area was dangerous and logically on her return one might have expected her parents to be concerned about her safety. Instead, they demanded a blow-by-blow description of her sexual activity. The implicit messages they gave their daughter was a high degree of interest in this; the explicit message was of course, disapproval. The girl obeyed the implicit request and was highly promiscuous.

Although family therapy had been tried for two years, the impotence of the husband was not known to the family therapist nor was it discussed. Thus, the adolescent daughter acted out the parental need for sexuality (Johnson, 1949).

In some controlling families, the parents may have an excessively strict conscience and may force their children to behave in highly conformist ways. If they do not allow their children to "act up or act out" within the family nexus, and if they do not allow behavior which relieves some tension which the age group inevitably produces, action outside the home may then be produced. A picture of an adolescent who is highly conformist within the nuclear family and antisocial within the community at large or in school may appear:

> A 17-year-old boy had an excellent educational and social record, never giving a moment's trouble until he reached grade 11. He was then rapidly involved in three successive car accidents associated with speeding; at the same time his school work rapidly deteriorated in both quality and quantity. As the boy was growing up, his rigid, demanding, apparently scrupulously honest father had always had him look out of the rear-view window of the automobile to check that there was no patrolman following the car when it was exceeding the speed limit.

An implicit contradiction to the overt demands for conformity may help produce antisocial behavior in adolescents, who may act out on the larger scene of the world the subtle techniques that parents may have taught them in the past. The adolescent may thus be used by the family to alleviate an excessively strict family conscience.

Generally, controlling families value a compulsive life style. Socially acceptable environmental mastery is highly esteemed, and typically there is conformity to the desired Puritanical ethos. Sometimes controlling groups may make it difficult for their late adolescent children to become autonomous, and when this occurs, late adolescent children may seek out pseudomaturity with drug abuse (Williams, 1970). This may appear as a significant issue in the first year of college and is a fairly common cause of academic drop-out at that time. This is more likely in large schools which offer little in the way of emotional support to students.

Controlling families are found in a variety of ethnic groups and their family style is related more to social class than to ethnicity. The middle class black family for example, may be more like its white counterpart than lower socioeconomic class black families.

Impulsive Families

Impulsive families may not consciously approve of violence, yet in this type of family parents may typically behave in a violent way toward their children. These families often use words as a preliminary to physical attack rather than as a technique of mediation. The amount of yelling, scolding, slapping, pinching, hitting and yanking seen within these family groups and acted out by parents on their very small children may appear shocking to people from controlling families (Steele and Pollock, 1968). Historically, such families have internalized the concept that aggression towards children is acceptable; whereas, in controlling families aggressive psychological disturbances may not show problems of physical violence:

> A 15-year-old boy was admitted to hospital with a history of severe drug abuse. He had a history of temper tantrums for which no organic cause was found and which had persisted until puberty. At that time, he began to use marijuana excessively and the tantrums subsided. In the hospital, he began to show clear symptoms of "affective rage," would swear and shout, but he never struck anyone, although, he threatened to "kill them." He was diagnosed as suffering from a depressive equivalent and these symptoms subsided on appropriate drug therapy.

He came from a family in which he recalled having been slapped by his mother only twice in his life and anger was generally mediated only by use of words.

On the other hand, when violence is used as a technique of parental control, particularly if this is reinforced in the local community and in the culture of the street, physical violence is almost automatically used by the aggressively disturbed adolescent.

A 14-year-old boy came to the psychiatric unit because he had violently assaulted his probation officer. He was suffering from one variety of affective rage disorder which responded to drug treatment. However, he attempted to control the other adolescent boys in the hospital by a variety of "strong arm" methods. He was unable to comprehend easily that this was not acceptable behavior within the adolescent program in which he was residing.

His rage attacks had been homicidal in intent and involved much physical brutality. He came from a family in which controls were exerted by the infliction of physical pain. Mother would beat him with a belt; before deserting the family father would use his fists. The boy lived in a deprived neighborhood in which survival required one to be "streetwise."

Within this type of family, aggression may become excessive violence when the head of the household suffers particular stress; this may occur either because of well-defined clinical syndromes or, sometimes, socioeconomic conditions. It is well known that in times of high unemployment, the incidence of alcoholism, child abuse, and wife beating increase. The less the head of a household, whose orientation is impulsive, has a socially valued activity within the community at large, the more likely is the family to become deviant and to produce deviant problem behavior in children and adolescents.

A Comparison of Family Types

Controlling families are less tolerant of experimental sexuality on the part of their adolescent children than the impulsive group. The latter may be ready to accept a heterosexual relationship of their children: by the time the middle stage of adolescence is reached they do not find this activity distressing. Masturbatory activity is disapproved of as infantile; whereas, this activity is generally more tolerated by the controlling family. Impulsive families may allow their children to have extramarital sexual relationships in the family home; they may also be ready to take in the illegitimate child of their daughter with little in the way of overt conflict, although, later, the child's mother may have to compete with her own mother to rear the baby. Within these families it is not suprising that incestuous relationships between brother and sister or father and daughter are not uncommon, particularly in more isolated areas of the country.

Whenever psychic pain is potentially present within impulsive families, the immediate family style is to act to remove it. This may be done either by the ingestion of alcohol or by immediate physical action. The cause of difficulties is generally projected; this type of nuclear family may sustain itself with the attitude that the enemy is without. Such families are likely to be overtly prejudiced and to dehumanize other groups with apparent ease.

Prejudice in controlling families is more clearly related to unconscious psychological conflict within its individual members. Thus, when white controlling families are antisemitic or anti-black, they have a variety of illogical reasons for not liking these minorities, reasons which clearly relate to unconscious conflicts over their own family norms. Thus, Jews are said to be "pushy"; blacks are said to be "oversexed" or "too violent." In impulsive families prejudice is more simplistic: "they take our jobs and our houses, and they are preferred by the government."

Since aggressive punishment within families does not eliminate aggression, but rather increases it, those families who use physical violence as a controlling technique teach their children that physical violence is acceptable and they train their children to be aggressive. Thus, behavior which controlling families may look upon as antisocial and delinquent, may be looked upon by impulsive families as acceptable.

Almost all symptoms of adolescents' psychological disturbance show in problem behavior. Neurotic illness in which psychological pain is internalized may be present in both controlling and impulsive families, although the latter are more likely to have adolescents with behavioral difficulties. If the children do suffer from a neurosis, symptoms such as school phobia or those of hysterical neurosis are common. Controlling families tend to have children who are likely to show more depressive types of illness or symptoms of emotional withdrawal.

Symptoms have value in the preservation of psychic equilibrium for individuals and they also develop meaning in the life of the family. The goal of symptoms is to maintain or restore psychological homeostasis when the personality is exposed to excessively perceived stress. Symptoms also help maintain equilibrium around which the family maintains relationships with its individual members and society at large.

DELINQUENCY

Delinquency is socially and legally defined and, broadly, it may be looked upon as problem behavior in which pain and frustration are inflicted upon others. The abuse of both drugs and alcohol is delinquent, but the latter is more regressive than aggressive.

In understanding such behavior, whether regressive drug abuse or aggressive delinquency, the relationship between the family and the social system in which it is placed may be as significant as the social organization of the family itself. This is the infrastructure within which the individual and his symptomatic behavior interact.

Whatever style of relationships may be used within the nuclear family, it is a basic socializing agent for children (Campbell, 1969). Historically, the family has been viewed as a central institution of human society which has the major responsibility for the socialization of its members. Desirably, the ethos of the nuclear family is reinforced by society, a "tribal" ethos. If the nuclear family's attitudes are dissonant with those of the society within which the family lives, if the bonds of the family are not excessively strong and the family tightly contained, the children in the family are constantly exposed to conflict. This explains some aspects of so-called cultural delinquency.

If the local adolescent group typically behaves in an antisocial way—for example, to become illegitimately pregnant, or to be placed on probation—not all the adolescents in the neighborhood will conform to this. Clearly, some family units are able to offer their adolescents enough support so that their sense of autonomous masculinity or femininity does not require conformity to an antisocial peer group norm.

The child has to relate both to adults who are not immediate family members and also to peers who are not siblings. When a family is isolated geographically from a group of caring adults or when it experiences intellectual isolation, it tends to become a less effective socializing agent. When the child begins to move psychologically from the family during adolescence, he may have conflicts for which he may not have been taught to cope by the family. These may be handled either by regressing back into the family and being unable to move from it; becoming violently antagonistic to family mores; or by the pseudomaturity of drug abuse.

Sometimes when a family lives in a community in which antisocial behavior is a generally accepted norm, the family ultimately may adjust to this behavior, although it may not be verbally accepted. As an example, many families do not notice when their children acquire stolen property or they may accept stories of acquisition through gambling and so on:

> A 16-year-old boy broke into a local school and stole all its audio-visual equipment. He took it to his room at home, dismantled it and sold many of the components. His parents did not notice that he was

spending excessive amounts of time in his room nor that he was clearly spending more money than was usual for him.

When adolescents live in areas in which antisocial behavior is acceptable to the peer group, the type of problem behavior that they may adopt often relates to family norms. For example, adolescents nowadays are likely to live in societies in which drug abuse and drug dealing is almost normative among their groups. This may be actively colluded in by the larger society and families being overly permissive about experimental and even regularly occurring drug abuse.

Adolescents who come from family groups in which the acquisition of profit and earning large sums of money are considered important are more likely to become drug dealers. Those children whose families do not transact their relationship to society in this way may sell or give drugs to friends occasionally, but do not acquire large sums of money by dealing drugs.

In the suburban area of a large mid Western city, a 17-year-old boy was reputed by his peers to make $30,000 a year dealing drugs. This was clearly an exaggeration, but he did buy an expensive automobile and from time to time flew on "vacation" to various parts of the United States. His father was a stockbroker and accepted the son's story that he made enough money as a checker in the local supermarket to support his life style.

The boy argued that there was little difference between the way he and that of his father made money.

In those adolescents with sexual behavior difficulties, it may be clear that the child carries this type of antisocial behavior into the family, reinforces a previously implicit communication and makes it explicit. This has been described with sexual acting-out by adolescents (Newman and San Montino, 1975), but violent sexual behavior may also mimic behavior which the adolescent observed in the family when he was a child. It may represent parental behavior of which the adolescent was in a sense a childhood victim.

John was arrested at the age of 17 for violent assault on women whom he would rape while threatening them with a knife. He would indicate to them that if they resisted he would cut off their breasts. After he had finished with the victims, he would slap their face, call them foul names and leave. Each attack was preceded by a hallucinatory experience and one aspect of the etiology was temporal lobe epilepsy. Another was in John's child rearing experience. He lived with his natural parents until he was 5, when he was removed from the family because of child abuse. However, apart from being a victim of direct violence himself, he had observed his drunken father having sexual relations with his mother on the floor of their living room. On these occasions the father would threaten to mutilate mother and then would beat her. Both mother and son independently described these episodes without knowing that the other had told a similar story.

Runaway behavior is one type of adolescent activity which is antisocial, but society is in conflict as to how delinquent it should be considered. In this type of activity, sometimes an adolescent may act as a delegate of the family to society at large and the disturbed behavior of adolescents may be, in a sense, for the sake of the family. Runaway adolescents may be partly satisfying the stated wishes of the parents to "get out of my life." They may also provide thrills for the family who have to live in a state of high tension while the adolescent is on the run. Finally, the runaway may bring back information to the family about the world at large.

The adolescent's problem behavior may meet an important family need. Runaway behavior, for example, is not uncommon just before or just after a family move. The parents may disown the child's behavior, but the child may be scouting out the new land for the parents. Thus, as with much delinquent activity, this symptom may demonstrate the interplay between the adolescent's intrapsychic conflicts and the family's interpersonal dynamics. The understanding of both are essential for the understanding of delinquency and drug abuse.

Both antisocial and drug-abusing behavior may occur because the family has failed to nurture satisfactorily. When this happens, personalities are produced that cannot tolerate frustration and are incapable of developing satisfactory techniques of gaining environmental mastery. Within a family there may be collusion, provocation and stimulation of aggressive antisocial and regressive drug-abusive behavior.

When an adolescent behaves in one of these antisocial ways, he may on the one hand be scapegoated by the family which cannot tolerate the acting-out of its implicit needs, but the problem behavior may also hold the family together (Erickson, 1962). An adolescent who behaves antisocially may give the family a coherence which allows the parents to relate to each other by externalizing parental tensions which otherwise would be internalized and played out in painful intrapsychic conflict. Alternatively, this behavior may give the parents a common focus both for concern and for the projection of their own anxieties. It is not unusual for a highly fragile marriage to fall apart when children are successfully treated for antisocial difficulties, whether regressive or aggressive.

The scapegoated adolescent may become the repository of parental projections, but secondarily may represent a common bond for the family. The parents may invite the behavior and then attack because of it. On the other hand, when the regressively and aggressively disturbed behavior of the adolescent assists the family in staying together, the child may be aware that his or her actions are providing a bond for the parents.

DRUG AND ALCOHOL ABUSE

A significant etiological determinant of drug and alcohol abuse is found in family relationships. An early study of cigarette smoking in boys demonstrated that it was associated in a statistically significant way with the maternal use of cigarettes (Emery, 1967). Amphetamine abuse in adolescents was initiated in some Western societies by medical prescriptions of diet pills to overweight parents. In impulsive families something "good" prescribed for mother may be used by the whole family. When adolescents were "bored," their mothers offered them their pills. In controlling families, medication prescribed for parents may be left lying around and the adolescent may steal them. Doctor's households are notorious dispersal points for drug abuse as the adolescent children of physicians may identify with their physician parent and "prescribe" stolen samples for their friends.

Often drug abuse in an adolescent has as a determinant the unconscious wish of parents to have the child remain sick, dependent or immature. It is not unusual for drug-taking adolescents to be unable to break the ambivalent tie with their mothers. Some parents who have been limited in the expression of their feelings have a powerful need to infantilize their child. Alcoholic adolescents, and those who have abused marijuana, by their gross incompetence, may bolster their mother's omnipotence.

In drug abuse, commonly, mothers play a dominant identification role. A passive orientation of the child is reinforced by drugs and, traditionally, passivity is still associated with the role of women in our society. Children who abuse drugs may in some ways both seek to be nurtured and to identify with a nurturing mother. The adolescent who looks after his or her peer who is on the drug-taking "trip," to some extent is adopting a pseudo-mothering role (Williams, 1970).

The prognosis for these adolescents who abuse drugs as a result of adolescent developmental difficulties is considerably better than for those who, because of earlier characterological difficulties, have become physically pubertal, but not psychologically adolescent. To some extent, drugs hold out the promise of magical solutions and their use is clearly related to the ambivalence of both the child and the parent about separation. Drugs offer a fantasy of autonomy. Within the transactional field of the family, drug use may reaffirm and preserve an infantile object constellation.

There is no evidence that drug abuse has a significant physiological determinant, but this may not be true for some types of alcoholism. Adolescent alcoholism, which is becoming epidemic, is almost certainly a function in all societies of liquor being made freely available to late adolescents who may then give or sell it to younger adolescents. If alcohol becomes a problem in the physiologically vulnerable when adulthood is reached, it has usually first appeared in early or middle adolescence.

SUCCESSFUL TREATMENT

Successful treatment of drug abuse and delinquency is difficult if the parents do not wish the child to be treated. If the antisocial behavior of the child preserves psychological homeostasis for the parents and an interpersonal balance for the family, then the treatment both of drug abusers and delinquents becomes difficult. Families that depend on an aggressively or regressively disturbed child for survival may find it inordinately difficult to allow the child to give up this mode of behavior.

The problem is compounded because in our society, drug experimentation has become almost as normative as an early adolescent's transient involvement in antisocial behavior. The issues in any individual instance for parents, physicians, and all others involved with youth are the nature of the act, its frequency, and its significance regarding future personality development (Miller, 1974). It is to these issues which we as professionals must address ourselves if the more immediate problems of delinquency and drug abuse as well as the long range problem of family survival are to find workable solutions.

SUMMARY

Drug abuse and antisocial behavior among adolescents have reached epidemic proportions. There has tended to develop, perhaps in part because of the urgency of the problem, sharply differentiated etiologic and treatment approaches from psychiatrists with different organic, psychodynamic, and sociocultural theoretical preferences. In this chapter, the family is offered as the nexus between the psychobiologic individual adolescent and the sociocultural matrix in which the additive or delinquent behaviors take place. The clinical vignettes illustrate the perspective that physiologic predispositions, intrapsychic conflicts, and societal pressures are, each of them, always involved to some degree in these behaviors, and that the site from which they may advantageously be observed is the family. Each transaction described is at the boundaries between the individual and the family, and between the family and society, which highlights the critical role of family process in determining the maladaptive behaviors addressed. The differentiation of "controlling" from "impulsive" families may provide a useful clinical rubric for psychiatrists who treat delinquent or addicted adolescents and their families.

REFERENCES

Campbell, J. S. (1969), The Family and Violence. In J. S. Campbell, J. R. Salud, and O. F. Stang (Eds.), *Law and Order Reconsidered.* Washington, D.C.: U. S. Gov't. Printing Office.

Emery, F. (1967), *Affect Control and the Use of Drugs.* London, Tavistock: Institute of Human Relations.

Erickson, K. T., (1962) Notes on the sociology of deviance, *Soc. Prob.* 9:307-314.

Goode, W. (1969), Violence Among Inmates. In D. Mulvilhill and M. M. Trimin (Eds.), *Crimes of Violence.* National Commission on the Causes and Prevention of Violence, Study Series 13, pp. 954, Appendix 17. Washington, D.C.: U.S. Gov't Printing Office.

Johnson, A.M. (1949), Sanctions for the Super-Ego Lacunae of Adolescents. In K. R. Eissler (Ed.), *Search Lights on Delinquency.* New York: Int. Univ. Press.

Miller, D. (1969), *The Age Between—Adolescents in a Disturbed Society.* London: Hutchinson.

——— (1970), Parental Responsibility for Adolescent Maturity. In K. Elliott (Ed.), *The Family and Its Future.* London: Churchill.

——— (1974), *Adolescence: Psychology, Psychopathology and Psychotherapy.* New York: Jason Aronson.

——— (1978), Early adolescence: its psychology and implications for treatment. *Adol. Psychiat.* 7: 434-448

Newman, M. B. and San Montino, M. R. (1975), Adolescence and the relationship between generations. *Adol. Psychiat.* 4:60-71.

Steele, B. F. and Pollock, C. B. (1968) A Psychiatric Study of Parents Who Abuse Infants and Small Children. In R. E. Helfer and C. H. Kempe (Eds.), *The Battered Child.* Chicago: Univ. of Chicago Press.

Stierlin, H. (1975) The adolescent as a delegate of his parents. *Adol. Psychiat.* 4:72-83.

Williams, F. S. (1970) Alienation of youth as reflected in the hippie movement. *J. Amer. Acad. Child Psychiat.* 9:251-263.

2

Families, Communities, and Rebellious Adolescents

JOHN W. C. JOHNSTONE
NANCY J. JOHNSTONE

ISSUES AND QUESTIONS

Of the many points of uncertainty in contemporary social science, few approach the heights of inconclusiveness which the role of the family occupies in the etiology of antisocial behavior among youth. On the basis of about half a century of empirical inquiry, one might be persuaded to either of the following positions: that the family is the major predisposing force in the emergence of contranormative behavior; or, that while there may be some association between family factors and problem behavior among adolescents, due to external or intervening influences, there is no direct causal link between the family and these behaviors. Few inquiries fail to turn up some kind of a family relationship, however, and few officials who deal with delinquent youth, or professionals who work with them, fail to note aberrant features of their family situations. As a result, popular notions prevail that weak families produce troubled youngsters. A cover story in Time (July 11, 1977) attributes the major cause of youth crime in the United States to the breakdown of the family. Perhaps so. Yet as a discipline, youth research finds itself neither with a coherent theoretical position, nor consistent empirical evidence on this matter.

Although the reasons are complex, the confusion seems to stem from a

17

number of sources. One clear source is a gap between the findings of clinical and field research. In general, clinical studies which have traced the backgrounds of troubled or delinquent youngsters (e.g. Jenkins and Hewitt, 1944; Glueck and Glueck, 1950) have been the ones which have accorded family factors a major causal role. Field studies based on population samples of young people (e.g., Nye, 1958; Hirschi, 1969), on the other hand, have usually reported only weak relationships between family characteristics and deviant behavior, and as a result have assessed the impact of the family more cautiously. One reason for this discrepancy is that referral systems are more likely to process young persons when there is no intact or stable family situation to which to return them. In the juvenile justice system in the United States, for example, youth who become official delinquents, and who are therefore likely to come into contact with the helping professions, tend disproportionately to be selected from less stable family backgrounds—so-called "broken" families, or intact but large and economically-depressed families (Nye, 1958; Williams and Gold, 1972).

A second source of confusion emerges when youth analysts fail to isolate different components of the family system—most notably, when they confuse family structure with family functioning. Although it seems hardly necessary to insist that broken families may not necessarily be unhappy ones, too often these dimensions are not kept separate. Some who deal with problem youth assume, uncritically, that intact nuclear families are more stable emotionally, generate fewer tensions, and are better able to control and set limits on the behavior of their adolescent offspring.

A related problem is that social scientists have paid very little attention to different types of broken families: the single-parent family; the three-generational attenuated family; families with one natural and one stepparent; or family situations which include unrelated adults. Systematic efforts to evaluate the impact of these different types of family structures on adolescent behavior have been lacking—in large part, perhaps, because the subtypes are rare, and may fail to turn up in sufficient numbers in investigators' samples.

In addition, clinical and field researchers have tended to define and measure problem behavior differently. In research on delinquents, for example, many clinical studies have developed typologies of delinquent acts, usually relating different expressions of deviant behavior to differences in socialization, personality, or unmet needs. Field studies of delinquents, on the other hand, have tended to conceive and measure contranormative behavior with some type of unidimensional behavior index, sometimes lumping together all those youngsters who end up in juvenile court. As a result, there has been a poor fit in youth research between the richness of insight afforded by clinical observation, and the representativeness afforded by scientific field studies. Where clinical investigators have been unable to link behavioral distinctions to the environmental, social or cultural contexts which generate them, field researchers have been reluctant to make distinctions in behavioral outcomes.[1] Neither tradition, in short, has been effectively able to address the very real possibility that family factors may well have a stronger impact on some types of deviant behavior than on others, or alternatively, that the impact of the family on adolescent behavior may be much more salient in some types of social environments.

A final source of inconclusiveness in the literature stems from the failure of investigators to analyze and interpret data within a sufficiently comprehensive theoretical framework—a tendency created in part by intense rivalries between different schools of thought on adolescence, but primarily by limitations and shortcomings in analytic design. For example, it is well known that there are more single-parent families in economically depressed areas of urban centers than in economically more advantaged ones. It is also known that juvenile arrest rates in urban areas are higher in communities of the former type. When a relationship is reported between family intactness and delinquency, then, it should be the burden of the investigator to determine whether the behavior can be attributed to the fact that the family is disrupted, or to the fact that the community is depressed. It could very well be that rates of delinquency among youth from both intact and disrupted families are higher in communities of the former type. Yet this kind of problem is seldom addressed, and many who have interpreted the relationship between family structure and delinquency as causal have ignored the possibility of spurious relationships.

STUDY DESIGNS, TARGET POPULATION, AND METHODS

It is these issues which provide a framework for the discussion which follows. In this chapter we examine the relationship between family factors and antisocial behavior among adolescents from a perspective which takes into account different components of the family system, different forms of antisocial behavior, and different community contexts within which both families and adolescents function. The focus is the high-school aged population at large, rather than some specific subset. We will first present a descriptive overview of the relationships in question, and follow this with comments on their theoretical and programmatic implications.

The empirical assertions we will present are based on the results of a large scale study of young people in Illinois.[2] This inquiry, which began in

1972, had two components: anthropological field studies of youth in 12 different Illinois communities, including three neighborhoods in Chicago; and a statewide sample survey of over 3,000 youngsters between the ages of 14 and 18. Although we will not here present systematically the evidence on which our conclusions are based,[3] some comments are in order regarding the nature and scope of the sample survey. The survey was based on an area probability sample of the state of Illinois, and field workers contacted over 19,000 households in order to locate eligible youth, who were defined as all persons 14-18 living in a household. The sampling frame covered 40 different counties as well as over 200 local neighborhoods (census tracts) in the Chicago area. Our observations thus pertain to adolescents in a wide variety of community settings, and include rural areas, small towns and cities, affluent suburbs and inner-city slums. The sample design excluded institutionalized delinquents, young people living in school or college residences, youth in the Armed Forces, and those housed in other institutional settings. It is likely that most runaway youth were also missed, so we can say less than we would like to about that group.

Data from young people were collected by means of anonymous self-administered questionnaires which respondents completed in their homes. Personal interviews were also conducted with adult members in a large number of households, in part as a tactic to ensure that youngsters could answer questions without interference from a parent. Seventy-five percent of the enumerated youth completed questionnaires. The questionnaire covered a wide range of topics relevant to adolescent life, including extensive sections devoted to family relationships, peer relationships, school experiences, self-attitudes, aspirations, and participation in illegal or contranormative activities of varying seriousness. Our principal concern here is with this latter behavior.

FINDINGS THAT CLARIFY THE ISSUES

Adolescent Family Situations

Before turning to the question of adolescent behavior, several features of the family situations of contemporary American adolescents should be clarified. Despite an apparent increase in divorce rates in the United States in recent years, it was still the case in 1972 that a large majority of Illinois adolescents lived with both of their natural parents. In our sample, 72% lived in intact nuclear families, and another 5% in extended families where both parents were present, thus leaving less than a quarter of the cohort distributed among family arrangements of other types. Of these, the single-parent female-headed family was by far the most common, representing the situation of about 13% of all Illinois adolescents. Another 6% lived in re-structured nuclear families, most typically where the mother had remarried. Only 2% of the population lived in single-parent families headed by the father, while the remaining 2% lived either with older sibs, other relatives or unrelated adults. We would estimate that in total fewer than 10% of the adolescent population in Illinois lived in extended family situations, al-though this pattern is known to be more prevalent among the black popula-tion (Billingsley, 1968). More often than not, then, the so-called "broken" family implies father absence without a related or unrelated male adult consistently present in the household.

An extremely important but often overlooked fact about the single-par-ent family is that it is much more prevalent in the lower echelons of the social-class ladder, as well as in economically depressed communities. For example, among adolescents from the lower third of the socioeconomic continuum, 27% were situated in single-parent families compared to just 5% from the upper third of the continuum. Comparable differences could also be reported for communities. In the heart of the urban slum, then, as many as a third of adolescents find themselves in single-parent situations, and only a little over half live with both of their natural parents. No serious assessment of the impact of family structure on adolescent behavior can afford to ignore these economic realities.

Our data also clarified several issues regarding the nature of adolescent-parent relationships in different kinds of family structures. In this analysis, we compared levels of both affective and instrumental integration within three types of structures: intact families—where both natural parents were present; single-parent families—either female- or male-headed; and restruc-tured families—where a stepparent had been added to the family nexus. Our findings here confirmed some popular notions about broken families, but challenged others.

Affective Integration Defined

Two criteria were used to define the level of affective integration within a family. The first of these was the quality of interpersonal relationships, and was measured by the following: how well young people got along with their parents; whether they could talk freely about personal things with their parents; and whether they felt understood by parents. The second criterion was actual interaction with parents, and was measured by the number of activities, such as visiting relatives, shopping or participating in recreational pursuits, that adolescents and parents did together. As defined here, then, affective integration refers to a combination of close relationships and shared activities. In all cases we defined a situation as affectively integrated if positive affect or shared activity was reported with at least one parent. On both measures we found that levels of integration were lower in single-parent than intact families, and in addition, that there was less cross-gener-ational contact in restructured than intact families. In short, both the quality and quantity of parent-youth interaction turned out to be greater in two-parent families. Popular impressions that broken families offer adoles-cents a less rewarding emotional environment may have some basis in fact. This is probably due in large part to the emotional support adults can give to each other in two-parent families, whereas the single parent may be fulfilling multiple roles and have little emotional energy left for the chil-dren.

Instrumental Integration Defined

With regard to instrumental integration, our findings are of a different order. Instrumental integration is defined by two components, control and respect, each having to do with the degree of structure in family life. The first of these components can be defined further as the efforts parents make to establish behavioral expectations for their children. This was measured by the number of areas of family life in which they had set definite expecta-tions, which included rules regarding curfews, school work, friends, knowl-edge of the youth and duties and chores around the house. On this measure we found no differences whatsoever among the family types. Single-parent and restructured families were neither more nor less likely than intact fami-lies to make efforts in this direction.

While one element of an authority relationship is tapped by the expecta-tions of those in control, the essence of effective social control lies in the extent to which participants regard authority sources as legitimate. The second component of instrumental integration was therefore defined as the extent to which adolescents regarded their parents as legitimate sources of authority, and was measured in the study by such things as the amount of respect they had for parental advice, how important they felt it was to please their parents, and how fair they thought their parents were in the way they set and enforced rules. Here our findings were revealing. They showed lower parental salience in restructured families than in either other type. Respect for parental authority, in short, was considerably lower in families which included a stepparent than in intact families or families with just one parent present. Since the challenging of parental authority is a central theme in adolescent development, the stepparent as an "outsider" would no doubt have great difficulty establishing himself or herself as a legitimate source of authority. One might speculate that the issue of legitimacy has a relationship with the length of time the stepparent has been in the home. In any event, our evidence suggested that families with a stepparent have more difficulty having their rules accepted as legitimate by their adolescent offspring. In these families, the greater the parental efforts at control, the lower the respect accorded. On this same criterion it was the single-parent family which seemed the most integrated, for these adolescents were the ones most likely to respond to increased control with increased respect.

Overview

In overview, then, while single-parent families face problems of affective integration, restructured families have more problems with instrumental integration. Where the dominant strain in the single-parent situation is parental availability, in the restructured family it is parental credibility. Weak ties and weak controls, in other words, may be conditions which describe different types of 'broken' families. Although the single parent has no special problem with credibility, he or she may find it difficult to generate a strong socioemotional climate within the family. On the other hand, while a stepparent may contribute positively to interpersonal communication, the person in that role may not be accepted by the adolescent as a legitimate authority source. Popular impressions that single-parent families are either less able or less willing to provide direction or exert control over their adolescent offspring would not appear to have a very substantial base of factual support in the population at large.

The Family and Rebellious Behavior

The types of rebellious behavior of concern to us here range from relatively trivial adolescent improprieties to serious delinquent pursuits. Our data in this regard are of the self-report variety, and come from the answers youth gave to a series of 30 questions regarding contranormative activities. This battery included several major violations of the law, such as breaking into a store or a home to steal, as well as commonplace adolescent status infractions, such as skipping school or consuming alcohol.

Although studies of undetected delinquency of this type must cope with very real measurement problems, it should be noted that validation studies of the self-report methodology (Gold, 1966; Hirschi, 1969) have concluded that most adolescents will in fact give accurate reports of their illegal involvements. Comparing self-reports with information obtained from informants, for example, Gold (1966) concluded that over 70% of his subjects had told him everything his informants had told him, and that fewer than 20% had concealed information. It should also be pointed out that one may face even more serious problems of validity using official statistics on delinquent youth, since it is known that official records overrepresent certain classes of offenders, in particular, minorities, lower-class youth, males and persons from disrupted families. Although we will not discuss this issue at length here, it can be reported that our data revealed some of these biases, the most interesting being that youthful offenders from single-parent families had been processed further through the juvenile justice system than had offenders from intact nuclear families. Self-report methodology may be far from ideal, but it may still be preferable to many other methods of studying violative behavior in a youthful population.

Six Subtypes of Violative Acts

On the basis of factor and cluster techniques, we were able to identify six empirically distinct subtypes of violative acts. The terms *empirically distinct* and *acts* have to be emphasized here, for we are identifying sets of concrete actions which distinguish actual groups of persons: we are not classifying behavior in terms of its underlying form or the dynamics which may generate it. Our criteria for sorting behavior, in short, are empirical patterns of convergence and differentiation. The labels we will assign the subtypes, accordingly, will be concrete rather than abstract.

The first cluster of activity consisted of *violent acts* where no reference was made to utilitarian gain, and included behavior such as fist fighting, fighting in a gang, and carrying or using weapons. Although almost half of the adolescent population had been involved in a fist fight at some point in the past, fewer than 20% had ever carried or used a weapon, or been involved in a gang fight.

The second distinct cluster consisted of three serious *proto-criminal offenses*, which legally would be classified as burglary, larceny and robbery.

Involvement in this category of behavior was rare in the population, and only one adolescent in seven admitted to having been involved even once.

The third category consisted of *automobile offenses,* which ranged from minor infractions such as driving without a license to automobile theft—an index offense in the FBI reporting scheme. Here, cumulative prevalence rates over time varied sharply with the seriousness of the offense.

Several types of *property violations* formed a fourth grouping, and included activities such as shoplifting, the use of stolen goods, vandalism and petty theft. Offenses of this type are more common in the adolescent population, and a majority said they had committed at least one of the four.

The fifth type of behavior, and the most readily identifiable, was the use of *illicit drugs*—principally marijuana, psychedelics, barbiturates and amphetamines. Although drug use within this population was not as high as some studies have reported, the impressive feature about the teenage drug culture is that it is so clearly recognized a subgrouping among youth themselves. Data from both the anthropological and survey phases of the research confirmed that of the various strands of youth culture distinguished within the adolescent world, drug users were clearly the most visible.

The sixth and final cluster of contranormative behavior consisted of *status violations,* basically school infractions such as truancy, sexual activity, violations of laws regarding alcohol use among minors, and other forms of behavior which are not law violative if committed by adults. A substantial majority of teenagers violate one or more of these norms, and there is some question as to whether this category of behavior is in fact contranormative.

For reasons stated earlier we will not discuss runaway youth here, but it should be noted in passing that runaways in our population did not fit as clearly within the status violation category as might be expected on the basis of the legal classification of this behavior. Many of those who had run away and then returned home had become involved in infractions of a much more serious variety, and behaviorally speaking, the adolescents who were closest to becoming runaways were those who had been involved in serious infractions of the law. We can only speculate that many runaways may either get into serious trouble after they leave home—or perhaps leave home after involvement in serious trouble.

Two Answers to the Question

To what extent are family factors related to these different forms of antisocial behavior? There are two kinds of answers we can give to this question, and they depend on whether the family (a) is viewed as a social system or cultural island unto itself—which is virtually the only way it has been treated in the literature on adolescence—or (b) is viewed as an institution nested within the context of a surrounding community and social environment. We will discuss this distinction in detail, for it turns out to be important.

As with many other studies on this topic, the Illinois study turned up moderate, yet statistically significant, relationships between adolescent violative behavior and family characteristics. In fact, all of the elements of the family system we have been discussing—its structure, its affective cohesiveness and its instrumental integration—turned out to be related to all six types of violative behavior just identified. Rates of norm violation were higher among adolescents from non-intact families, in families where relationships with parents were distant or strained, where levels of shared activity with parents were low, where parents set fewer limits, and where adolescents regarded parental authority more lightly. It was also the case that no single element of the family system could be singled out as dominant: all dimensions seemed to make a difference, and approximately to the same degree. There were hints in the data that the instrumental or control dimension might be more important than the affective as they relate to delinquent behavior, and that family factors had a stronger impact on behavioral violations of lesser seriousness. But at this level of analysis, the best interpretation would be that breakdowns, either in the family structure or in family functioning, could elevate levels of rebelliousness and delinquent expression among adolescents.

The second answer is more complex, but, we think, more realistic. It is based on a theoretical model in which adolescent behavior, either normative or contranormative, is viewed as the end product of three sets of forces: peer-group influence, family influence and community norms and pressures. The model is diagrammed in Figure 1. This formulation assumes first that the stability of the family and the level of its integration are affected by pressures from the external environment. At the same time, the family is also seen as a buffer which can mediate the impact of outside pressures on the adolescent. The family can influence adolescent behavior either directly, or by influencing the adolescent's choice of peer attachments, indirectly. In this model, community norms and pressures, which we label here as the environmental press, include such factors as the level of poverty or affluence in a community, the adult crime rate in an area, the quality of the school the adolescent attends, and opportunities, real or perceived, for upward social mobility. Insofar as adolescent behavior is concerned, we also interpret the economic position of the adolescent's own family as part of the environmental press. In this model peer-groups can influence behavior in either normative or contranormative directions.

This formulation is admittedly synthetic, and draws from a variety of extant theories of delinquent behavior. It articulates well with ecological perspectives on crime and delinquency (Shaw and McKay, 1929, 1942), with so-called "opportunity theory" (Cloward and Ohlin, 1960), with differential association theory (Sutherland, 1947), and at certain points with control or containment theories (Nye, 1958; Reckless, 1966; Hirschi, 1969). For present purposes, the real advantage of the formulation is that the effects of the family can be specified independently of the effects stemming from

Figure 1. A Contextual Interpretation of the Impact of the Family on Adolescent Rebelliousness

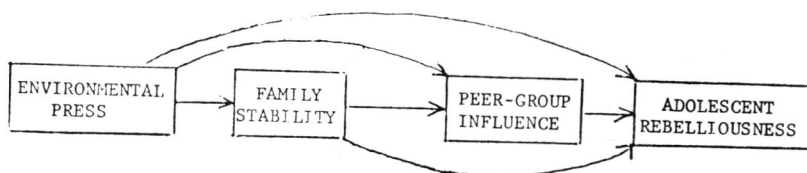

other sources. Indeed, the logic of the model insists that if family characteristics are to be considered causal, the empirical relationships must persist
after the impact of the environment and the peer-group have been taken
into account.

Viewed in this light, several new insights emerge, some contrary to popular wisdom. The contextual analysis [4] showed that the influence of the family varies both with the type of norm-violative behavior involved, and with
the setting in which the behavior takes place. With regard to the first point,
there was an inverse relationship between the seriousness of an offense and
the importance of the family in accounting for it. Family factors had a
definite impact on less serious kinds of norm violations—status offenses,
drug infractions and property violations—but had virtually no value as pre-
dictors of proto-criminal and violent behavior. It was precisely on these
latter types of behavior, moreover, that environmental factors had their
strongest effects. Both offense patterns, the criminal and the violent, were
predicted better by characteristics of the community than by characteristics
of the family. Adolescent participation in "heavy" delinquent pursuits, in
short, simply had no connection with family structure or with the quality of
family life experienced. As such, these patterns of behavior should probably not be interpreted, as many would have it, as expressions of hostile
impulses generated from a bad family situation. The behavior is rooted
primarily in the wider social environment; in slum communities it can en-
trap youngsters from both stable and disrupted family situations. There was
some secondary evidence that two-parent families can help create a buffer
for the adolescent against a hostile environment, but the best interpretation
of the data is that in depressed communities the press of the environment
supersedes the capacity of the family to counteract it.

On the other hand, several forms of adolescent rebelliousness do seem to
be a direct response to family malfunctioning. Status violations, drug use,
property offenses, and to a degree automobile offenses, are all better interpreted as reactions to family problems than as reactions to a hostile external
environment. Indeed, community characteristics had almost no impact at
all on these forms or rebelliousness.

What these patterns suggest is a shifting balance between the role of the
family and the role of the community in explaining adolescent contranormative behavior. Where the external environment is stable and provides a
modicum of safety and security, disrupted family conditions can and do
generate adolescent rebelliousness. Where communities and neighborhoods
are crowded and deteriorated, and where the economic press of life is constant and ubiquitous, however, the net impact of a bad family situation is
minimal. Paradoxically, then, it is not in the heart of the inner-city slum

that family disintegration plays its most significant causal role in the etiology of adolescent violative behavior. Deteriorated families have a much stronger impact on youth in benign than in hostile ecological settings.

It was also evident from the analysis that adolescent antisocial behavior is determined more by the peer group than by the family. Although this suggests clearcut support for differential association theory, the results also indicated that family factors are important determinants of the type of peer-group to which adolescents become attached. Membership in a delinquency-prone peer culture was better predicted by family than by community malfunctioning. The family therefore has important secondary effects on adolescent behavior through its influence on peer attachments. In this regard, the key element in the family system was the level of instrumental integration, parental effectiveness in setting behavioral limits and in generating respect. Adolescents who were attached to delinquent peer-groups were more likely to come from families where authority relationships had broken down, but whether or not a family was intact mattered little in this regard.

Our second answer to the question is therefore more qualified, and is situationally based. The impact of the family on adolescent rebelliousness depends in large part on the community context. In a stable social environment a malfunctioning family can have a strong impact on adolescent rebelliousness: if the external environment is a hostile one, where survival is the key issue, even a well-functioning family may not be able to protect its youngsters from serious contranormative involvements.

CONCLUSIONS

While there seems little doubt but that the family has a disposing influence on delinquent behavior, our main conclusion is that the net impact of the family varies inversely with the quality of the social environment. Although families in poverty-stricken communities are more disrupted themselves, they do not play the major role in determining delinquency. In these settings, pressures from the street far overshadow negative influences from the home. In more stable and affluent communities, on the other hand, poor family relationships have a stronger and more direct impact on delinquent behavior. A related conclusion is that families have a greater impact on less serious patterns of acting-out than on hard-core delinquency.

It is striking how well these results fit within a needs-hierarchy frame of reference (Maslow, 1954), for they suggest that explanations of adolescent rebelliousness which focus on higher-order social and affiliational needs make sense only in situations where lower-order needs for survival and security are likely to have been met. Before pointing to the relational system within the family, in other words, one should be fairly certain that the critical factor is not what happens to the child outside of the family. In hard-core poverty areas, family problems, though real, seem to be the second order of business to be attended.

We would also conclude that the impact of the family on delinquency is not as strong as the impact of the peer group. Families do exert influence on the types of peer-groups adolescents become attached to, however, and in this sense the family has both a direct and an indirect relationship to delinquent behavior.

Finally, we would conclude that family structure by itself is of little importance in explaining delinquent behavior. Structural features may be related to how far youthful offenders are processed through the system, but they do not account for the actions which bring youth to the attention of authorities in the first place. Single-parent families have more strength and resilience than they are often given credit for, and it is more important to know if an adolescent-parent authority relationship is viable than to know whether two parents are present in the household. Single-parent families appear to have just as much control over their adolescents as intact families, although families which include a stepparent may well have less.

For the practitioner these relationships add a new dimension, the community context, to the process of defining the problem of delinquency and developing relevant intervention strategies. This is not a substitute for a carefully developed individual diagnosis, but it suggests a three-pronged evaluation focused on the physical and emotional health which a child brings to adolescence, the presence or absence of serious pathology within the family, and pressures emanating from the larger community, including peers and major institutions such as schools.

Two conclusions seem particularly relevant to the practitioner: first, that in communities characterized by poverty and high delinquency rates, adolescents from even the most stable families may not be able to resist the pressure to engage in delinquent acts; and second, that the family's ability to maintain effective controls is more important in preventing delinquency than the quality of interpersonal relationships within the family.

GUIDELINES FOR DELINQUENCY INTERVENTION PROGRAMS

In designing delinquency intervention programs, it becomes critical to allocate limited resources where they will be most effective. Based on the observations presented here, we would suggest the following five guide-lines:

(1) Family therapy is more likely to be effective, and in fact may be the only intervention necessary, when the acting-out youth comes from an affluent community. There is some evidence that this may also be the preferred technique for the less serious offender.

(2) In hard-core poverty communities, family therapy will probably have little impact on preventing or solving problems of delinquency. If resources are available, family therapy may be useful as one component of a broad service package, and it may also be necessary in those situations where the family system clearly contributes to the child's problems or blocks any efforts the child makes to improve. As a general rule, however, we would suggest that other types of programs for parents would be more relevant in these settings. Examples would be parent effectiveness training focused on controls and limits; social or recreational activities which bring parents together and break down the isolation many of them experience; and involvement of parents in community groups which meet to study and solve problems in their communities.

(3) In hard-core poverty areas substantial resources should be allocated to a wide range of services geared to helping youth deal better with the negative influences of their environment. These services would include individual and group treatment, job training and placement, career counseling, recreational activities, educational programs and leadership training.

(4) In any community the coordination of available services is important, but in hard-core poverty neighborhoods it is critical. Here the needs for food, shelter, protection, medical care and other concrete services must be addressed if one hopes to have any impact on delinquency. Since no one agency has the capacity to address all of these needs, it is imperative that public and private institutions work cooperatively toward the solution of the problem.

(5) Finally, the program implications of this research would not be complete without a word of caution to the juvenile justice system. Those persons, such as police officers and judges, who are responsible for decisions as to whether a child is put on probation, goes to a correctional institution, or gets a lecture and sent home, would be well advised to look at the total family system. Too often these decisions are based on a superficial evaluation of a family, in combination with stereotypes and biases. The tendency to look only at family structure, and the failure to look deeper into the quality of life in the family has led to grave injustices and inequities in the juvenile justice system.

SUMMARY

The role of the family in the etiology of delinquent behavior among children and youth has been persistently elusive to social and behavioral scientists. This chapter discusses reasons why the connection has been clouded in the research literature, and reinterprets the relationship on the basis of results obtained from a large-scale field study of adolescents in Illinois. The relationship is found to vary both with the form of norm-violative behavior in question, and with the type of social environment within which the behavior takes place. Serious delinquency is found to be rooted in conditions in the wider community, and to have little connection either with family structure or with the quality of family life experienced. On the other hand, several forms of adolescent rebelliousness which are less serious in legal terms are found to be a direct response to family malfunctioning, and to be more or less impervious to environmental circumstances. The patterns are interpreted from a needs-hierarchy perspective, and policy implications regarding intervention with the family are discussed from this frame of reference.

NOTES

1. There are notable exceptions, of course, on both sides. See in particular Offer (1969), Stein (1971), Cloward and Ohlin (1960) or Short et al (1963).
2. The research was supported by Grants A-70-52R, 2-09-25-0410-02, 2-09-25-0410-3 and 2-09-1138-04 from the Illinois Law Enforcement Commission, and by Grants 75NI-99-0013 and 76JN-99-0004 from the Law Enforcement Assistance Administration.
3. Readers interested in the statistical analysis can obtain a copy of the technical report (Johnstone, 1976) by writing the Institute for Juvenile Research, 1735 W. Taylor Street, Chicago, Illinois, 60612.
4. Our interpretations in this section are based on the results of multivariate analysis. The specific strategy was to fit the data to a path analytic model in which (a) measures of antisocial behavior were regressed against measures of peer-group involvement, family characteristics and economic-environmental factors; (b) participation in a delinquency-prone peer group was regressed against the family and environmental variables; and (c) family factors were regressed against the economic and community variables. Technical discussion of the methodology of path analysis may be obtained from a variety of contemporary sources, including Land (1969) and Nie et al. (1975).

REFERENCES

Billingsley, A. (1968), *Black Families in White America*. Englewood Cliffs: Prentice Hall.
Cloward, R.A. and L. Ohlin (1960), *Delinquency and Opportunity*. Glencoe: Free Press.

Glueck, S. and Glueck E., (1950), *Unravelling Juvenile Delinquency*. New York: Common-wealth Fund.

Gold, M. (1966), Undetected juvenile delinquency. *J. Res. Crime Delinq.* 13: 27-46.

Hirschi, T. (1969), *Causes of Deliquency*. Berkeley: University of California Press.

Jenkins, R.L. and Hewitt, L. (1944), Types of personality structure encountered in child guidance clinics. *Am. J. Orthopsych.* 14: 84-94.

Johnstone, J.W.C. (1976), The Family and Delinquency: A Reappraisal. *Research Report, Institute for Juvenile Research,* Chicago.

Land, K.C. (1969), Principles of Path Analysis. In E.F. Borgatta (Ed.) *Sociological Methodology.* San Francisco: Jossey-Bass.

Maslow, A. (1954), *Motivation and Personality*. New York: Harper.

Nie, N., Hull, C.H., Jenkins, J.G., Steinbrenner, K., and Bent, D.H. (1975), *Statistical Package for the Social Sciences*. New York: McGraw-Hill.

Nye, F.I. (1958), *Family Relationships and Delinquent Behavior*. New York: Wiley.

Offer, D. (1969), *The Psychological World of the Teen-Ager*. New York: Basic Books

Reckless, W. (1966), A New Theory of Delinquency and Crime. In R. Giollombardo (Ed.) *Juvenile Delinquency*. New York: Wiley.

Shaw, C.R. and McKay H., (1929), *Delinquency Areas*. Chicago: University of Chicago Press.
——— (1942), *Juvenile Delinquency and Urban Areas*. Chicago: University of Chicago Press.

Short, J.F., Tennyson, R.A. and Howard, K.I. (1963), Behavior dimensions of gang delinquency. *Am. Sociol. Rev.* 28: 411-428.

Stein, R.F. (1971), *Disturbed Youth and Ethnic Family Patterns*. Albany: State University of New York Press.

Sutherland, E.H. (1947), *Principles of Criminology*. 4th Edition, Philadelphia: Lippincott.

Time (July 11, 1977), The Youth Crime Plague.

Williams, J.R. and Gold, M. (1972), From delinquent behavior to official delinquency. *Soc. Prob.* 20: 209-227.

3

Parens Patriae—*The State as Parent: A Case of Child Abuse and Neglect*

WILLIAM E. RITTENBERG

This chapter will focus on how well the state acts as a family and how it also can threaten a family. We shall examine how we have traditionally institutionalized and neglected children under the concept of acting in their best interests and what a lawsuit has done to change this system in one state. This state is Louisiana, but it should be noted that Louisiana is fairly typical, and clearly not unique.

HISTORY

Our laws have distinguished between children and adults for less than 200 years. Prior to the nineteenth century, children were tried, convicted, and sentenced in the same manner as adults. Children went to adult jails unless the jury found the child too young to know the difference between "good" and "evil" (Law and Tactics in Juvenile Cases, 1977).

During the nineteenth century, reformers began to claim that children were "bad" because of "bad environments." It was argued that one should remove the child from the environment to "cure" the child. The idea of "curing" the environment or family was not discussed. One of the first experiments with this idea was the House of Refuge in New York in 1824.

35

It was argued then, as now, that not all children were eligible for reform, that some must be written off. "Those that could not be rescued were to be prevented from contaminating the saving process. The reformers were convinced that it was necessary to close their House to prematurely corrupted and corrupting young persons" (Fox, 1970).

The concept that the state could separate a child from its parents to be placed in child institutions or refuges was given judicial approval in 1839 (Ex Parte Crouse 4 Whart. 9 Pa.). The American version of *parens patriae* began with this case, which gave the state power to be a superior parent and allowed the separation from parent, and regulation of the child for the welfare of both the child and the state. It is not surprising that when the needs of the state (its institutions) were in conflict with the "best interests" of the child, the state's needs won.

This reform movement reached its final state in 1899 with the development of juvenile court in Chicago. Juvenile courts removed children from the criminal process entirely, including the constitutional due process protection afforded those charged with crimes. Juvenile courts practiced *parens patriae* with a vengeance. If it was decided a child should be removed from his parents, the child was placed in an institution. Juvenile courts made this decision at a secret hearing and did not afford the child or its parents a right to legal counsel. Traditional due process concepts of fairness, such as being presumed innocent until proven guilty beyond a reasonable doubt, were deemed unnecessary since the actions were done "in the child's best interest."

In Kent v. United States (1966), and In Re Gault (1967), the United States Supreme Court recognized that juvenile courts did not always act in the "best interests" of the child, and the system could in fact be punitive in spite of the theory. With these cases, children began to obtain some rights such as: to counsel, to remain silent, and to have a chance to confront and cross-examine witnesses. The Supreme Court in 1970 finally held that children were innocent until proven guilty beyond a reasonable doubt (In Re Winship, 1970).

These decisions and due process are inconsistent with the theory of *parens patriae*. They suggest a rejection of the theory that the state can be a parent. Today, many people argue that the state cannot act as a parent, but can give due process. These people urge that the state also abolish the large primitive institutions and encourage programs that support the family and treat the child in the community.

A major flaw in the concept of *parens patriae* is that the courts have lacked the tools to act as a superior parent. The court has traditionally had only two choices: institutionalization or noninvolvement. The state has not tried to be a parent, and it has not had the availability of truly professional counseling for the child or child's family. The juvenile court was mandated to "treat" and "cure" the child without a proper evaluation and diagnosis of the "illness." The court has not had the necessary services available.

Many children are labeled retarded or brain damaged without the examination of a neurologist. If a child scores low on an I.Q. Test, he may be retarded because of brain damage. On the other hand, a child may score low because of cultural deprivation and lack of stimulation. Obviously, a culturally deprived child should not be treated the same as a brain-damaged child, yet lack of diagnostic tools prevents the court from distinguishing the difference.

It is presumed by "the best interests" test that the parents or the court will represent the best interests of the child. Yet, there is no reason why we should presume this. This is not to say that we should presume the state's or parents' intent is to harm the child; it is just that the state or parent has other interests. The state is concerned with protecting society or making the parents happy. The parents may have conflicts with their child. These conflicts may easily be remedied by seeing that the child is represented by counsel and taking the role away from the state. If the court is neutral and not charged with protecting anyone's "best interest," it avoids having a conflict of interest. The parties in court, if fairly represented, can have all sides heard. The court should rule only after hearing all sides and weighing all interests.

THE STATES' CHILDREN

The New Orleans Police Department recently arrested a "16-year-old Negro male" for threatening a white man. The man had entered a mostly black housing project. When asked, "Why did you do it?" Joseph G. said, "That white man should have known better than to come in here." This same teenager had also been caught stealing, fighting and lying. The experts think he is dangerous. Fear of children like him is the reason many people will not walk the streets at night. The paradox is that we as a society are the parents of many of these kids. Our jails are filled with people who first started going to state and private institutions at a very early age, but their first experience with an institution was not for committing a crime, unless it is a crime to do a poor job choosing your parents or to be handicapped. These institutions of first experience were built for our neglected, retarded, or disturbed children.

Who are these children that threaten our security? Many are children whose nurturing and education have been the responsibility of society, children who have been separated from their parents under the doctrine of *parens patriae* so that the state shall act as parent.

Gary W.

Gary W. is 20, has trouble finding a job, and spends most of the time in a New Orleans housing project. He spent five years at Dyer Vocational Training Center in Leona, Texas, at the expense of the taxpayers, and was given thorazine daily. He wasn't retarded when he was sent to Texas, but after taking thorazine and having no treatment or education for five years he became retarded.

His problems with the state began in 1969. At thirteen, he was arrested by the juvenile authorities for shoplifting. He was a truant from school, had no contact with his father and had a mother with problems of her own. Gary probably was emotionally disturbed.

The Juvenile Court's evaluation of Gary at a Louisiana mental hospital found him to have a 76 I.Q. and to be mentally disturbed. He was placed on 400 mg. of thorazine a day and sent to Dyer Vocational Training Center in Leona, Texas. He remained there from 1969 until his mother retained this author to investigate the case and secure his release in 1974. That year, Gary's I.Q. was tested at 65, a drop of 11 points while the state was responsible for his care.

Placing a child in an institution usually does one thing: it creates an institutionalized, regimented adult who is told day after day when to sleep, dress, bathe, play or relax. The institution takes on total responsibility for the individual. Therefore, the individual never learns to take responsibility for himself. Even the best institution cannot "love" a child or be an object of the child's love as a parent. Large childrens' institutions train our children to fit into institutionalized life, but give them no preparation for life in the more chaotic "real world" in which we live.

I was the advocate for Gary W., Joseph G. and Clifton P. in a class action suit (Gary W., 1976). Following are some of the experiences which formed the basis of the lawsuit.

Joey

In 1964, when Joseph G. was 2½ years old, his parents divorced and his father stopped supporting the family. Joey's mother had three other children and no money to support them. When she applied for assistance, she was told she was ineligible because her husband had not been gone six months. The welfare department suggested that she should surrender the children to the state so they could be placed in foster homes until she was able to support them. At this point in Joey's life the state stepped in. According to the law, it was to act as his parent. The first step of the welfare department was to remove Joey from his loving mother and place him in a home run by a stranger who kept several foster children. According to the law, the welfare department was only to do what was in Joey's best interest. As we see, this welfare bureaucracy does not always respond to meet the needs it was designed to remedy.

When Joey was placed in foster care, according to the Office of Family Service's rules, his mother was only allowed to see him one hour each month. During his first year away from home, Joey lived in three different foster homes. At the end of a year, Joey's mother was told that Joey was emotionally disturbed and should be sent to an institution in New York.

While Joey was in foster care, his mother attempted to visit him often, but the "rules" limited visits to once a month. When Joey's mother would end a visit, Joey would start screaming that he wanted to go home with her. These "temper tantrums" were used as evidence of his emotional disturbance. We suggest that it is emotionally disturbing to 2-year-olds to be taken away from their parents and placed with total strangers. We are not quarrelling with the diagnosis, but would have suggested a more conservative treatment. We wanted Joey returned home. The state wanted him sent from New Orleans to New York, and so he was.

Joey spent about six years in the New York institution. There is no evidence that anything was wrong with this institution; on the other hand, there is no explanation as to why a child from New Orleans, with family in New Orleans, should be sent to an institution in New York. Perhaps Louisiana had no explanation because they never visited him. The only thing the welfare department knew about Joey was that every month $1,100 of Louisiana money went to New York for his care. But very few taxpayers in the State of Louisiana knew about this practice until the lawsuit was filed in 1974.

In 1971, when the welfare department discovered they could save money by sending Joey to the East Texas Guidance Center in Tyler, Texas, he was sent there. He remained in Tyler, Texas, until his mother asked me to seek a court order demanding his return to Louisiana in 1974.

Joey spent 10 years away from his mother as a ward of the State of Louisiana. For nine of those years, Joey's feet never touched Louisiana ground, and no one from the state saw him. Joey's mother asked the state to pay for her visits, but it would not.

The state provided no support or counseling to Joey and his family when he was returned home at age 13. The welfare department spent well over $100,000 in direct payments for Joey's care in New York and Texas. Joey's main problem was that his mother was poor.

As a society, we actually spend too much money on cases such as Joey's. The state, as parent, spent nothing on preparing Joey to live a self-sufficient life in New Orleans when he grew up. If it prepared him for anything, it was to live life in state-supported institutions. But at what cost to his chance of developing into a responsible citizen with a life of his own? And at what cost to us?

Clifton

Clifton P. was luckier than Joey and Gary since he was not institutionalized as long. At 15, his parents' marriage began to break up, and he had problems in public school, got into fights, and skipped classes. Clifton's mother sought help for her son. She was advised by Louisiana officials that her son would be better off giving up public school and getting into a vocational training program. Although Louisiana had no such program for children under seventeen, Clifton could go to Dyer Vocational Training Center in Leona, Texas, and Louisiana would pay for all the costs. Since Clifton wanted vocational training, his mother agreed to allow him to go to Texas.

Clifton was picked up at his New Orleans home and driven to Leona, Texas. He noticed immediately that the other children in the car seemed retarded. At Leona, Texas, he found himself in an institution for the retarded. The only vocational training in Dyer Vocational Training Center was in its name. The Louisiana officials sending children to Dyer and other Texas institutions knew nothing of the programs offered. One high Louisiana official did visit Leona, Texas, to meet Robert Dyer and go hunting with him. There is no evidence that he ever checked on their program or the children his agency placed.

Clifton only spent nine days in Texas. During that time he witnessed a sexual assault and was corporally punished for trying to call his mother to get him out. Finally, Clifton's mother received an anonymous telephone call from a Dyer employee telling her that this was not a suitable place for her son.

Clifton's mother and father reunited for the emergency, and drove immediately to Leona, Texas. When they arrived at approximately 9:00 p.m., they found the institution padlocked and they were not permitted to enter. Clifton's parents were told at first they could not see their son. Later, after a long wait and the threat to call the police for help, Clifton was allowed to go home with his parents.

Clifton now works in New Orleans with a rock band, and seems happy and well-adjusted. Unlike Gary and Joey, he spent days instead of years having the state as parents, and he did not become adapted to life inside an institution. The state spent less on Clifton and harmed him less.

THE COURT CASE

In the summer of 1974, several parents (including those of Gary and Joey) approached me about wanting to see their children. They knew their children were in profit-making instituions in Texas, paid for by the State of Louisiana.

I discovered that Louisiana was spending $18 million a year on out-of-state child-caring institutions for hundreds of Louisiana children in Texas and other states. The Children's Defense Fund agreed to be co-counsel with me. In September, 1974, we filed a class action lawsuit in United States District Court against the responsible Louisiana officials and 44 Texas child-caring institutions. This case has come to be known as Gary W. v. Louisiana (1976). We alleged that Louisiana was banishing children to faraway institutions where they were literally being "warehoused." After investigation, the Civil Rights Divison of the United States Justice Department joined us in suing the State of Louisiana.

After 18 months of preparation, we went to trial in March, 1976, and parents and children testified with horror stories. National experts in mental retardation and psychiatry from all over the country testified about the impropriety of Louisiana practices for which Louisiana had no defense. The New Orleans Director of Catholic Charities testified about facilities in New Orleans which would have been more appropriate for Gary, Joey and many other children who were instead sent to Teaxs. The New Orleans institutions at the time of the trial were being given $430 a month to care for children. Since they were spending $200 per month over this rate, they refused to take more children. They testified that for $630 a month, they would expand their services and take in more children. Meanwhile, Louisiana was spending twice this amount in payment to Texas "warehouses."

The experts testified that children can be more adequately cared for if they are not institutionalized. In fact, by separating children from their family and community, problems are usually aggravated. It was agreed by all of the experts that usually problem children are not problems in isolation, but their problems relate to their family and community. By banishing children from family and community, the real problems are ignored. The child is more likely to be treated successfully if his family is involved in the treatment and chances of rehabilitation in the community are greater if there is no separation from the community.

The state was also unable to rebut the shocking charge that institutionalized child care was more expensive than de-institutionalized care. Experts testified that almost all of the Louisiana children sent to Texas could be cared for in a non-institutional setting, and parents of severely retarded children could care for them at home with proper training and the availability of day-care centers. If foster parents received more money, training and supervision, they could care for many "hard to place" children. Community treatment centers and group homes could care for other children. In fact, there is a great variety of treatment alternatives that would keep the child in its community and be less expensive than institutionalized care. The state offered few of these alternatives, causing more people to be locked up as the only available alternative. The experts testified about a variety of innovative alternatives being used in other states. These de-institutionalized alternatives cost less than the Texas institutions.

The experts at the Gary W. trial suggested a way of dealing with our problems that would work and be a savings to society. They showed how our traditional method of putting our problems "out of sight, out of mind" came back to haunt us.

After spending most of March, 1976, listening to parents, children, and experts, United States District Court Judge Alvin B. Rubin took the case under advisement and issued an opinion on July 26, 1976. The state conceded that all Louisiana children would be brought home from Texas; the Court did not need to order their return. Judge Rubin ordered their more immediate return from the worst institutions, set up minimal constituional standards for caring for the children and decided that children in state care should have a constitutional "right to treatment" (Gary W., 1976).

The court did document substantial child abuse occurring in Texas institutions. At Bartley Woods House it found that: "Patients have been tied, handcuffed, or chained together, to fixtures or furniture as a means of control and discipline." At Children's Cottage, "The Administrator has abused children by hitting them with her hand or a soup ladle and by tying one child to her bed and keeping her in a high chair all day." Many of the institutions lacked an adequately trained staff to provide humane care.

At Dyer Vocational Training Center, the former home of Gary W. and Clifton, the court found excessive use of psychotropic drugs and no training for even the most elementary matters, such as self-feeding. As a result of the inadequate care that Dyer provided, the court held that some children had actually regressed.

Judge Rubin documented the inadequate state monitoring of these Louisiana children and held that their constitutional rights had been violated. The court ruled that the state may not place children with just anyone that would take them; that children whose liberty is deprived, even because of a handicap, are entitled to something in return for their deprivation of liberty. They are entitled to treatment to cure the need for that confinement.

The July 26, 1976 order was 42-pages long. The following excerpt from the opinion will give an idea of the reasons for the ruling (Gary W., 1976):

No compassionate human being could fail to be moved by the plight of the children who are the plaintiffs. . .

What is required is that the state give thoughtful consideration to the needs of the individual, treating him constructively and in accordance with his own situation, rather than automatically placing in institutions, perhaps far from home, and perhaps forever, all for whom families cannot care and all who are rejected by family or society. . .

Accordingly, the decree will require the development of a treatment plan for each individual held, and will set forth some basic standards for the development of that plan. . .

The persons preparing the treatment plans for each child will be required to consider the least restrictive alternative for that child. . .

The opinion was a clear mandate ending the historical practice of "warehousing" children. Whether this mandate becomes a reality remains to be seen.

The Louisiana children sent to Texas were evaluated psychiatrically under the court order. From that evaluation, Coddington, Tabor and McMillan (1978) made the following observations:

(1) The state spent more money on brighter children. This amounted to approximately $600/month more for the child with an I.Q. over 85 than for a child with an I.Q. under 35;

(2) The state contributed a greater amount of money for the care of children from wealthy families. This came to about $200/month more for the very rich than for the very poor;

(3) The state contributed about $130/month more to the care of a black child than of a white child with similar characteristics.

However, these factors were all interrelated. Eighty-eight percent of the black children compared to only 36% of the white children came from families in the two lowest socioeconomic classes. Of the black children in the program, 62% had I.Q.'s below 52. Only 25.7% of the white children fell into this category.

. . . . a disproportionate number of black children were in the worst institutions, as were more children from poor families and more children with limited intelligence. Furthermore, the average length of stay was almost 1½ years longer in the poorer institutions. Generally speaking, there were two programs, one for mentally retarded youngsters and one for children with higher I.Q.'s. The first was long-term and had an over-representation of black children from poor families. In the second, the stay was shorter and the majority of the participants were white children from homes of a higher economic class. The former were housed in the worst institutions, while the latter were housed in the best.

This phrase "with similar circumstances" is crucial since the determination that $130 more was spent monthly on black children than white children was based on a multiple regression analysis in which the effect of I.Q. and socioeconomic class was held constant. Since Louisiana also spent more for children with higher I.Q.'s and for children from families of higher socioeconomic classes who were able to seek out the best and the most expensive programs, and since, as we have seen, more of these children were white, it turned out that the state actually spent an average of $170.75 *less* on blacks than on whites.

This practice of inappropriately and unnecessarily placing children in institutions is not unique to Louisiana. A study of child-caring practices in seven states by the Children's Defense Fund concluded that states provide the money for institutional placement, but provide little money to support the family staying together. Children get placed where the money is available, away from their homes. A movement has begun to encourage community services that would reverse this trend.

The implementation of this order has helped many children in Louisiana. Congress has held hearings investigating the out-of-state placement of children. Language from the Gary W. (1976) lawsuit mandating minimal constitutional standards and the "least restrictive alternative" has found its way into federal legislation. Because of Public Law 94-142, local public schools must educate all handicapped children and even children in institutions must be educated, as much as possible, with children who are not handicapped.

The importance of stimulating and nurturing children was well documented by Skeels (1966), who compared a group of neglected normal I.Q. children, given stimulation and nurturing from surrogate retarded mothers, with a group of children of normal intelligence who were raised in a relatively nonstimulating environment and became retarded. The nurtured and stimulated group made an average gain of 28 I.Q. points, while the nonstimulated group lost an average of 26 I.Q. points. The experimental group married and held jobs as adults. Over a third of the contrast group reached adulthood institutionalized and few of them married or held regular jobs. Skeels (1966) found that the cost to the state for providing custodial care to the contrast group was five times the cost for the group provided with stimulation and love. He concluded:

> It seems obvious that under present-day conditions there are still countless infants born with sound biological constitutions and potentialities for development well within the normal range who will become mentally retarded and noncontributing members of society unless appropriate intervention occurs. It is suggested by the findings of this study and others published in the past 20 years that sufficient knowledge is available to design programs of intervention to counteract the devastating effects of poverty, sociocultural deprivation, and maternal deprivation.

Provence and Lipton (1962) showed that infants develop best with a family model and that the farther we stray from this model, the more difficult development is. They concluded that it is perhaps impossible to adequately meet the needs of infants in group care. At the end of the first year, Provence and Lipton found institutionalized infants different in many ways from family-raised babies. Institutionalized babies had general impairments to their relationships with people. "They rarely turned to the adult for help, comfort, or pleasure. There were no signs of a strong attachment to any one person, nor any signs of the development of a sense of trust in the adults who cared for them." The institutionalized children did not develop the ability to communicate or physical coordination that family-raised babies developed.

Love cannot be provided in an institution the way parents give it. Institutions have three shifts of employees with different personalities. There is no way this could substitute for a mother's love.

A child's need for love is no new discovery. It was perhaps accidentally discovered 700 years ago by the Emperor of the Holy Roman Empire, Frederick II (Stone and Church, 1957). He wanted to discover what language a child would speak, if no one spoke to it. Thus, he had some children raised, fed, bathed, but never spoken to by their foster mothers. He expected the children to start speaking Hebrew or Greek, or perhaps the language of their parents. The children all died. They could not live without attention and loving words. Seven hundred years later, our research confirms the experiment of King Frederick II, yet some children in America are still warehoused in ways that injure their lives.

Study after study supports the importance of the family for child development and the fact that institutionalization retards that development. The witnesses for the plaintiffs in the Gary W. trial (1976) all emphasized treating the whole family. Separating the child from its family made that treatment impossible. The defendants tried to get their experts to say that sending the child far away was not harmful. The experts would not say that. The defendants asked their experts, "Isn't corporal punishment an acceptable disciplinary method under certain circumstances?" Their experts (and the plaintiffs') said, "No!"

Large institutions are not the place to leave children for long-term care. Of course, hospitals are necessary, but for acute care, not chronic or long-term care. Institutions cannot provide love. Individuals give love. Children need to develop binding love with individuals over a long period of time. This is difficult in an institution run on three eight-hour shifts with the typical staff turnover.

Children, and especially older children, must be gradually given more and more responsibility to prepare them for their day of independence. To become an adult, is to learn to take responsibility for our own actions. Institutions do not provide encouragement to take chances or accept responsibility. Inmates know when they must wake, sleep, eat, or do chores. There is no room for flexibility. When one becomes institutionalized, that person becomes dependent on the institution and takes no responsibility for himself.

I have interviewed many children in state institutions who have told me they plan on being in the penitentiary when they grow up. By treating them the way we do as a society, we promote business for adult corrections.

The Office of Juvenile Justice and Delinquency Prevention (a federal agency) is trying to encourage states to de-institutionalize hard-core delinquents. O.J.J.D.P. cites studies showing hard-core delinquents are less likely to be a recidivists if they are kept in nonsecure facilities as opposed to secure facilities. There is much resistance on the state level where building contracts for institutions are so politically attractive. Massachusetts de-institutionalized successfully in the early 1970s because of the leadership of the head of the state's child-care bureaucracy, Dr. Jerome Miller. Miller incurred the wrath of the AFL-CIO and the child-care workers who are dependent on the institution, but he freed the children.

CAN GOVERNMENT BUREAUCRACY ACT IN A CHILD'S BEST INTEREST?

It has always been the law that the state act in the "best interest" of the child, which is the doctrine of *parens patriae*. It has, unfortunately, been used by welfare bureaucrats to justify the separation of parent from child and the state regulation of that child. This is the doctrine that got children into these child care "warehouses." Can Judge Rubin's opinion and federal legislation solve the problem? I have serious reservations.

So many government regulations encourage the breakup rather than the promotion of the family entity. Children outside of their homes get cut off from their families by the agencies created to serve them. Although the government spends thousands of dollars a month per child for institutional care, the same states offer the parents little help to support that same child in the natural home.

In New Orleans, the foster care system places as many as 14 emotionally disturbed adolescents in the home of one foster mother. That foster mother probably didn't graduate from high school, and clearly has received no training in the treatment of emotionally disturbed adolescents. It seems that this is a system designed to fail.

The Louisiana Department of Health and Human Resources administers the child-caring business in Louisiana. Much money is spent on institutional care, yet they pay that mother with 14 emotionally disturbed foster children only $120.00 a month per child. Those same children are on their way to $3,000- and $4,000-per-month institutions. They end as failures with the help of numerous regulations and practices. We, as a society, pay the bill.

The foster father is not part of the system. We run our foster care system sending the check each month to a foster mother. The welfare worker does not ask about the father even though, in some cases, he's there. Brothers and sisters are sent to separate foster homes. When natural parents die or are otherwise not available, the relatives are not eligible for support payments. A child gets total strangers for foster parenst while the state refuses to give his aunt or uncle $120 a month for the child's care.

Many regulations discourage the continuation of the family relationship.

The structural design of the bureaucracy seems to create failure. There is duplication of effort and incredible gaps in service, and several state agencies can have jurisdiction over the same type of child. One agency may pay twice as much as the other for the same service. Each different agency will have a different response. We have no overall government policy on children.

Bureaucracy has been rewarded for failure. It has grown larger and fatter each time a child goes from the natural home to foster care to an institution. Foster care may only pay $120 per month, but foster care workers must be hired to administer the program. When the child graduates to the institution, we start talking about big money: construction contracts, doctors, social workers, guards and patronage jobs. Just the fire insurance on the institution can be lucrative to someone. An institution has a contract with a janitorial service who may be a political friend. Because we have not made clear a philosophy of child care, bureaucracy has developed a haphazard system that meets the needs of those who run the bureaucracy, but not that of the child.

RECOMMENDATIONS

We need to develop a national policy on children based on open public debate which must consider the needs and various alternatives to meet the needs. State and federal governments should spend more money encouraging the family unit to continue, and less on institutional care. Our track record as individual families is mixed in child rearing abilities, but our track record as a government caring for children is less than zero. America is a greatly diversified country, and its diversity makes it great. Variety of experience must be encouraged. Homogenized, unstimulating institutions stifle life and creativity. The separation of child from family is an extreme measure, and it should be done only after all other alternatives have failed. When the child is removed, it need not include removal from its community. The debate should discuss the need to develop alternatives and mechanisms to encourage continued varieties of educational and treatment modes.

Yet the immediate problem with the public attitude toward children is the pull the bureaucracy has on these attitudes. Many sincere and good people are afraid of change because of what it will do to their jobs, since restructuring the bureaucracy would threaten many jobs, and successfully reducing the bureaucracy would mean the abolition of jobs. The people working in this system understandably have a tendency to defend the institutions.

The coming public debate on a government policy towards children is inevitable. The lines are already drawn. On one side is the status quo of institutions. On the other side the battle cry is "deinstitutionalization." The manner in which we treat our children determines our future as a society. The outcome of this debate should have a major effect on our destiny.

SUMMARY

The movement to provide care for children in need now seems to have come full circle. We began by removing children from their homes and placing them in institutions for "the child's best interest." More likely than not, we neglected the child once he was institutionalized and turned our backs on the family and community that was the child's real home.

Now we realize the harm caused to the child by removing him from home instead of supporting the family. We are moving in a direction away from large "warehouse" institutions towards a policy of emphasizing keeping families together. It is ironic, yet a very important historic lesson, that the biggest obstacle to reform is a previously radical idea cast in concrete. The innovative treatment ideas now being suggested are hoped to replace the institutionalized result of our predecessor's radical ideas. We should work toward models that are more accepting of the reality of change.

REFERENCES

Children's Defense Fund (1977), *Children Without Homes.* Washington, D.C.

Coddington, B. D., Tabor, R. and McMillan, H. (1977), *The "Texas Children Children Project."* Presented at the American Orthopsychiatric Assoc. meeting, San Francisco, California, March 1977.

Education for All Handicapped Children Act (1975), Public Law 94-142.

Ex Parte Crouse (1839), 4 Whart. 9 (Pa.)

Gary W., et al. v. Louisiana (1976), 437 F. Supp. 1209.

Gault, In Re (1967), 387 U.S. 1.

Fox, S. J. (1970), Juvenile Justice Reform: An Historical Perspective. *Stan. L. Review* 22:1187-1239.

Juvenile Justice and Delinquency Prevention Act of 1974 (1974), 42 U.S.C. ⁵5601, et seq.

Kent v. United States (1966), 383 U.S. 541.

Law and Tactics in Juvenile Cases (1977), third edition, National Juvenile Law Center.

Provence, S. and Lipton, R.C. (1962), *Infants in Institutions.* New York: Int. Univ. Press.

Skeels, H. M. (1966), "Adult Status of Children With Contrasting Life Experiences," *Monograph of the Society for Research in Child Development,* 31(3):1–56.

Stone, J. and Church, J. (1957), *Childhood and Adolescence.* New York: Random House.

Winship, In Re (1970), 397 U.S. 358.

PART II
The Schools

4

Improving the
Relevance of Secondary
Education for Adolescent
Developmental Tasks

IRVING H. BERKOVITZ

Many professionals in mental health as well as in education have in recent years questioned whether the social organization of junior and senior high schools (grades 7-12) and the structures of the social systems that have been created meet the developmental needs of adolescents. Certainly the rise in rates of difficulties in relation to self and society in the teenage population cannot be attributed entirely to the state of educational practices. Yet the school must accept part of the responsibility. It is the institution after the family, where the majority of young people first find social and personal definition and meaning.

Therefore, the psycho-educational practices of schools deserve to be examined for both positive and negative influences. Secondary school personnel will be the first to identify correctly that they inherit the problems created or passed on by parents and elementary schools. Still, as many have stated (Blos, 1967; Pumpian-Mindlin, 1965) the adolescent years also provide the opportunity for repair of some of these earlier damages, or the possibilities for aggravation.

Educators have perennially tried to effect change in secondary education ever since the establishment of the first American public high schools in the

1800s. One of the recent attempts was the California Commission for the Reform of Intermediate and Secondary Education (RISE). This commission included 50 percent school personnel. Its 1975 report stated that

> Increasing numbers of young people find schooling boring and ineffective, unable to challenge their abilities, meet their goals, or prepare them for adulthood. Growing numbers of students, educators, parents and others find that education as a whole is out of step with real world needs and far behind current social changes.

> Mounting numbers of students are being "turned off" rather than "turned on" to schooling; these students are disinterested, not motivated, and many are actually doomed to failure in schools today.

These are indeed severe indictments! In this chapter, I shall attempt to examine some of the schools' attitudinal and structural features which may contribute to this unfortunate state of affairs and present some suggestions for possible remedies.

The developmental needs of adolescents have been described extensively in numerous writings. Berkovitz (1972, p. 6) described them as follows:

> (1) a greater enabling of interdependent autonomy. This would include emancipation from disabling attachments to parental demands and expectation but allow for a respectful appreciation of and reconciliation with positive qualities of parents and other adults; (2) reduction (but not crippling) of childhood narcissism, so that there is greater ability to respond to the worth of other individuals, beginning with peers; (3) enhancing appreciation for personal creative energies so that sustaining life goal and zest for what is available in living become more stable features in the personality; (4) a greater sense of sureness of self, in terms of familial, sexual and social identity, with a minimum of arrogance and rigidity.

A relevant question which some occasionally ask is, "Do adolescent's needs have to fit the school's needs, or should the schools meet the adolescent's needs?" This is a complex provocative question and not easily answered. In many ways it certainly is true that both adolescents and adults have to have needs met in schools. Ideally, the student should come first, but the educational establishment is an important employer of large numbers of adults who need to work for economic reasons, to gain self-realization, a feeling of importance, to express love and concern for children as well as other goals. Some school persons, it is true, become embittered and then turn anger on to students, or do their job in a less than ideal way. Just as with other professional groups in society, e.g. the legal, military, medical or judicial, etc. change, improvement and self-correction is slow.

Any large, complex system changes slowly. The educational system is unique in that it deals with young people, a part of society that has the fastest change rate. As a result, school practices often have difficulty keeping step with changes in student's needs. On top of this, the change rate for most adolescents is greater and more energetic than that for the younger children. Therefore, we often find a greater imbalance and clash between the needs of the adolescents and the secondary schools trying to provide for them. We in the mental health profession often are called upon to assist young people who have become the casualties of a seemingly insensitive, impersonal and rigid educational apparatus. However, rather than concentrate on individual cases, I would like to attend to reconciling needs of adolescents and adult staff in the systems of secondary schools.

Sociopolitical issues complicate the efforts of any parent, school person or consultant who enters schools to change the quality of school life for student or staff. But the need is present for constant efforts to effect change. In this connection, Berlin made the point relevant to all mental health professionals that we have to pay attention to the effects of schools on children's mental health or "we risk our credibility as professionals concerned with the mental health of children" (Berlin, 1975).

SOCIOPOLITICAL FACTORS

In trying to make changes one has to be aware of the many sociopolitical factors which often prevent well-intended educators from doing an optimum service for young people. It should be stressed that schools cannot be expected to correct all the evils of society. Schools are one more structure of society which by design, or accident, brings adults and young people together to transmit the learning of mankind and the tools developed in a society to help young people cope and grow in life. However, as with any structure devised by men, there are good, bad and changeable features. Some of the more specific sociopolitical elements which complicate changing this institution are as follows:

1) The quantity and pattern of financing public education which is influenced by legislators, governors, political lobbies and the voting public.

2) The teacher certifying process and the institution of teacher tenure which provides essential job protection for teachers, as well as influencing

quality control, training for new teachers and maintaining skills of experienced teachers.

3) The kinds of training provided by schools of education, as well as the in-service programs offered in school districts for teachers currently practicing, and,

4) The courses which colleges require for high school graduates to enter college, as well as those involved in the requirements of graduate and professional schools.

As an example of these sociopolitical and structural factors consider the following:

One of the traditional structural features of secondary schools often questioned, as well as defended, is the five period per week course schedule. It is of interest to learn the origins of this structure. In 1909 the Carnegie Unit was introduced into American secondary school education, related ironically to organizing a pension plan for college professors. It was decided that 14 units of secondary school work should be a minimum preparation for college work, and a unit was defined as a five-period-a-week class that was pursued throughout the school year.

Gorman, an educator, writing about the "high school America needs," stated,

> The Carnegie unit appears to rest upon an assumption that may be stated something like this: The learning of a high school student in a given field is directly proportionate to the hours he spends in an organized class in that field. This assumption remains unsubstantiated to this day. On the other hand, much has been learned about negative learnings since 1909. It has been demonstrated, for example, that additional hours spent by some students in the classes of some subjects may result most notably in a mounting distaste for the subject, that is, in a determination not to study the subject anymore, anywhere, under anyone. (Gorman, 1971, page 119).

Some schools have experimented with "modules," where 2-3 periods were allotted to selected subjects, e.g. art, and then not necessarily five days per week. I begin with these sociopolitical details not to discourage efforts at change, but to stress that effective attempts to change need to occur at several levels. Now the focus will briefly be on the psychodynamic part of adolescence.

It is not possible to discuss here in detail the developmental needs of adolescents of different ethnic minorities, i.e. multicultural needs, or the needs of the disadvantaged, handicapped and gifted adolescents. These teenagers have special needs and raise special issues which are important and significant. However, it is likely that the school situations to be discussed do apply equally to influencing the relevance of secondary education also for these groups of teenagers.

PSYCHODYNAMIC ASPECTS OF ADOLESCENTS IN SCHOOLS

The adolescent years, especially ages 12-15, involve a growth from dependence on previous adult authority. This growth may be minimal and unobtrusive, or maximal and violent. The pubertal hormonal change is related to this emancipatory thrust and provides as well a new reservoir of urgent energy which pushes for closeness, alternating with distance, to peers as well as adults. These new qualities could be concisely labelled the push to (1) action, (2) peer relations and (3) autonomy.

After age 16 (approximately) there are additional needs which show themselves, depending on the degree of resolution of the earlier needs. Issues such as identity, responsibility, commitment, management of job and possibly car, heterosexual relations, and college plans become more clearly defined daily issues. Cognitive, verbal intellectual interests *may* become stronger as well. The earlier period (12-15) coincides with junior high school (or intermediate school) and is closer to childhood. The period 16-18 coincides with high school, usually a more mature period.

A feature of "normal" adolescence which perplexes and often aggravates so many adults, especially parents and teachers, is the occurrence of regression, i.e. a return to younger, less mature behavior alternating with progression, i.e. an advance to new, more mature behavior. How often adults will say: "You were so grown up yesterday, why are you so childish today?" Anna Freud (1965), as well as others, have postulated that adolescents who cannot allow themselves to regress (within limits) are prone to rigidities and difficulty experiencing "normal" development in later years.

Many professionals feel that one of the contributants to adolescent difficulty is the loss of the extended family (Miller, 1970). Disruption of a relationship with parents results also in the disruption of relationships with other significant adults. In this hiatus, school systems, especially but not exclusively, are organizations of society that could provide adolescents with contexts in which they could continue to grow. In this regard, Miller (1970) made the relevant point that

A preoccupation with the way subjects are taught can ignore the importance of human relationships in the schools: of children to each other, of staff to children, and of teachers and pupils to parents.

The educator will usually stress the cognitive side of the adolescent development and the role of enhancing intellectual abilities. I would agree that pride in learning and growth of intellectual mastery can enhance self-esteem, a feeling of control and a satisfying sublimation of impulses for many adolescents. However, in many places, the traditional secondary school classroom of 30-50 adolescents who are seated five periods per week per subject listening restlessly or attentively to the respected teacher is under criticism (cf. RISE Commission) of not engaging the minds of the majority of adolescents. Possibly the three needs previously cited are not sufficiently fulfilled.

What James Coleman wrote in 1964, seems equally, or more, relevant today:

> Good grades and concentration upon studies are seen by the adolescent community, and rightly so, as acquiescence and conformity to adult constraints. By contrast, social affairs extracurricular activities, and athletics are activities of their "own," activities in which adolescents can carry out positive actions on their own, in contrast to school work, where they carry out "assignments" from teachers. Such assignments are galling to any community which feels itself at all autonomous.

This does not mean a call for a completely permissive non-demanding school setting. An essential need of young people in secondary schools is to find a group setting which accepts, supports and enhances each as a worthy individual, as well as teaching acceptance of reasonable demands and limits. Intrinsic to this will be the provision of cognitive training necessary to self-esteem as well as to understanding oneself and others, and finding a useful, rewarding place in adult society. Important additional needs would be developing relationship skills to facilitate enjoying intimacy needs in dyadic relations, as well as altruistic involvement in social goals.

SCHOOL PERSONNEL ATTITUDINAL FACTORS

In pointing out the need for structural changes in schools, clinically oriented professionals must observe judicious cautions. Understandably, educators may feel resentment and offer resistance, unless a mutually respecting dialogue has been achieved. It is always easy to tell the other guy how to do his job. Also, while at times structural changes can facilitate attitudinal changes, more often attitudinal changes are elusive, and hard to mandate. Too often educators are arbitrarily mandated to make changes decided upon by anonymous higher authorities. Often these changes are superficial and effect little change in pervasive problems, such as student-teacher relations, or intergenerational misunderstanding.

In secondary schools, an especially relevant attitudinal need often eludes well-intended structural changes—namely adolescent-adult communication. Educators especially those over 30, have the same difficulty as do others of that age group, when relating to adolescents who present other than cooperative and reasonable behavior. Mental health personnel do not always have perfect ease in this respect either. At times, the educator's cognitive, task-oriented, health-oriented, less emotionally oriented approach is effective and will engage, reorient and help the depressed or rebellious teenager to sublimate difficult feelings. At other times, the ability to empathize and briefly provide an interested ear may relieve a stress of the moment and allow clearer attention to the cognitive task. Many adults have difficulties moving easily between these two types of interaction. As well as a flexible assortment of relating techniques, personal knowedge of the individual student would certainly be of help. However in the average large urban secondary school the latter, especially, is often not available. In addition, if ethnic barriers are present between staff and students, effective communication, while not impossible, is that much more difficult.

This is but one of the several attitudinal difficulties common to adults working in any context with adolescents. Naturally they are also prevalent in school interactions. Change in these types of attitudes are often difficult and elusive. Some interventions which have been successful will be described. It is tempting when talking about schools to consider mainly changes in structure, financing, organization etc. These topics are certainly more tangibly subject to change. However it would be self-deceptive and lead to frustration to ignore certain important culturally prevalent attitudes. Let me start with the intergenerational issue.

SCHOOL ADULTS IN MIDLIFE

Most adults in schools are in the mid-life part of their development (ages 35 to 65). In mid-life one is, comparatively speaking, beginning to slow down. One has made commitments about such things as marriage, career, family, personal style, and standard of living. There still may be change going on, but for the most part ideas, value systems, and expectations are fairly firmly established. Sometimes there may be hopelessness and stagnation. Usually there is peaceful working at a job and a firm feeling about one's place in life. The emphasis can be labelled conservative, for the most part protecting one's investments, one's family, a more or less materialistic concern, a desire for stability, lesser change, and only moderate innovation. Of course there are exceptions to any of these generalities. Contrasting especially to the teenage period, is the fact of commitment involved in having made identity, career and other choices. Commitment involves giving up many other options. Many teenagers often feel omnipotential, immortal, beyond physical harm and able to do anything, "if I just want to do it, I can if I put my mind to it." This is the exciting and also at times aggravating aspect of teen attitudes. As an adult, one discovers that one has to specialize, focalize, concentrate, and give up some other interests, or at least limit them, occasionally painfully. Working in a school system often involves this narrowing, plus financial limitation.

Therefore, when an adult who has acquired some of these more conservative traits, comes face to face with a teenager whose life may still be somewhat in fantasy, there may be a discrepancy in understanding, if not an overt clash. It may be difficult for some adults to allow the adolescent testing of options or to tolerate somebody else having these options, without feeling envious, competitive, and over-concerned. Of course, teaching reasonable limits is often desirable and necessary.

In their attempt to expand freedoms many teenagers will challenge established limits and values in whatever system they may be involved. This challenge may be of a serious destructive nature, depending on the amount of anger a teenager is carrying into this period from earlier conflicts and situations. Or the challenge may be simply flexing muscles, especially if in other settings they were encouraged to ask questions and test limits. They may test limits to gain esteem in the eyes of peers, or be distracted from a temporary period of crisis by the excitment of the challenge. How to differentiate which elements may be involved in such a challenge is a very trying question for many adults, especially if they themselves have suppressed urges to challenge and needs to challenge.

Another more diffuse attitude is that unfortunately there is disrespect for teenagers in many parts of society. This may be due to larger size and the physical threat, the greater energy, the narcissistic push to make a place for oneself even at the expense of others, the pseudo-maturity and deceptive ability to use words and concepts of adulthood, masking the child part which is still operating internally, or numerous other reasons.

KNOWLEDGE OF PUBERTAL EFFECTS

School consultants have often been impressed by findings that many educators have lesser awareness and/or denial of the emotional and behavioral consequences of pubertal effects in young teenagers. This may be a useful, necessary blindspot to allow concentration on the intellectual functions, or the indication of defenses against these feelings, for individual personal reasons. Often, it indicates a gap in current educational training. Certainly the comfortable integration of sexual impulses and behavior with intellectual knowledge has not yet been achieved in many parts of American society, as well as in schools. In schools however, the result is that many efforts at sex education in the curriculum are inadequate or absent. This pressing, urgent part of adolescent development is then ignored or stigmatized. The opportunity for teaching responsible management and enjoyment of the new sexual ability is lost. The vital need for parent and family management training is gradually receiving greater acceptance and provision in many secondary schools, but not yet enough. Certainly community sensitivities and financial constraints play a part, but not entirely.

It is of interest that Inhelder and Piaget (1958) give puberty a status secondary to the intellectual. They deemphasize puberty as the "distinctive feature of adolescence," but highlight the "development of formal structures linked to maturation of cerebral structures. The individual begins to take up adult roles." I would agree that the changes of adolescence are too multiple and complex to be reduced only to the manifestations of hormonal changes. Role expectation and school experience do have a strong reciprocal influence on timing and type of entry into adulthood, and probably also on postpubertal impulsive action demands. These authors, so prominent in educational training, may well give support to educators' often unfortunate, minimizing of pubertal energies as a force in their student's actions, other than in obvious sexual activities.

ANGER BETWEEN ADULT AND TEENAGER

A greater knowledge and comfort with these parts of adolescent behavior, could well reduce feelings of threat in the educator. Spontaneous defensive behavior by the educator at times may provoke reactions which can escalate into dangerous and/or mutually defeating outcomes.

The following example, shows how a potentially minor incident can be inflamed to major proportions by inadvertent adult misjudgment.

Gail comes storming down the hall in school yelling that someone has stolen her Parker pen. The language is unbearable. A teacher stops her and starts to yell at her about her language. They both yell at each other for a short period of time. Students gather. The teacher grabs the student by the arm to take her to the office. She resists, calling the teacher names. In fact she attempts to hit the teacher and finally does. Other teachers join in and they take the girl to the office. The principal hearing the story suspends the girl because of her language and because she struck the teacher. Parents, teachers union, civil rights leaders, etc., enter the situation until finally she (the student) is reinstated. (DeCecco and Richards, 1974, p. 118)

DeCecco and Richards (1974) made a valid point that the same aggression aroused by conflict can be the well-spring for creative resolutions of it. They, along with many others, criticized the modern American high school, but recognized the potential for change. They stated (p. 14):

The clashes between young people and the school can result in apathy, bitterness or reform. They result in apathy and/or bitterness when the school denies students opportunities to express their frustration, impatience, and criticism, and fails to confront them. They can result in genuine reform when the school recognizes and respects both the conflict and compatibility in the goals of adults and young people.

Hacker (1972, p. 221) argues for controlled expression of aggression to reform and repair social institutions. The high school appears to be the social institution with greatest impact on the people who will run all the social institutions of the future. It makes its impact on these people in terms of teaching them to handle their aggressions in the way that will be appropriate for them as adults. The choice is whether to teach students that verbal aggression should be stifled (with the potential increase in violent physical expressions of aggression) or to show them how to use their aggression in verbal forms that serve the varied purposes Hacker suggests.

DeCecco and Richards (1974) conducted interviews during 1969 and 1973 with 6,783 urban and suburban elementary, junior and senior high school students and staff of many socioeconomic and ethnic levels from which they analyzed the ingredients of conflict in secondary schools.

The findings are disturbing: school authorities used force in 716 incidents (about 11%), while students used force with other students in 376 incidents (about 5%) of the time. Against school authorities the students used force in 192 incidents (about 3%).

A follow-up study (DeCecco, 1971) showed that teachers, when given explicit choices of negotiation vs. decision by authority or force, choose "negotiation" as a way of getting the student to "cooperate," and then, when the student resists, resort to force before they consider mediating the conflict with the help of third parties. This study also found that outside of school, teachers resort to force in dealing with children more often than they do in school.

MENTAL HEALTH CONSULTATION

These findings are not cited to place prime responsibility on the adults in the situation. Many teenagers have acquired skills in knowing how to manipulate, provoke and otherwise "press the buttons" of adults, especially educators. Educators (as well as parents) need mutual support groups to help pool knowledge and techniques on how to deal with the wily, provocative or needy teenager, especially in the difficult outnumbered context of the classroom. It is all too easy to lose control. If one has been a camp counselor or a parent, one may have become more versed with effective self-control and action. In some cases mental health consultation (Berkovitz and Newman, 1980; Berkovitz, 1980) can help develop these skills. Occasionally, consultation may provide help for educators who carry unresolved issues from their own adolescences which color and interfere with their reactions to adolescent students. Personal psychotherapy at times would be useful (Jersild and Lazar, 1962). Mental health consultation cannot serve as personal therapy, but at times may facilitate the comfortable surfacing and amelioration of maladaptive attitudes to adolescents, especially in group consultation where peer support can foster gradual change. For more specific examples of the ways mental health consultation can effect change in school personnel attitudes, the reader is referred to other more extended articles (Berkovitz and Newman, 1980; Berkovitz, 1980).

FEMALE ROLE CHOICE

Another attitudinal and curricular part of school practices which frequently does not answer the needs of adolescents is the stereotypic and biased role choices offered to female adolescents in many secondary schools.

Societies and schools often foster limiting stereotypes which restrict choices for optimum individual female development. Many of these stereotypes are changing in schools, especially since Title IX of of the Higher Education Act of 1972.

Restrictive stereotypes may occur in peer group and faculty attitudes, textbooks, tests and counseling assistance, among other places. These stereotypes often involve a view of the female as passive, submissive, less assertive and less competitive, pleasing others more than self, less active physically, often less capable than males generally, but especially in math, science, and technical subjects. In addition, vocationally, women are often depicted as mothers, nurses, secretaries, teachers, etc. rather than in a wider range of occupations. Often some of these stereotypes are related to and reenforced by what seems required to obtain a man's regard and companionship.

For education to prepare women for freer, less conflicted adult roles and personalities, many of these prevalent stereotypes and rigid role-options need to be modified. A more conscious examination of changing societal roles and unconscious cultural biases needs to be a part of every woman's education to facilitate optimum choice making. Men should have this available as well, since reciprocal stereotypes occur for men and hamper comfort of male choice as well (Berkovitz, 1980).

STUDENT INFLUENCE ON SCHOOL MILIEU

An essential goal of adolescent development is the ability to be able to make responsible decisions and have the courage to seek and accept leadership positions which will then be exercised in an honest and nonarrogant manner. Above all it is desirable that the adolescent enter adulthood with the feeling that speaking one's mind is meaningful and that this will be given appropriate respect by peer and adult communities. Many students will find arenas for these abilities in elections for student government positions and other campus activities, e.g. newspaper, drama, sports, etc. In recent years many students have felt disinterested or hopeless about the real effectiveness of traditional student offices. During times of ferment, informal nontraditional organizations have been organized, e.g., Brown Berets and Black Student Union. In these organizations many students who felt excluded from or opposed to traditional organizations were able to develop the ability to exercise leadership. One psychiatric consultant (Black, 1975) was able to provide a discussion forum for leaders in these groups and help them to see the extent of their power and how to develop effective methods. Several students of this group then made plans to attend college, partly as a result of these discussions. Occasionally educators fear the formation of these types of groups and isolate the leaders and members to peripheral positions rather than to include them in the legitimate educational process. The alienated student will occasionally rejoin the peer group after an experience in such an indigenous group.

There certainly will be times when students' actions will be inflammatory, militant, crude or in poor taste. Some monitoring is necessary, but the degree of censorship can often determine whether a campus is muted and repressive or open, exciting and bubbling with new ideas and discussion. One such experience of opening up discussion in a previously troubled school is described by Sarchet, et al. (1975). Here, groups consisting of one administrator, four teachers, and eight students met in discussion weekly, during their free period, to discuss various aspects of school life, e.g. dress codes, teaching methods, student behavior, or campus cleanliness. The evaluation after 10 meetings was as follows:

> Some students told teachers how they "turn them off." The teacher began to work on ways of avoiding this.
>
> A senior observed: "I've noticed teachers thinking at a younger level. They don't just go by the book. They deal with you as a person and try to find out about the problem. Not that they're more lenient—they have found another way to think out the problem. What we asked for we got. Younger teachers are being hired. The whole attitude has a younger look. At other schools you can't see the change; at this one you can. Teachers are like jailers elsewhere."
>
> Another student said, "I have a chance to talk in these groups to a kind of student I'm never in touch with otherwise."
>
> Students said they would rather discuss matters in the group than with their counselors.
>
> A freshman reported, "I told the teachers some kids getting F's are the teacher's responsibility—the class is not interesting. They listened!"

Later evaluation concluded that

> During 1969 and the hectic early '70s, when militance was a feature of many campuses, discussion groups allowed straightforward communication and personal contact to take place between staff and students. The open communication which resulted from the groups was effective in deterring destructive confrontations that might otherwise have occurred.
>
> Survey of the groups has shown that students have continued their positive feelings about group participation longer than have teachers. Students value the groups as providing them with an opportunity for personal communication and a place to have an effect on the institution. They can accept the low-key discussions, but the teachers tend to feel a stronger need for demonstrated results.
>
> Several spin-off programs have come from the personal interest generated by the groups. One of these is a teacher-advisor program in

which teachers select from their classes 10 students for whom they provide more educational and personal support when needed. More personal involvement of classroom teachers with individual students has resulted.

By utilizing skills in discussion techniques gained by staff members, it has been possible in several instances to bring together students from varied backgrounds for a series of discussions aimed at solving specific problems. For example, to deal with some of the hostility between neighborhood gangs in the attendance area, a series of meetings was held which included student leaders from several of the gangs. Two other schools in the district have developed their own versions of this group program.

STRUCTURAL PROBLEMS

Without losing sight of the primacy of these attitudinal factors, let me focus on some structural changes which might possibly reduce obstacles to school personnel providing more ideally for the necessary adolescent developmental needs. The move from the smaller elementary school to the larger secondary school gives the maturing teenager objective validation of maturation and accomplishment, as well as a new adaptive challenge. However, there also occurs the unfortunate, and to some students a troubling, disruption of social and intrapsychic stability. In the words of Miller (1970):

It appears reasonable to assume that when early adolescents are undergoing acute internal upheaval, they should remain in a stable social environment. If a school change occurs from grade school to junior high school at the age of about 12, for grades 7, 8, and 9, most adolescents will change school at a time of maximum internal conflict.

Fortunately many students are able to reestablish a stability with the help of available understanding teachers, counselors, peers, etc. However, there then may be the loss of these new relationships by relocation from junior high school to the high school:

A move from junior to senior high school at 14 to 15 means that many adolescents give up on the possiblity of making relationships with adults. As a result, the early adolescent over-preoccupation with their own age group continues and the intergeneration gap is really under way (Miller, 1970).

Miller (1970) suggested that changing school location at grades 5 and 9 would be preferable to the traditional changing at grades 6 and 10. In addition, he recommended that

1) To facilitate better relations with the adult staff some teachers should stay with the students for two or three years, and not always to have the day broken into five or six periods which prevents any sustained prolonged relationship.

2) To make the lunch breaks longer and have recess periods through all the school grades for more learning and significant contact with teachers and peers.

3) Divide the large school into smaller social units covering all grades.

It is of interest that the RISE Commission (1975) without knowing of Miller's suggestions, came up with a set of similar suggestions. In addition, they added emphasis on providing more community activities as a part of the curriculum, but without ignoring traditional library and classroom formats.

Community locations might include business and industrial sites, public service agencies, and cultural centers. For example, an art appreciation activity might be conducted at a public museum and/or a private gallery; or a consumer education program might take place at a city office for consumer affairs.

Learners should have the opportunity upon request to be assigned to an actual work situation related to that learner's interests, career objectives, and maturity. For example, a learner interested in veterinary medicine or in caring for confined animals, might gain experience at a municipal animal shelter, learning while performing a public service and possibly earning a salary.

School times (hours, days, months, even years) should be flexible, extensive, and varied enough to accommodate a diversity of learner interests, styles, needs, and choices. Instruction and all other educational services—such as counseling, libraries, learning centers and recreational facilities—should be available to learners throughout this expanded time schedule. (RISE, 1975)

These changes would of course make the need for numerous costly changes in existing school practices. Some school districts have already made steps in these directions. The RISE Commission made other recommendations for relaxation of attendance requirements.

School attendance requirements should allow a learner to leave school temporarily with the approval of the learner's parents and the school. These furloughs should be of flexible duration, of educational value to the learner and consistent with the learner's educational needs and objectives. Local guidelines should be developed to provide continual contact between the learner and the school to ease the reentry of the learner into the school system when the furlough is completed.

In talking generally about adolescents, or secondary school students, we must keep in mind the diversity of individuals in such a large group. This group will probably include the gifted, retarded, and delinquent. Special school programs will be necessary for many, and already exist in various degrees of quality and adequacy. This is especially so for the unique individuals at each end of the spectrum i.e., the gifted and the retarded or handicapped. Recently, Public Law 94-142 authorized more school services for the latter group. These programs merit a special discussion of how schools do or do not meet the developmental needs of handicapped or gifted students. Space does not allow this discussion in this chapter.

The 60-80% in the middle section of the bell curve are the ones on whom I am focusing. Many of this group have the potential for involvement, gaining joy in learning and the exercise of mastery. Many of these will find a good teacher (or several) even in traditional classrooms and go on to learn. Many will become scholars, enter professions, white or blue collar jobs, etc. However, many more turn off, or just get by. Many schools have discovered that some turned off students will gain new motivation in smaller, more open, and occasionally community-oriented learning environments. More will be said of these structural innovations later.

It may be clear, also that to achieve the previously described goals and changes, would require retraining of many school staff, as well as obtaining additional staff and finances. Tenure rules often prevent release of some staff and obtaining new personnel. Some have suggested allowing voluntary course selection by students. However, this is feared as possibly resulting in a popularity poll by students, as well as teacher salesmanship and unfair pressure in competition. Opening the structure as described above might allow more flexible use of some staff.

At times, community activities of students may lead to conflict with the community, so that containment in the classrooms may be preferred by some adult members of the community. For example, one eighth-grade class studying urban renewal and housing construction patterns uncovered political questions which caused uncomfortable feelings in some members of the school board and the city council. However, the improvement in school attendance and learning in this, as well as the other experimental classes, was so striking that the program was preserved despite the uncomfortable feelings (Berlin, 1972).

Role of Support Staff Personnel

The support staff, i.e. psychologists, counselors, nurses, counselor aides, even administrators, are personnel who could help classroom teachers and adolescents more than is currently being fostered in schools. Many investigators feel that an insensitive school structure can push sensitive vulnerable young people into more acute difficulties. Support staff could ameliorate some of these. Unfortunately, finances and level of mental health expertise often interfere.

Most often these support personnel confine themselves to rescuing casualties, and dealing with psychopathology, rather than helping with those not yet in difficulty. Yet the help they do provide can rescue many young people from needing clinical services. The previously described role of the mental health consultant from an agency outside the school system, who has become a trusted guest and friend is important here. The consultant can assist this group of personnel to provide some buffer to the previously described shortcomings in providing adequately for adolescent developmental needs.

Further Structural Change

Considering all these criticisms and suggestions for modifying the traditional structure of the secondary schools, one might ask, what is there to maintain about the existing structure? Certainly some would like to change this radically (Holt, 1976). For example, Illich (1970) felt that "deschooling" society is desirable. He would distribute children in the community to work individually or in small groups with chosen individuals who could be considered good teachers, very much in an apprenticeship relationship. Illich's recommendations have been criticized as impractical in many places, especially for educating the present large number of children, and considering the technical needs of our society. However, it does raise the question of differential education, namely, a work education for some, and an academic technical education for others, very much as once occurred in England and possibly other European countries (Scharff, 1975).

Without being planned as deliberately, this may be already occurring in the United States. For example, in 1967 approximately one fourth of America's youth did not acquire a high school diploma (Statistical Abstract, 1967). An additional 15-25% were psychological dropouts.

They are forced by social and economic pressure to hang on and secure the symbol of persistent attendance although they never really enter into the mainstream of the schools' opportunities (Gorman, 1971, p. 5).

This 40-50% however may be making a less confident entry into the work force than if this entry had been structured more deliberately at the beginning of their secondary school careers. In rebuttal to the advocacy for more vocational and community types of education, Gorman (1971, p. 39) defended providing a general education to all children.

In the last analysis, the truck driver whose formal education ended with high school and whose job for hours on end often demands little mental energy, has both more time and perhaps more inclination to reflect upon a Hemingway novel or Socrates' theory of immortal life than has the insurance executive who acquired a B.S. in Business Administration.

There is one outstanding feature of too many American secondary schools, especially in larger cities which may offer inherent obstruction to optimal development for many adolescents in schools. This feature is large size, especially above 1,500 students. It is likely that units of 400-500 (or less) within a large student body can more easily provide the feeling of kinship to allow a less harried, more individualized learning experience, and a more considered chance to work on life goals or personal development issues. If large secondary schools are necessary, building them up from units of this size and providing central audio-visual, laboratory, gym, etc. facilities would provide the advantages of a large campus, as well as the more manageable immediate environment. The RISE Commission (1975) saw this as a relevant need.

Groupings of learners should be small enough to offer a psychological atmosphere that promotes the development of the learner's self-worth and identity within the school and community. For example, a school with a large enrollment might be divided into several smaller schools within a school to insure a more personalized setting.

This structural change is one that may well allow for the correction of several of the undesirable features described above. However, as with any change, without appropriate safeguards and cautions, old problems can simply be reestablished in new structures.

The plan could involve several small units on one campus. Large lectures can be provided as a balance to the smaller study and work groups. The possibility of a narrow inbred quality, dominated by 1-2 stronger teachers is possible and would require scrutiny by a central leadership. But the differences from the busy city square atmosphere to the calm deliberative learning atmosphere is a meritorious possibility.

Too much staff energy is today directed into elements of control with the result that problems are as often made as solved (Gorman, 1971).

The ethnic and racial conflict on many urban campuses could be less inflamed by the chance to know each other as persons rather than anonymous skin colors. There have been several examples of ethnic confrontations in small groups leading to better understanding (Kaplan, 1975) and exploration of alternatives to violence (O'Shea, 1972; Leong, 1975).

Gorman (1971) in his speculations about the high school needed for the year 1990, cited the need for several features:

1) Encouragement of a sense of personal and social responsibility.
2) Faith in pupil desire and capacity.
3) Cultivation of self education.
4) The house plan of about 200 students—to build better "identity with a unit with a solid social community, to facilitate "more fully the degree to which students learn from each other, the ways in which they support and give confidence to each other. This is not to neglect the cognitive task: "teacher knowledge of learner interest and activity facilitates the introduction of many more student projects that cross subject-matter boundaries."

The effects of current college placement testing practices cannot be overlooked. The heavy emphasis in these crucial tests of verbal, cognitive knowledge forces high schools to promote learning these abilities. The more esthetic, creative, spatial, nonverbal abilities and parts of adolescent thinking are therefore given secondary importance. No doubt many other changes than those mentioned may be possible and needed to help schools promote more healthy, productive development in adolescent students. While I have underlined many of the less helpful features of secondary school experience, let us not overlook some of the positive values which do exist. Certainly prime practical goals for most adolescents are vocational or college preparation and planning. As important but unfortunately often more difficult is the task of equipping young people with the maximum self-realization, adjustment, sense of responsibility, well-rounded general knowledge, and the judgment to be informed citizens. An important part of this is the opportunity for teenagers to learn optimum ways of relating to each other, for achieving dyadic intimacy as well as wider altruism.

SUMMARY

Secondary school experience provides important support and enhancement for adolescent development. However, educators and mental health professionals have been aware for many years that secondary education has also had defects in providing relevant education for a large number of teenagers. Schools alone are not at fault but they may share society's difficulties in providing adolescents with a meaningful, participatory role. Yet, possibly schools could contribute more effectively to adolescent development, if certain attitudinal and structural changes could be implemented.

It is especially relevant that mental health personnel become instigators of some of these change attempts. Various sociopolitical realities of school operation need to be kept in mind as well. Some of these realities are school financing, teacher certification and tenure practices, in-service training, programs in schools of education, college requirements for high school graduates, and other factors.

Often the academic and organizational emphasis of school procedures interferes with necessary attention or opportunity for adolescents to learn optimal relating with peers, adults and self. Yet, attention to academic skills is equally important to development of self-esteem and coping skills. Various attitudinal positions of school personnel can at times interfere with mutual satisfaction and beneficial relations to students. These attitude difficulties relating to teenagers are prevalent in many adults, but are especially crucial in school personnel.

Some of these attitudes relate to the fact that most school personnel are adults experiencing midlife types of readjustments, which can reduce the ability to have the necessary tolerance, understanding and reactivity for the more energetic and more self-centered adolescent behavior. Appropriate knowledge of the effects of pubertal development on younger teenage behavior is often deficient especially in school personnel. Anger between adult and teenager can often get out of control and interfere with adolescent development as well as school function. The adolescent's need for education in negotiation and the processing of anger is furthered when adults know more about their own anger.

Mental health consultation is a technique which has been used to effect change and improve some of the attitudes which can interfere with optimal communication between school personnel and adolescent students. Some structural features of school function also can interfere with facilitating optimum adolescent development. Some of these structural difficulties relate to stresses in junior high school and adequate support systems for relating to peers and teachers.

While the recommendations may be of specific value in helping secondary education be more relevant to adolescent development, there are many other efforts and suggestions continuously offered by educators and non-educators. The process of adult-adolescent intergenerational mutual learning and teaching is a vital, endless part of every generation's maturation.

REFERENCES

Berkovitz, I. H. (1972), *Adolescents Grow in Groups: Experiences in Adolescent Group Psychotherapy,* I. H. Berkovitz (Ed.), New York: Brunner/Mazel.

Berkovitz, I. H. (1979), Effects of Secondary School Experiences on Adolescent Female Development. In M. Sugar (Ed.), *Female Adolescent Development,* New York: Brunner/Mazel.

———— (1980), School Interventions: Case Management and School Mental Health Consultation. In G. P. Sholevar, R. M. Benson, and B. J. Blinder (Ed.), *Treatment of Emotional Disorders in Children and Adolescents,* New York: Spectrum Publications (In Press).

———— and Newman, L. E. (1980), School Consultation—Techniques of Primary Prevention. In D. P. Cantwell and P. E. Tanguay (Ed.), *Clinical Child Psychiatry,* New York: Spectrum Publications (In Press).

Berlin, I. N. (1972), The school's role in a participatory democracy. *Amer. J. Orthopsychiat.* 42:499-508.

Berlin, I. N. (1975), Child psychiatry perspectives: Professional competence, public confidence and children's rights. *J. Am. Acad. Child Psychiat.* 16:748-752.

Black, S. (1975), A High School Leadership Group. In I. H. Berkovitz (Ed.), *When Schools Care,* New York: Brunner/Mazel.

Blos, P. (1967), The second individuation process of adolescence. *Psychoanal. Study Child* 22:162-186.

Coleman, J. S. (1964), The Competition for Adolescent Energies. In F. R. Cyphert, E. W. Harmer, and A. C. Riccio (Ed.), *Teaching in the American Secondary School.* Selected Readings, New York: McGraw-Hill.

DeCecco, J. P. (1971), Attitude change in the classroom. *Encyclopedia of Education,* New York: Macmillan, 1:396-402.

DeCecco, J. P. and Richards, A. K. (1974), *Growing Pains, Uses of School Conflict,* New York: Aberdeen Press.

Freud, A. (1965), *Normality and Pathology in Childhood,* New York: International Universities Press, pp. 62-107.

Gorman. B. W. (1971). *Secondary Education, The High School America Needs*, New York: Random House.

Hacker. F. J. (1972). Sublimation revisited. *Int. J. Psychoanal.* 53:219-223.

Holt. J. (1976). *Instead of Education*, New York: Penguin Books.

Illich. I. (1970). *Deschooling Society*, New York: Harper & Row.

Inhelder. B. and Piaget. J. (1958). *The Growth of Logical Thinking*, New York: Basic Books.

Jersild. A. T. and Lazar. E. A. (1962). *The Meaning of Psychotherapy in the Teacher's Life and Work*, New York: Columbia University Press.

Kaplan. C. (1975). Ethnic Issues in School Group Counseling. In I. H. Berkovitz (Ed.). *When Schools Care*, New York: Brunner/Mazel.

Leong. W. (1975). A Total Commitment Group Counseling Program in an Inner City High School. In I. H. Berkovitz (Ed.). *When Schools Care*, New York: Brunner/Mazel.

Miller. D. (1970). Adolescents and the high school system. *Comm. Men. Health J.* 6:483-491.

O'Shea. C. (1972). "Two Gray Cats Learn How It Is" in a Group of Black Teenagers. In I. H. Berkovitz (Ed.). *Adolescents Grow in Groups*, New York: Brunner/Mazel.

Pumpian-Mindlin. E. (1965). Omnipotentiality. youth and commitment. *J. Am. Acad. Child Psychiat.* 4:1-18.

Report of the California Commission for Reform of Intermediate and Secondary Education (1975) California State Department of Education. Sacramento. California.

Sarchet. J., Jines. J., and Haines. G. (1975). Fostering Hope and Responsibility in the High School by Student-Teacher Administrator Discussion Groups. In I. H. Berkovitz (Ed.). *When Schools Care*, New York: Brunner/Mazel.

Scharff. D. E. (1975). The Transition from School to Work: Groups in London High Schools. In I. H. Berkovitz (Ed.). *When Schools Care*, New York: Brunner/Mazel.

Statistical Abstract of the United States. Bureau of Commerce (1967) Washington. D. C. Government Printing Office. p. 118.

5

Cultural Degradation and Minority Student Adaptations: The School Experience and Minority Adjustment Contingencies*

GEORGE W. NOBLIT
THOMAS W. COLLINS

The recent controversies over school desegregation have largely focused upon the problems of whites in desegregated schools and the problems of school systems in successfully implementing desegregation. These controversies have largely overshadowed the original concern of desegregation with providing equal educational opportunity for minorities. Somehow we have assumed that school desegregation has solved the educational problems of minorities. Unfortunately that is not the case. The many concerns that emerged in the urban education debates of the 1960s are still quite salient. Schools still are somewhat alien and alienating for minorities. Their cultures are degraded and they respond. This chapter examines this situation in a southern desegregated high school.

* The research upon which this article is based was performed pursuant to Contract 400-76-009 with the Field Studies in Urban Desegregated Schools Program of the National Institute of Education. It does not, however, necessarily reflect the views of that agency.

RESEARCH PROCEDURES

The data for this investigation were drawn from an ethnographic study of a desegregated high school with approximately 500 students in the south. The study, funded by the National Institute of Education, took place over two years, and was primarily geared to investigate the process of interracial schooling. The data were gathered via intensive, unstructured interviews, observations, and document review conducted primarily by the authors of this paper.

It is important to review the nature of ethnographic research, since it is a technique often misunderstood by nonanthropologists. Spicer (1976) argues that ethnographic research is emic, holistic, historical, and comparative in nature. That is, it gathers data directly from the people involved in the categories that are relevant to them (emic); it places events in context of the total experience under study (holistic); it incorporates history as a natural event in the studied experience (historical); and it considers and compares the various classes of events that make up that experience (comparative).

Further, the collection and analysis of ethnographic data is conducted under rigorous rules of analytic induction. The most significant of these rules for data analysis concerns data exhaustion. Simply put, a hypothesis that is inductively derived must explain all the data relative to the relationships and classes of events contained in the hypothesis. If the "heuristic" hypothesis does not meet this standard, then either it must be modified so that all data are exhausted by it or a substitute hypothesis must be formulated that satisfies the standard. In short, an ethnographic analysis and/or synthesis is "true" for all relevant data collected, even though it may not be generalizable across other settings. Further discussion of the ethnographic technique and a response to its critics can be found in Noblit (1977).

Finally, it should be noted that ethnographic data is best used to gain an interpretive understanding of an experience or event, and as such is vital to deriving a scientific proof concerning the nature of the experience or event. Both interpretive understanding and causal explanation (as derived from enumerative research strategies) are necessary to satisfy the notion of a scientific proof (Turner and Carr, 1976).

The School

Crossover High School (a pseudonym) was built in 1948, and graduated its first class in 1951. The structure was built on a 35-acre tract of land for the expanding residential areas of a southern city. From the beginning, its program, kindergarten through twelfth grade, was established as a sort of college-prep school for the children of this economically affluent area of the city. In reflection of the political character of the community, the district boundaries were simply gerrymandered to exclude most children of working-class parents. And, of course, the dual system that existed under total racial segregation excluded the black children from the neighborhood of Crossover located two blocks to the north, just across the tracks.

With this highly homogeneous school population, the academic program of Crossover High School (CHS) developed a reputation for excellence. Regularly, 95% of the senior graduating class enrolled in college. In one year during the 1950's, there were eleven Merit Scholar students in one graduating class. Many of the local influential middle-management executives, professional people, and political leaders are graduates of CHS. During the 1950s and 1960s competition at the school was intense across the gamut of academics through the available social activities, and parents supported the school financially and spiritually.

The all-white faculty found the teaching situation highly attractive at Crossover. They received the best equipment and generous volunteer support. Only select teachers were permitted to transfer to Crossover, and only the very best maintained a position. Hence, the teacher turnover up until 1969 was minimal.

In a 1972 desegregation plan, the black neighborhood of Crossover, located just across some railroad tracks from CHS, was included in the school district. Not unlike other black enclaves in residential areas of southern cities, the community was established early in the century to house a labor force for service in white homes and businesses. While the sense of community is strong in the neighborhood, it is plagued by property, violent, and victimless crimes. In many ways, it can be characterized as a "street corner society."

The former black high school (now a feeder junior high school for CHS) was a source of pride for the neighborhood. Business and parent groups, as with the segregated CHS, were active supporters of the school.

Needless to say, both black and white communities were apprehensive about pairing and desegregation of Feeder School and CHS, and responded with mixed emotions. When desegregation was ordered in 1972, most white parents with children in the senior high permitted them to remain and graduate. But many parents with students in the junior high, particularly girls, removed them to private schools rather than send them to what was considered an inferior black junior high school. The black community had no choice but to comply. The white principal at Crossover High School resigned rather than face the inevitable problems of desegregation.

Thus, the black principal at Feeder, with half his staff, moved to take charge of a desegregated Crossover High in September 1972.

Results

The incompatability of the education and desegregation goals for education led to interesting patterns in Crossover High School. As it turned out, the efficacy of the desegregation efforts became highly dependent upon keeping whites, students and instructors, in the school, for without them no desegregation would have occurred. This requisite had two effects. First, it prompted the principal to allow the white students and teachers some disproportionate influence in the school setting. Even as the school became majority black, the student council, clubs, and honors remained controlled by an elite white student network while the athletic program became largely black. The white, "old guard" teachers became the protectors of academic standards ("education") and the accelerated courses which provided the skill backgrounds that were of use to those who planned to continue on to college. The black teachers and a network of inexperienced teachers, black and white (whom we came to call the "motleys"), were relegated to the standard curricular offerings and, as the principal saw it, to "integration." The net result of the incompatible goal was simple resegregation essentially along lines of ability. The "old guard" taught the elite, white students and a smattering of black students, and advised the school organizations that these students controlled. The black teachers and the "motleys" taught classes populated by lower class whites and blacks, with the latter being in the majority. Desegregation had its most meaningful test in the standard curriculum since there were few selection criteria for such courses. The accelerated courses had more stringent criteria and included few blacks.

The resegregation was the result of two factors: the requisites for selection and success in the accelerated curriculum and the contingencies that faced the minority students who wished to satisfy those requisites.

Negotiating Success

Obviously, it can be argued that there are formal and informal requisites for selection to, and success in, the accelerated curriculum. However, the students, particularly those students who had some difficulty in negotiating the attainment of the requisites, were most likely to "ground" these formal requisites in their interactional context and thus saw the distinction between formal and informal as blurred if not nonexistent. The "old guard" and elite white students saw a high grade point average, teacher's recommendations and a determination of the students' interest and abilities (often by the guidance counselor) as the formal requisites, and promoted strict adherence to these standards even when it resulted in the enrollment in these classes being so low that they could no longer be offered. When accelerated courses began to be eliminated because of low enrollments, the "old guard" held their standards and watched their curriculum dwindle. In this context, the minority students suffered not only from degradation, but also from the emergent contingencies that were imposed on them by the school.

Suttles (1968, p. 58) argued that the ethnic ownership of schools defines the adaptation expected of the less powerful group:

> Schools . . . are consigned to ethnic groups on multiple criteria: location, precedent, the ethnicity of staff and the ethnicity of the student body. Where all these criteria coincide, the minority group students may take on the ingratiating manner of a humble guest. With this behaviour they can survive and sometimes even advance. . . . If they do not accept this status they must fend for themselves.

His analysis is especially poignant in the case of CHS, as suggested by two comments by black students: "If we had stayed at Feeder (the former black high school) none of this would have ever happened. Everybody wouldn't be turning black and white," and "Once we went to Crossover everybody cared about what the white folks were doing." The black students were rarely admitted to the accelerated courses; the grade point averages, teacher recommendations, and the counselor's estimation of interests and abilities were sufficient to relegate most black students to the basic or standard course offerings. However, many blacks wished access to the college preparatory curriculum, and those who desired such access "understood" that their success required "acting white." These students made a conscious effort to "take on" or emphasize those attitudes and traits that characterized elite white students. This emulation included behavior, dress, and linguistic patterns. Membership in certain school clubs and participation in selected school activities were seen as mechanisms to solidify their claim to academic and, ultimately, economic success. Nevertheless, the whites controlled the advanced curriculum and the prestige clubs and activities. All in all, the proficient black student was required to publicly renounce his or her ethnic heritage for the chance of success. Those students who had few prospects for the accelerated curriculum, high social status, and college saw this transition. As one of these students argued:

> Carl—his kind is trying to act white. Do you know Susan? She forgot she is black, she dresses white, she acts white, she even talks white.

Darryl is an Oreo, he's busy getting his titles. Blacks working in the office ain't really black, just look at Greg. Paulette turned white for a while but now she has turned back black. David is just like a white boy.

However, this is not just the biased account of one of the losers, for the school continued to be a threat even for the more successful. For example, even if admitted to the accelerated curriculum the sucessful black student still had to face standardized college entrance examinations, often noted for their cultural bias. As one of the more successful students explained:

I know I'm just a token for the whites as chaplain for the Student Council. I want desperately to go to college but there's no way I can pass the ACT. I belong to several clubs so it will look good on my college application and in the yearbook. I made a 7 on the ACT but I will retake it and if I can make a 12 I want to go to the State University. If not, I will try for the local community college and transfer to the State University.

Another successful black student concurred:

I belong to several clubs because I need this for my application for college. I have a 3.0 grade average.

The proficient black students found it necessary to manipulate the building of their credentials in as many ways. Almost universally, however, it was required that these students "act white." A commonly expressed opinion by black students was

White students have more freedom and are disciplined less. If you want to get ahead you have to act white. The teachers like you if you act white. If you act white you get better grades.

The relatively proficient black students found success and their ethnic heritage to be in direct contradiction. They had to reject their culture for the purposes of schooling; the contingencies of success at CHS required it and they adapted. Nevertheless, the adaptation taught many lessons, not the least of which was to distrust whites:

This is all in just learning how to deal with these devils. Even in petty things . . . they will use trickery if need be.

The examples of the distrust of whites were many in the accounts of the interviews with these students:

He said black students loved to participate in club meetings, but the majority of meetings where you really had fun or really got into something were held at white students' houses that were far from the school. These meetings were usually held at night and black students did not have transportation to get to them. He thought this was just another extension of the white people being tricky. He felt that they knew that black students couldn't come out to their houses, so therefore they couldn't have that much input into the clubs the whites wanted to control.

Even tokenism was thought to indicate trickery:

Cordette Crane was a black student. She was on the student council, she was a majorette and homecoming queen. She had lots of activities. She was the only black asked to participate on the prom committee. She was appointed, it was believed, as a joke. It was argued that these white people knew Cordette would not actively participate on the prom committee because she was out for popularity. She just had too many activities to want to really get into the prom committee.

One of the black members of our research team commented in her account of an interview with one of the highly successful black students,

These are my personal comments on Clark Dane. Clark is not a bitter student; he may seem so from the conversation given you, but this is taken out of context. Clark is not bitter, does not hate white people. He likes white people, but it stresses him that you have to treat these people with a long-handled spoon. Anytime you get a white friend, you just cannot trust him. He talked about Mary Wells. This was one of the so-called white liberals. He said that even he had caught her at certain things that she wouldn't want her black friends to know. He said he would never want to go back to the segregated environment because integration had taught him how to deal with white people, what they expected. He felt they had taught him how to smile and at the same time be able to stick them in the back. He said he was now able to do this—now able to play their games, of smiling on the front and having no good intentions on the back. I (the black researcher) think this is a realistic observation. This is an observation that I carry to this day, and I do not include all white people in this category, but there are a lot of white people that you have to treat with a long-handled spoon as Clark is saying.

Peer Pressure

The successful black student has to pay more costs than personally denying his or her cultural heritage by acting white and developing a distrustful
eye for those whom he/she had to emulate. The successful black students
were subject to derogation by their own who had not achieved academic
success. Those who were relegated to the basic or standard curriculum, as
noted earlier, chided their more successful peers for "acting white," and
occasionally attempted to call for ethnic allegience. These students had
generally developed street repertoires and were regarded as a threat to the
proficient black students who had cultivated an image contrary to the stereotypes of blacks held by whites. The proficient blacks argued:

> That bunch in the low-income housing projects don't like whites and
> just hate them to death. They are always smoking dope in the projects.
> Almost every girl in the projects has a baby.

The peer pressure was great and often forced the students to choose
between acting black and acting white not only in school, but more holis-
tically. The unsuccessful black students would not allow their more successful compatriots the luxury of degrading black culture for school purposes.
They saw it as an either-or proposition: either you act black or you act
white. Ethnicity was behavioral and cultural in their minds; one's genetic
heritage was not sufficient to define ethnic identity. One female black student explained her experience of these pressures:

Student: I'm kind of paranoid. You know people give me such a
              hard time, I just kind of stay away from people that I'm
              not sure about or I know don't like me.
Interviewer: Why do you think the black students are like you say?
Student: They won't give you a chance. This started in the tenth
              grade. This white girl in my classroom was very talkative,
              very pretty, and you just couldn't be mean to her. And
              her name was Mary, and she lived in the nicest block in
              this white community, and we became very close. If you
              saw one of us, you saw the other. And after that. . . . Well,
              no one liked me anyway because my momma dressed me
              real nice. They used to say I thought I was white before I
              ever talked to a white person. When I started being with
              her, they were just getting all motivated . . . and they beat
              me up every evening anyway and this gave them even
              more reason. But after that they wouldn't speak to me. I
              could count my black friends on one hand. That made

> me feel bad, because I know I'm black, but, you know,
> after you start being with people so much, you start act-
> ing like them and talking like them. I became changed,
> using kind of white slang and dressing like Mary did. I
> just thought because my black friends weren't giving me
> a chance. . . .

Another student commented, "You know, it's weird, nobody likes me at
school, and it's more blacks than whites. . . ."

DISCUSSION

In the late 1960s and early 1970s, the dialogue concerning education was
rather focused on the problems of minority students in a middle class
school. It was in that era that critiques of public education were common
and that the academic problems of minority students often were framed
more as structural problems with the organization and process of schooling
than problems with student capabilities (cf. Pearl, 1972; Carnoy, 1972).
These critiques have continued to today, but little has resulted from them in
the way of educational change. In part, this can be attributed to the reluctance and probable impotence of educational institutions to change their
fundamental logic of sorting (Katz, 1971), and in part to a lack of specificity
on the part of the critics to provide guidelines so that small-scale educational innovations could be designed that would challenge that fundamental logic.

Perhaps the most direct challenge to the sorting logic of public schooling
that emerged from these critiques has been court-mandated desegregation.
Seemingly, this desegregation has imposed an imcompatible goal upon
public schools.

Education and Desegregation

Obviously, it is necessary to demonstrate that the goal is compatibility of
education (as embodied in American public schools) and desegregation.
There are many ways to do this, but probably the succinct argument is
based in history. Katz (1971), Karier, Violas and Spring (1973) all demonstrated historically that public education in the United States was designed
and functioned to serve the industrial and economic order, and not to promote equality since its goal was to maintain stratification while prompting
industrial skills.

The Interaction of Stratification and Schooling in the United States

Katz (1971) has argued most convincingly that the "Great School Legend," as Greer (1972) calls it, does not seem to have much historical veracity. In fact, Katz portrayed the origins of public education in the United States as part of a movement to maintain Protestantism over Catholicism as the dominant form of religion in this country. The force of this movement was bolstered by the demands of a Protestant-controlled economy that was rapidly becoming industrial.

The industrialists saw the urban immigrant masses as a potential source of workers. However, most immigrants had come from agrarian backgrounds, and simply were lacking in skills that industry needed. Yet even more problematic than this lack of skills, since experience could easily give skills, was the potential of these masses for urban unrest, and more specifically an attitude that was not conducive to working in industry. The necessary attitude, according to the industrialists, was one of acceptance and docility. Mass production required workers who not only had skills, but who also accepted their lot and were not divisive elements in a work setting that required acceptance of routine and authority. The Protestant industrialists, according to Katz (1971), viewed public education as the appropriate vehicle through which to inculcate these skills and attitudes in the poor.

There was some dissension, however, over how to best provide these educational services. Katz documented the range of experimentation and discourse to highlight the significance of the final choice of "incipient bureaucracy" as the organizational form that was believed to be most able to achieve the desired goals.

Intriguingly, bureaucracy has been seen as the most "rational" form of organization (Weber, 1964). This "rationality" was precisely what the industrialists saw. Bureaucracy maximizes order and control. It more nearly regularizes the distribution of power and authority than do other forms of organization. Thus, when looking at the task of instilling a particular set of skills and values into an extensively heterogeneous mass of immigrant groups, the selection of bureaucracy by those in control was indeed "rational" for their interests. They were pushing integration into the industrial order, if not American society.

It could be argued then that the history of mass education in this country is a history of conflict over the meaning of integration. As Katz (1971) showed for the nineteenth-century origins of public schooling in this nation, Karier, Violas and Spring (1973) and Spring (1976) demonstrated for education in the twentieth century; the persistent logic of the public school movement has emphasized assimilation over intellectual development, with the often explicit goal of teaching "the norms necessary to adjust the young to the changing patterns of the economic system as well as to the society's more permanent values" (Karier, Violas and Spring, 1973:7).

The assumption of bureaucracy as the organizational form for public education was, thus, a design to forcibly, but subtly, assimilate the newly immigrated into an emerging industrial order that was dominated by Anglo-Saxon Protestants. Further, this "assimilative logic" has persisted and often seems to have been heightened by the increasing bureaucratization of public education.

It may be argued that, if anything, the "assimilative logic" may have been heightened over time through an institutional accrual of power. The assumption of bureaucracy as the organizational form for public education seems to have led to an insulation and isolation of the institution from those which it serves. Inasmuch as the preeminent feature of bureaucracy is internal control, problems that emerge within the organization are routinely resolved internal to the bureaucracy with only gross incidents referred to the formal linkage to the community, the school board. Further, given that the pattern of democracy in this nation is simply majority rule, it is often the case that the school board is more representative of local industrial interests than of the general community. Even when this is not the case, school board decisions are often based upon information and recommendations of the "experts" who staff the bureaucracy. Even the formation of state accrediting regulations reflect this pattern.

The institutional accrual of power by education seems to have been supported by the professionalization movement among educators. As with other occupations, professionalization appears to be a mechanism which "cools out" outside influence and control through the development of colleges of education that determine, under legislative mandate, who can be a teacher and who can be an "expert" in the field of education.

Interestingly, some of the characteristics of bureaucratization, differentiation and specialization in particular, have seemed to neutralize the possibility that anyone can be "expert" on all facets of the educational process. (Not only are educators specialists but schools have differentiated various curriculum blocks, administrative specialists, and levels of authority.) This trend seems to have been effective not only in reducing community influence and involvement, but also in thwarting the emergence of any large body of intellectuals who are "knowledgeable" across the gamut of educational philosophy, theory, policy, curriculum, instruction, and so on.

In short, public education, seemingly through increasing bureaucratization, has accrued such power over the past century that it may consciously only minimally represent even the industrialists. Yet the mold seems to have been cast in the 1880s, and education may never be able to escape its allegiance to the early industrialists, and its assimilative logic, if it never escapes bureaucracy as the dominant organizational form.

Desegregation is a challenge to the assimilative logic of public education because it serves the interests of those who have been denied a quality education because of their lack of assimilation. It represents a direct attack on public schools because it puts the burden of proof, and therefore accountability, upon them for "integrating" those who have not been "assimilated." Further, given that bureaucracies by design maximize control, "integration" into the conventional world and the promise of economic sufficience are the rewards for being assimilated and accepting the parameters of behavior and style promulgated by the institution. The threat of punishment used by public schools for promoting "assimilation" is the denial of access to conventional economic opportunity by denying access to educational certification. As a result then, desegregation, when imposed as a goal for public schooling, challenges the major social control mechanism of public schools. The goal of education as embraced in the American public schools is in direct contradiction with desegregation and equality of educational opportunity. The implementation of these incompatible goals has effects upon the everyday life of a public school, and upon the adaptations of minority students to the public school.

Contingencies and Adaptations

Minority students face many contingencies in attempting to negotiate schooling successfully. Many who do not meet the "standards" find an ethnic identity available to them, but those minority students who more-or-less meet the standards are in a more precarious position. First, the standards are a constant threat. Not only must one make the grades, but one must do well on standardized tests. Not only must one compete academically, but one must compete socially for club memberships, honors, and teacher recommendations. Second, one must also challenge ethnic boundaries. The white-controlled activities often are the most prestigious, and the striving black student must emulate whites to be socially acceptable. Nevertheless, they will not escape their ethnicity as far as the whites are concerned; white students have employed the blacks for their own ends. Therefore, the striving black student dares not trust those whom he/she emulates, while on the other hand, he/she loses the trust and respect of those less successful students who are of the same ethnic heritage. While they are not allowed to be white, they are also not allowed to be black.

The proficient black students are isolated when most adolescents are consumed by the peer group. They are threatened because there can be little trust. They are alienated and anomic in the classic sense of the concepts: without norms, they guardedly tread upon schooling; without available identification, they must structure their personal selves; and without participation, they must attach themselves to the strictures of a somewhat alien culture. Adaptation seemingly requires of them the degradation of their culture and the emulation of another in which they will never be granted full status.

Responding to the Costs of Success

Unfortunately, educational programs are based upon a naive assumption that those who publicly appear to be assimilated in the mainstream of our society have fewer problems that need attention than those who are not being assimilated. It seems appropriate to reconsider this assumption on at least two grounds. First, those who are not being assimilated seemingly have different problems than those who are. The high priority for the unassimilated should be in the procurement of "hard" services like income and health care which directly affect the quality of their lives. Those who are being "successfully" assimilated into a majority culture have different needs. They may well need the support of "soft" services like counseling and guidance, for they are in a situation where guidance and understanding is hard to come by. Second, it may be that we have conceived the problem incorrectly. Usually, most professionals would argue that, in some form or another, lack of access to success is the problem, although this may be the result of our own ethnocentrism concerning assimilation. Because we were able to negotiate success, we believe it must be a problem of those who were not able to do so. If the results reported here have any validity, the problem is more the assimilative logic employed in our society and in our schools, whether they be desegregated as in the case here or segregated by race. The black students respond to the contingencies they face due to assimilation. Some fail the test of assimilation, cultural degradation, and resolve it by adopting a larger "street" repertoire that is available to them. Some degrade their culture, and find none fully available to them.

If the assimilative logic is the problem that ultimately needs remedying, this, obviously, would be a monumental task. It involves restructuring American schooling, if not the economy, and seemingly requires some form of cultural pluralism that as yet has not found easy reception in our society. As we explored earlier in this paper, desegregation was a challenge to the

assimilative, stratifying logic of education. The data presented unequivocally demonstrate that even that has not been successful in its challenge. All
in all, both remedial services and a concomitant change effort would probably be the most effective strategy at this point. Nevertheless, more emphasis
on their adaptations to those contingencies seems to be appropriate. People
adapt readily, but society changes slowly. The latter needs more of our
attention.

SUMMARY

In this chapter we have tried to better understand the situation of minority youth in the desegregated schools that are constitutionally mandated.
These students, as our data reveal, are under great pressure both from the
requisites for academic success and from their culture as embodied in their
peer group. Schools seemingly coerce the minority student to modify the
significance of his/her culture and the minority student adapts by developing new cultural routines.

Desegregated education has done little to reduce such pressure upon the
minority student. In part, this is because desegregation as conceptualized
and enforced by federal courts has not been able to successfully modify the
assimilative logic of public schools. Desegregation has resulted more in
blacks and whites engaging in a competition of cultures than a more pluralistic respect for diverse cultural styles. The minority student is still disadvantaged in these settings.

This disadvantage is rather complex. Not only are there actual skill differences, but also differing definitions of appropriateness of behaviors and
linguistic patterns. Further, the minority student is buffeted between desires
for socioeconomic ability and the heritage and support of his/her family
and culture. The black students' legacy, their disadvantage, and their emotional survival are all contingent upon how well they are equipped to resolve these competing demands.

REFERENCES

Carnoy, M. (1972), *Schooling in a Corporate Society.* New York: David McKay.
Greer, C. (1972), *The Great School Legend.* New York: Basic Books.
Karier, C., Violas, R., and Spring, J. (1973), *Roots of Crisis: American Education in the Twen-
    tieth Century.* Chicago: Rand McNally.
Katz, M. (1971), *Class, Bureaucracy and Schools.* New York: Praeger.

Noblit, G. (1977), "Ethnographic Approaches to Evaluation." Presented at the National Conference on Criminal Justice Evaluation, Washington, D.C.

Pearl, A. (1972), *The Atrocity of Education.* St. Louis: New Critics Press.

Spicer, E. (1976), Beyond analysis and explanation? *Human Organization* 35:4: 335-343.

Spring, J. (1976), *The Sorting Machine.* New York: David McKay.

Suttles, G. (1968), *The Social Order of the Slum.* Chicago: University of Chicago Press.

Turner, S. and Carr, D. (1976), "The Process of Criticism in Interpretive Sociology and History." Presented at the American Sociological Association meeting, New York.

Weber, M. (1964), *Theory of Social and Economic Organization.* New York: Free Press.

PART III
The Law

6

The Expanding Right to Treatment for Minors: The Legal Implications for the Enabling Adults and Disciplines

SOL GOTHARD

This appeared in a New Orleans newspaper (Times/Picayune, Nov. 17, 1976):

AFTER 16 HOMES, BOY DOUBTS ABILITY TO LOVE

Oakland, Calif. (AP)—Dennis Smith doesn't know who his parents are or how he got his last name. And after being shuffled to 16 foster homes, the 17-year-old says he doesn't know if he could ever love anybody again.

"It's like a scar on your brain," Smith said. "If I had known I was going to spend the first 16 years of my life this way, I'd rather have been dead. I'd have wished my mother could have aborted me."

Smith is suing the Alameda County Social Services Agency and a school district for $500,000 for failing to put him up for adoption in all those years and for inaccurately labeling him retarded.

"One of the reasons he brought the suit is Dennis' concern with the way foster care operates and the hope that as a result of the suit other foster children will not be left in limbo as he was," his attorney, Robert Walker, said Tuesday.

"I don't think there's any specific reason why he was never put up for adoption," Walker added. "I don't know what happened except there are a lot of kids who get lost."

The suit filed Monday also contends that Smith was saddled through much of his life with a wrong diagnosis of mental retardation. The Hayward Unified School District, another defendant, allegedly placed him in classes with retarded youngsters for several years. He now is taking regular high school classes and maintains an average record.

Alameda County Officials have refused comment on the case, but Librado Perez, director of the social services agency, said:

"Regardless of the outcome, we are re-examining our operation to determine whether improvements càn be made or if preventive steps can be taken."

Files show Smith was born on October 5, 1959. After a 2½ month period which is unrecorded, he began his journey through limbo from foster home to foster home.

Early in 1960, he met his second set of foster parents—and soon after that his third, a couple who specialized in mentally disabled children.

"When the social worker came out I couldn't explain my feelings very well," Smith said. "I would cry and sort of have her hug me, that was the only way I could tell her I wanted to leave very badly."

Other homes, other places followed. On July 12, 1973, Dennis was placed with a 71-year-old "father" and a "mother" in her mid-60s. He is with a new foster family now and doing well.

"There's no excuse for Dennis except inefficiency," said Mrs. Marian Love, secretary of the California State Foster Parents Association and Dennis' court-appointed guardian for the lawsuit.

"On the other hand, you have hundreds of childless parents waiting to adopt children," she said. "And on the other, you have hundreds of parentless children seeking stability and hoping against hope they'll be adopted. The chief impediment to bringing these two groups together seems to be the courts and the Department of Social Services."

As for Dennis, he says that his wandering has soured him on the chance of being adopted by a good family.

"I really don't know," he said. "I don't know if I could love anybody anymore." (p. 1)

We cannot speculate on the merits of this case until much more is known, but it could very well portray a dramatic failure to meet the fostercare and mental health needs of the adolescent involved. The purpose of this chapter is to present selected areas of the law of the United States as it attempts to address these issues and that of the expanding legal implications for those who are charged to deliver the mental and physical health services to minors.

HISTORICAL OVERVIEW

Humanity's attitudes towards its young people have been most inhumane. Various cultures of antiquity practiced abandonment or infanticide of weak or deformed infants for religious reasons, magic and superstitious sacrifice, as a form of population control, and for cultural reasons wherein males were often preferred over females. In Babylonia and Athens, the outright selling of children was legal. During the Renaissance, children were held as political hostages and security for debts in order to release parents from debtors' prison.

Throughout the history of colonial America, and on through the mid-1800s, children were treated as chattel; they were sold as indentured servants and enjoyed no separate status or privileges under the law.

The rights of parents received much earlier attention in the courts of the United States than the rights of children. For example, the United States Supreme Court protected the rights of parents to have their children taught a foreign language (Meyer v. Nebraska, 1923) and to direct their children's upbringing (Pierce v. Society of Sisters, 1925).

One of the earliest Supreme Court cases that recognized the right of minors, separate and distinct from that of their parents, was the case in which the Massachusetts Child Labor Law was upheld against the claim of a 9-year-old Jehovah Witness of a right to practice freely her religious convictions (Prince v. Massachusetts, 1944):

Parents may be free to become martyrs themselves . . . But it does not follow that they are free . . . to make martyrs of the children before the children can make that choice for themselves.

In Wisconsin v. Yoder (1972), the United States Supreme Court ruled in favor of members of the Old Order Amish who, for religious reasons, chose to discontinue formal education of their children at age 16. The decision was based on the parents' paramount right of responsibility to guide their children where the issue of religious freedom conflicted with the compulsory school attendance law.

The early 1960s brought drastic and far-reaching changes in the expanded rights of adults, particularly in criminal law, in such areas as confessions, illegal search and seizure, notification of rights on arrest, etc. As is usually the case, similar changes in juvenile law followed thereafter.

From the landmark case of Gault (1967), the major provisions of the ruling by the United States Supreme Court were that juveniles, during delinquency hearings, were entitled to:

(1) fair notice of the hearing, in writing, advising of the charge and with sufficient time to prepare a defense;
(2) notification of Right to Counsel;
(3) notification of Right against Self-Incrimination;
(4) notification of Right to Confrontation and Cross-Examination of Adverse Witnesses.

In Winship, (1969), the United States Supreme Court decreed the standard of proof in delinquency hearings must be proof beyond a reasonable doubt, rather than the lesser standards of clear and convincing evidence, or the preponderance of evidence. The McKeiver (1971) and Breed v. Jones (1975) (United States Supreme Court) cases dealt with the issues of jury trials (which states are free to employ or not in juvenile hearings) and double jeopardy testimony at juvenile delinquency hearings (not admissible later in adult hearings with same defendant and same charge).

DEVELOPMENT OF FURTHER RIGHTS IN SELECTIVE AREAS

I. Rights to Medical Care

In the Jehovah's Witnesses (1968) case the United States Supreme Court upheld the Washington statute declaring children dependent for the purpose of authorizing blood transfusions against the express religious objections of their parents.

In Hudson (1942) the Washington Supreme Court said the juvenile court had no power to order an operation (amputation of arm), adding:

(We) have not advanced or retrograded to the state where, in the name of mercy, we may lawfully decide that one shall be deprived of life rather than continue to exist crippled or burdened with some abnormality. That right of decision is a prerogative of the Creator . . .

No court has the authority to take a minor child, over objection of its parents who have not been deprived as unfit and unsuitable persons to have the custody and control of the child, and subject it to a surgical operation.

Since the Jehovah's Witnesses (1968) case, it has often been held that medical intervention in behalf of the child, over the objections of the parent, will be granted by the courts when the issue is life or death (McNulty, 1978). There is divided opinion where the issue is not so clear. If all medical and other authorities agree that a relatively minor operation will cure the debilitating effects of a hairlip, for example, should a court order it over the objections of the parents and their sixteen year old child? What if the child, however, asks for the operation, or is only eight years old? Should a court grant a sterilization request of parents, supported by a host of medical and mental health professionals, upon an attractive 14 years old girl with an I.Q. of 40? Most would agree that the "best interests" of the child should prevail, but there is a great divergence of opinion as to what is in the child's best interest, especially with respect to medical intervention. The physician is cautioned to have a court order authorizing said intervention.

II. Abortions, Venereal Disease Treatment, Drug Abuse Treatment and Birth Control

In the Danforth (1976) case the United States Supreme Court ruled unconstitutional that part of a Missouri Abortion statute that required the written consent of the spouse, or where the woman was unmarried and under 18 years of age, the written consent of at least one parent. The Court said that a State does not have authority to give a third party an absolute, and possibly arbitrary, veto over the decision of the physician and his patient to terminate the patient's pregnancy, regardless of the reason the parent or spouse withhold the consent. The Court emphasized that they were not suggesting that every minor, regardless of age, could give effective consent for abortion.

Many states now have statutes that allow physicians and clinics to treat juveniles generally, and for VD and drug abuse specifically, without the necessity of parental consent or sometimes even without their knowledge. These statutes generally hold that consent for such treatment by spouse, parent or guardian is not necessary; that the physician or member of a medical staff may inform said spouse, parent or guardian, but is not obligated to; and that the physician or medical staff member may advise above parties with or without the minor's consent. The rationale for these laws is that many minors would refuse treatment if their parents were told; and that quite frequently it is better that the child be treated without parental consent, and even without parental knowledge, than to let the medical condition deteriorate, especially with critical situations of drug abuse and venereal disease.

Birth control information and devices, however, have generated more controversy. Central to this controversy is the balance between rights and responsibilities of parents vis-a-vis the minors, and responsibilities and possible liability for the treating physician.

In the Doe (1973) case the Utah State Supreme Court said the best interests of children are not served by providing them with contraceptives without consent of parent or husband, since to do so would cause them to become immoral delinquents, perhaps even "strumpets or streetwalkers" infected with venereal disease. This conclusion appears to rest on the assumption that fear of pregnancy effectively deters teenagers from engaging in sexual intercourse. The Court also cautioned against the diminution of the duty of parents to "teach and instruct."

In contrast, the Supreme Court of New Jersey has noted in the case of State v. Baird (1967):

> The social gain (from the deterrence of sexual promiscuity) achieved is not worth the tragedy of unwanted pregnancy or venereal disease in the cases in which the law (prohibiting the display of contraceptives) fails in that purpose; and to prescribe such pregnancy or disease as a punishment for illicit intercourse would be a monstrous thing.

The United States Supreme Court considered the issue in the Carey (1977) case. A New York statute which contained a provision prohibiting distribution of nonprescription contraceptives to anyone under the age of 16 was declared unconstitutional. But the question of state power, parental rights, duties and responsibilities, and minor's rights once again proved so "vexing" (p. 2020) that in addition to the main opinion, there were three concurring opinions in which various justices only agreed on certain issues, and two dissenting opinions. The main opinion stated:

> The question of the extent of state power to regulate conduct of minors not constitutionally regulable when committed by adults is a vexing one, perhaps not susceptible to precise answer. We have been reluctant to attempt to define "the totality of the relationship of the juvenile and the state."

> ... Whatever may be their precise impact, neither the Fourteenth Amendment nor the Bill of Rights is for adults alone, *In Re Gault,*

supra, 387 U.S. at 13, 87 S. Ct. at 1436. On the other hand, we have held in a variety of contexts that the power of the state to control the conduct of children reaches beyond the scope of its authority over adults.

. . . The State's interests in protection of the mental and physical health of the pregnant minor, and in protection of potential life, are clearly more implicated by the abortion decision than by the decision to use a nonhazardous contraceptive.

. . . Moreover, there is substantial reason for doubt whether limiting access to contraceptives will in fact substantially discourage early sexual behavior. Appellants themselves conceded in the District Court that "there is no evidence that teenage extramarital sexual activity increases in proportion to the availability of contraceptives." . . . It is enough that we again confirm the principle that when a State, as here, burdens the exercise of a fundamental right, its attempt to justify that burden as a rational means for the accomplishment of some significant State policy requires more than a bare assertion.

The dissenting opinion stated:

I would describe as "frivolous" appellee's argument that a minor has the constitutional right to put contraceptives to their intended use, notwithstanding the combined objection of both parents and the State.

A concurring opinion stated:

There is also no justification for subjecting restrictions on the sexual activity of the young to heightened judicial review. Under our prior cases, the States have broad latitude to legislate with respect to adolescents. The principle is well settled that "a State may permissibly determine that, at least in some precisely delineated areas, a child . . . is not possessed of that full capacity for individual choice" which is essential to the exercise of various constitutionally protected interests.

Second, this provision prohibits parents from distributing contraceptives to their children, a restriction that unjustifiably interferes with parental interests in rearing their children.

. . . Constitutional interpretation has consistently recognized that the parents' claim to authority in their own household to direct the rearing of their children is basic to the structure of society. It is cardinal with us that the custody, care and nurture of the child reside first in the parents, whose primary function and freedom include preparation for obligations the state can neither supply nor hinder.

Subsequent to Carey (1977), the case of Doe v. Irwin (1977) was heard by a United States District Court in Michigan. The court felt that a majority of the United States Supreme Court would support a state statute requiring prior parental notice and consultation before even nonprescription contraceptives are distributed to unemancipated minors. Therefore, a Michigan Family Health Clinic that supplied the contraceptives to unemancipated minors, with no contact at all with the parents of said minors, violated parental rights protected by the 1st, 4th, 9th, and 14th amendments.

III. Mental Health and the Right to Treatment

A 1966 Pennsylvania statute provided inter alia that a minor under eighteen might be admitted to a state mental health facility upon application of his parent but, unlike an adult, the admitted person was free to withdraw only with the consent of the admitting parent. This applied only to voluntary admissions of minors, as opposed to court-committed, involuntary admissions. In Kremens v. Bartley (1977) this statute was declared unconstitutional as violative of the due process clause of the 14th Amendment. In briefs filed in the United States Supreme Court review of the case, various mental health groups raised other issues, such as children not being removed from the family and community without a formalized and searching inquiry into their needs, alternatives to institutions and parental motivation for the institutionalization of their children (treatment center or depository).

In *Parham v. J. R. et al.* (U.S. 1979), the United States Supreme Court outlined a constitutionally acceptable procedure to be used in the voluntary commitment of minors by their parents. The court held that the risk of error in such commitments is sufficiently great that an inquiry should be made by a "neutral factfinder." That factfinder must have the authority to override the parents' decision and refuse to admit a child who does not satisfy medical standards for admission. To the dismay of civil libertarians, the court clearly stated that a formal or quasi-formal hearing is not required. Furthermore, the inquiry need not be conducted by a law-trained or judicial administrative officer.

From the mid-60s on, various cases were heard by the Federal Courts, some by the United States Supreme Court, pertaining to adults in institutions via civil or criminal commitment. The main issue in the case of criminal commitment is whether the individual's rights of due process and equal protection of law, under the 14th Amendment, were safeguarded.

The Humphrey (1972) case held that the defendant was entitled to a jury determination of his "dangerousness" to the community, which was afforded to persons under the Mental Health Act but not under the Sex Crime Act.

With respect to adults under civil rather than criminal commitment, the United States Supreme Court stated in O'Connor (1975):

> The jury found that Donaldson was neither dangerous to himself nor dangerous to others and also found that, if mentally ill, Donaldson had not received treatment. A finding of "mental illness" alone cannot justify a State's locking a person up against his will and keeping him indefinitely in simple custodial confinement.

The new recognition of the right to, and requirement of, treatment, was then applied to minors in various situations. The grounds most often mentioned are the due process and equal protection clause of the 14th Amendment and the prohibition against cruel and unusual punishment in the 8th Amendment. One of the earliest reported cases arose in a detention home in Washington, D.C., alleging a minor needed psychiatric treatment and was not receiving it. The United States Court of Appeals, in Creek v. Stone (1967), held that a right of treatment exists in detention centers.

The United States District Court, in the landmark Morales (1971) case, found that in some of the Texas Youth Council Schools conditions were inhumane, brutal and repressive and ordered the closing of two of the schools. This decision is as important to the area of right to treatment as the Gault (1967) case was to Juvenile Court hearings:

> ... the commitment of juveniles to institutions under conditions and procedures much less rigorous than those required for the conviction and imprisonment of an adult offender gives rise to certain limitations upon the conditions under which the state may confine the juveniles. This doctrine has been labelled the 'right to treatment,' and finds its basis in the due process clause of the 14th Amendment ...

> ... Expert witnesses testified that the results of continual violation of a juvenile's dignity, privacy, pride, and possessions is inevitably the exacerbation of delinquency rather than its cure, for such treatment teaches the juveniles that they are considered to be less than full human beings, and that their personal property is unworthy of respect. Worse, they are thereby tutored in the abuse of power over those weaker or gentler than themselves.

> ... No matter how well-intentioned and professional a juvenile's treatment plan, it will be rendered worthless by an accumulation of daily indignities, discomforts and harassments, such as were documented at the trial.

... It would be ironic indeed if the law may require that every juvenile prior to incarceration be aided by a lawyer devoted to the fierce protection of his individual rights, yet may consign the child after incarceration to the status of a cipher, lost among hundreds of other children.

The Morales (1971) case was followed by the federal case of Nelson v. Heyne (1974):

... The District Court was unanimous in condemning the practice of corporal punishment. The uncontradicted evidence of the authorities suggests that the practice does not serve either as useful punishment or as treatment. Testimony adduced at the trial shows that it actually breeds counter-hostility resulting in greater aggression by a child. Among the other child-correctional institutions discussed during the hearing, none continues the practice of corporal punishment.

... Accordingly, the Court finds the defendants' present practice with respect to corporal punishment to be in violation of the plaintiffs' 8th Amendment rights and orders an immediate cessation of the practice.

Tranquilizing drugs were excessively administered:

The Court finds as shocking to the conscience and violative of the plaintiffs' 8th and 14th Amendment rights the defendants' present policy with respect to tranquilizing drugs ...

While the Court believes that these drugs may be used occasionally to calm states of excitation which are found to be potentially dangerous to life and property, the defendants' policies are far afield of minimal medical and constitutional standards.

Solitary confinement (euphemistically called "cottage detention") was employed—on one youth for 57 consecutive days:

Expert testimony offered during the course of the hearing revealed that prolonged and total isolation such as that practiced at the Boys School is emotionally and psychologically debilitating and serves neither treatment nor punitive goals. Although exclusion may be required in an institutional setting, it must be closely regulated. At a minimum this initially requires that the choice to commit one to solitary be an informed decision; the child must be aware of the reason for his detention, and the committing authority must demonstrate that isolation for a given period of time in each child's case meets the best treatment interests of the child. Secondly, the decision must be subject to regular, periodic review by professionally competent treatment personnel familiar with the effect continuing isolation has on the detainee. Lastly, the detained child must be given reasonable access to his peers and treatment staff, a reasonable amount of reading and/or recreational material, and opportunities for daily physical exercise throughout the duration of detainment.

The Court finds the practices now employed by defendants with respect to cottage detention both cruel and unusual punishment and totally devoid of the most rudimentary notions of procedural due process . . .

The right to treatment started with adults in civil commitment, spread to adults in criminal commitment, and then to minors in institutions. There are many more cases from various states which have not been referred to relative to children in various institutions. But the idea of "treatment" for children and youth in need or distress and of providing qualitative service for them, most especially when they are involved with some sort of public agency, or in care away from their home, has spread beyond confinement in institutions. This newer legal right of treatment, together with the ever-expanding rights of children and youth in general, has led the courts to new areas of concern.

IV. Foster Care

There is growing concern for children in foster care, their needs and rights, together with those of natural parents and foster parents. Children have too often been removed from abusive parents and placed with abusive foster parents. Therefore, many states and juvenile courts now call for periodic evaluation of these cases.

Whenever children are in foster care for long periods of time, many courts are now terminating the rights of the natural parents, making the children available for adoption by the foster parents. The concept of the "psychological parent," has been widely used as an authority in cases by various state courts (Goldstein, Freud and Solnit, 1973). The Smith case (1977) recognized the issue that children in foster care are not furniture in storage to accommodate parents. This and subsequent cases (W.C. v. P.M., 1978), while limiting the rights of foster parents and encouraging the return of children in foster care to their natural parents, acknowledges the role of foster parents, and the care and treatment that children in foster care are entitled to receive. A case has also been made for the "permanent foster placement of dependent, neglected and abused children (Derdeyn, 1977) in the quest to individualize children in foster care. These recent cases represent new areas of concern and scrutinize, for the first time, the "rights" of foster children as well as foster parents. In the Roy (1977) case, the mother of a 16-year-old boy who had lived in a foster home from age 1 year on, sought, not the child's return but, to maintain her title to the child and prevent his adoption. In rejecting the mother's "possessory claim," the Court said that "to refuse to consider the child's best interest because of an adult's title to him, albeit a biological parent's, seemingly would be unconstitutional."

A different result was reached in In Re Jacqueline F. (1977), wherein a 6-year-old who had lived most of her life with an aunt and uncle had custody returned to the parent. The least important consideration was the superior economic status of the foster parents. Regarding the time spent with the foster parents, the court said:

> In the instant case the infant is only six years of age. While she has spent most of her life with respondents, she was placed with them because of problems of the parents which were overcome by the time the infant was 3 years of age. Since that time, the parents have been endeavoring to obtain her return. The passage of time has established that the parents have succeeded in overcoming their earlier problems. The time required for the parents to establish this fact should not now serve as an impediment to their success in regaining their child who, the expert testimony concedes, is still at an age when she is capable of making the adjustment of permanent transfer to her natural parents with whom she has not established a relationship. That this transfer will be somewhat disruptive does not alone offer a basis for permanently depriving the parents of their child.

These cases are but a sampling of the reported cases. The debate that has been generated by the issue of children in foster care has led to articles such as "Babies are to Foster Care as Cars are to General Motors" (Greenberg, 1977). Involved in the great debate have been the American Civil Liberties Union, Mobilization for Youth, Legal Aid Societies and numerous other individuals and groups from various disciplines.

Part of this question reached the United States Supreme Court in the Smith case (1977). The main issue was the denial of the 14th Amendment rights of foster children being removed from foster homes:

> In this litigation appellees, individual foster parents and a foster parents' organization, sought declaratory and injunctive relief against New York State and New York City officials, alleging that the statutory and regulatory procedures for removal of foster children from foster homes violated the Due Process and Equal Protection Clauses of

the 14th Amendment. Under the New York Social Services Law, the authorized placement agency has discretion to remove the child from the foster home and regulations provide for 10 days' advance notice of removal. Objecting foster parents may request a conference with the social services department where the foster parent may appear with counsel to be advised of the reasons for removal and to submit opposing reasons. Within five days after the conference, the agency official must render a written decision and send notice to the foster parent and agency. If the child is removed after the conference, the foster parent may appeal to the department of social services, where a full adversary administrative hearing takes place, and the resultant determination is subject to judicial review. We deal here with issues of unusual delicacy, in an area where professional judgments regarding desirable procedures are constantly and rapidly changing. In such a context, restraint is appropriate on the part of courts called upon to adjudicate whether a particular procedural scheme is adequate under the Constitution. Since we hold that the procedures provided by New York State in S392 and by New York City's SSC Procedure No. 5 are adequate to protect whatever liberty interest appellees may have, the judgment of the District Court is to decide as it sees fit whether and when a child shall be returned to his natural family or placed elsewhere.

LEGAL IMPLICATIONS

New rights of minors and adults are being created by the courts, while previously recognized rights have been greatly expanded. We have discussed the evolution and development of the rights of minors in selected areas and presented the highlights. There are other areas, of course. For example, the concept of managing a "status offender" has altered drastically in recent years. Restricting the liberty of minors after dark, or curfew laws, has been held unconstitutional by a state court (People v. Chambers, 1975). A deformed son was able to maintain a medical malpractice action against the doctor who delivered him by alleging that the mother's consent to the delivery procedure was invalidated since she was not adequately advised of the possible risks (Shack v. Holland, 1976). Physicians and hospitals may be held liable for injuries sustained by a child if they negligently failed to diagnose and report the battered child syndrome, resulting in the child's being returned to her parents and receiving further injuries at their hands (Landeros v. Flood, 1976). Psychotherapists face liability to third persons who are assaulted or killed by the patient, where the therapist had knowledge of the potential for violence or homicide towards that third person, and when the third person was not forewarned by the therapist (Tarasoff v. Regents of University of California, 1976; Merchants National Bank v. United States, 1967).

The major legal implication, then, is to provide accurate diagnosis and treatment because of the right to receive treatment, and also to protect against malpractice which is a specialized form of negligence.

The treating person faces a variety of new potential risks that this sampling of situations illustrates and must determine what the duty is, and then perform the duty by delivering the service. It is a negligent breach of duty that forms the basis of malpractice suits. The physician should carefully document all steps in the diagnosis and treatment process, as good practice, and as possible evidence for the defense in the law suit.

In a negligence action, the following, as summarized by Prosser (1971), must be established:

1. A duty, or obligation, recognized by the law, requiring the doctor to conform to a certain standard of conduct, . . .
2. A failure on his part to conform to the standard required . . .
3. A reasonably close causal connection between the conduct and the resulting injury . . .
4. Actual loss or damage resulting to the interests (health, finances, and emotional or psychological stability) of another.

Lawyers do not guarantee that a case will be won. They do guarantee that they will use training and skill in identifying the legal problems and quality efforts to resolve them. Similarly, the physician must be aware of these newer issues raised, as they pertain in a given situation: Has the minor given informed consent? Should the parent be contacted? Has the minor been advised of possible dangers of treatment? Has unjustified force or coercion been used? How long has the foster child been in care without review, without seeing his parents? In each situation there are a myriad of new concerns, and it behooves the treating adult to have written legal opinion and authority whenever possible, because he or she is being held, with greater frequency, legally accountable to deliver certain services.

The determination of these "services," however, could also very well result in sharp disagreement between the physician and the minor's attorney/advocate. For example, a physician might be convinced that there are youngsters too ill to function, yet because of overzealous interpretation of their "rights," these youngsters are not being hospitalized or are being prematurely released from hospitalization. The minor's need to be helped to become responsible and accountable might be getting lost in the shuffle, with improper balance of equities. However, the physician, with proper legal as well as medical authority and argument, must be able to show, in court if necessary, that he is indeed responding to the minor's need as well as right to treatment.

SUMMARY

We are witnessing the recent revolutionary change of attitude towards the needs and rights of minors which has followed this development for adults. The changed legal attitude has been influenced greatly by the contributions of mental health professionals. The needs and moral rights of minors have become recognized and sanctioned by law so as to become legal rights. We have seen the creation of new rights and expansion of existing ones—in courts, schools, medical care, venereal disease treatment, drug abuse treatment, birth control programs, commitment to mental facilities, state training schools, and in foster care.

The enabling professions and the courts are addressing complex and conflicting issues such as the right to self-determination versus the need for guidance and restrictions. How do we free minors from arbitrary and adverse parental or societal domination, while protecting the right of the parents and society to guide, provide constructive discipline and necessary limits? There is great difference of opinion by people of good will as to what is in the best interests of the child in any specific situation.

However, it may be that overzealous advocacy has often resulted in unnecessary law suits, with the needs of an individual child being lost in the concern for the larger class action issue. Many individual trees may be unrecognized in our concern for the forest. As evidenced by the number of cases heard by the courts, the variety of issues presented, and the timeliness of the case, the rights of minors have become a major concern of the law today with many contradictions still present. As the rights of minors have become identified, the treating adult has likewise been held much more responsible and legally accountable. Therefore the treating adult needs more legal awareness of the new issues and concerns, and of what he or she must do to deliver suitable service to youth while protecting his or her personal and professional integrity.

REFERENCES

State v. Baird, (1967), 235 A. 2d 673.
Breed v. Jones, (1975), 421 U. S. 519.
Carey, et al v. Population Services International, et al., (1977), 97 S. Ct. 2010.
Creek v. Stone, (1967), 379 F. 2d 106.

Danforth v. Planned Parenthood of Central Missouri, et al, (1976), 96 S. Ct. 2831.

Derdeyn. A.. (1977). A case for permanent foster placement of dependent. neglected. and abused children. *Amer. J. Orthropsych.* 47:604-614.

Doe v. Irwin, (1977), 4 FLR 2079.

Doe v. Planned Parenthood Association of Utah, (1973). 510 P. 2d 75, stay denied 413 U. S. 917.

In Re Gault, (1967). 387 U. S. 1.

Goldstein. J.. Freud. A.. and Solnit. A. J.. (1973). *Beyond the Best Interests of the Child,* New York: The Free Press.

Greenberg. D.. (1977). Babies are to Foster Care as Cars are to General Motors. *Childrens Rights Report,* Juvenile Rights Project of the American Civil Liberties Union Foundation. New York. Vol. 1, No. 6 March.

In Re Hudson, (1942). 126 P. 2d 765.

Humphrey v. Cady, (1972). 405 U. S. 504. 92 S. Ct. 1048.

In Re Jacqueline F., (1977). 3 FLR 2556.

Jehovah's Witnesses in the State of Washington v. King Co. Hospital, (1968). 390 U. S. 598. 88 S. Ct. 1260.

Kremens, et al. v. Bartley, et al. (1977), 97 S. Ct. 1709.

Landeros v. Flood, (1976), 131 Cal. Reptr. 69.

McKeiver v. Pa., (1971), 403 U. S. 528.

In Re McNulty, (1978), 4 FLR 1071.

Merchants National Bank & Trust Co. v. United States, (1967), 272 F. Supp. 409.

Meyer v. Nebraska, (1923), 262 U. S. 390.

Morales v. Turman, (1971), 326 F. Supp. 677.

Nelson v. Heyne, (1973), 355 F. Supp. 451; cert. denied, 417 U. S. 976 (1974).

O'Connor v. Donaldson, (1975), 95 S. Ct. 2486, 45 L. Ed. 2d 396.

Parham v. J. R. et al., (1979) 99 SCt 2493.

People v. Chambers, (1975), 335 N.E. 2d 612.

Pierce v. Society of Sisters, (1925), 268 U. S. 510.

Prince v. Massachusetts, (1944), 321 U. S. 155.

Prosser, W. L., (1971), *Hornbook of the Law of Torts,* 4th ed., St. Paul, Minn: West Publishing.

In Re Roy, (1977), 3 FLR 1097.

Shack v. Holland, (1976), 4 FLR 2147.

Smith v. Organization of Foster Families for Equality and Reform, (1977), 97 S. Ct. 2094.

Tarasoff v. Regents of University of California, (1976), 529 P. 2d 553.

The Times Picayune (New Orleans), (1976), November 17, p. 1.

W. C. v. P. M., (1978), 4 FLR 2334.

In the matter of Samuel Winship, (1969), 397 U. S. 358.

Wisconsin v. Yoder, (1972), 406 U. S. 205.

7

Due Process and Protection: The Juvenile Court's Response to Adolescent Needs and Rights

M. A. BORTNER

The very existence of the juvenile court is predicated upon the needs of children. Traditional juvenile justice philosophy depicts the court as non-punitive and therapeutic, a legal institution whose espoused goals are protection and guidance of children. Accordingly, it has been praised as a socialized court offering individualized consideration and treatment on the basis of juvenile needs and characteristics.

Although not without detractors (Waite, 1921; Mack, 1909; Paulsen, 1957; Tappan, 1946), the juvenile court enjoyed an extended period of widespread acceptance and support within American society. For over sixty years the dominant interpretation of the court characterized it as the expression of humanitarian sentiments in which children are not truly capable of criminal intent, and the state, embodying the principle of *parens patriae,* is their benevolent protector. In this role of "substitute parent," the court has been charged with the responsibility of meeting the needs of neglected, dependent and delinquent juveniles.

Traditionally, court personnel have envisioned themselves as providing the protection necessitated by juveniles' inexperience and age, i.e., from adult exploitation and abuse, as well as from their own youthful indiscretion. Few would deny the importance of this function, for in modern American society childhood and adolescence are accorded a unique status, one for which most adults express concern and sympathy (Aries, 1962). Few would deny that children need and have a right to be shielded from abuse and exploitation by adults and to receive reasoned counsel from mature, experienced advisers.

Nevertheless, increasingly vocal critics have accused the juvenile court of failing to provide the protection and guidance needed by juveniles. Equally damning, opponents charge that the court's unique structure and organization have provided the rationale for the abridgement of juvenile rights (Blumberg, 1970; Fox, 1974; Schullenberger and Murphy, 1973; Ellis, 1976; Simpson, 1976). Critics also charge that the vast discretionary power wielded by court personnel has permitted and encouraged discrimination on the basis of race, sex, or economic status (Martin, 1970; Schur, 1973; Platt, 1977; Flicker, 1977).

U.S. Supreme Court decisions acknowledged these criticisms by calling for greater uniformity in the granting of juvenile procedural rights. It is erroneous to suggest that all juvenile courts denied procedural rights prior to these decisions; nevertheless, these rulings mandated uniformity in the granting of such rights. *Kent v. United States* (383 U.S. 541, 1966) dealt exclusively with the rights of juveniles being considered for transfer to the adult court. The Court ruled that a formal hearing is required before the juvenile court can waive jurisdiction and transfer a juvenile to the adult court for prosecution. It further stipulated that during such a proceeding a juvenile must have the right to counsel, defense attorneys must have access to all relevant court records, and a judicial statement must specify reasons for the waiver decisions.

In Re Gault (387 U.S. 1, 1967) and *In Re Winship* (397 U.S. 358, 1970) dealt with the rights of juveniles during the adjudicatory ("fact-finding") portion of juvenile proceedings. *Gault* stipulated that juveniles have the right to notification of the specific charges against them, the right to counsel, the right against self-incrimination, and the right to confront and cross-examine accusers. And although not specifically stated, it implied the right to recorded proceedings and appellate review. *Winship* stipulated that proof beyond a reasonable doubt is necessary for the charges against juveniles to be ruled true.

Although these decisions have been heralded as indication of the ascendance of procedural rights, they cannot be construed as a mandate for the juvenile court to alter its basic orientation. Although the Supreme Court has ordered that juveniles be granted certain rights, it has also instructed the juvenile justice system to maintain informality, flexibility and expediency in processing youthful offenders. Equally important, all of the rulings pertain to the transfer of juveniles to adult court or the adjudicatory portion of juvenile proceedings. No new guidelines have been established for disposition, i.e., the sentencing or treatment phase.

Thus, the juvenile court is instructed to combine the procedural safeguards of the adult criminal court and the informality and treatment ideals of the traditional juvenile system. Many question whether both objectives can be accomplished simultaneously. Others, such as Judge John Stekette (1973), suggest that only through strict separation of adjudication and disposition can both objectives be realized: due process should be carefully observed during adjudication and treatment considerations should dominate the dispositional phase.

Much of this debate fails to address the crucial controversy engulfing the court. Judges, lawyers and social workers are accused of abusing and abdicating their responsibilities as protectors. They are indicted as vengeful prosecutors and punishers, not benevolent advisers and protectors. Juvenile court personnel can no longer ignore these devastating accusations. Assertions regarding the protective potential of the juvenile system will no longer suffice; court personnel must also acknowledge the coercive and punitive potential of their actions. To assess the merits of this debate the author recently conducted extensive research within a large metropolitan juvenile court. The research encompassed a nine-month study, including observation of 250 formal delinquency hearings, in-depth interviews with key court personnel, and statistical analysis of 10,000 delinquency referrals. Observations derived from this study form the basis for this chapter.

ADOLESCENT NEEDS

Adolescents need and have a right to protection and guidance from emotional and physical harm. The frequent inability of parents, schools and society to afford that protection makes the court's role more essential than ever. But to meet this challenge, court personnel must acknowledge their limitations, demonstrate a new sensitivity to the needs of juveniles, and create a revitalized system which no longer rests on past rhetoric or visions of glory.

An initial step toward the achievement of these goals is systematic implementation of procedural rights for juveniles. Such rights are not antithetical to the protection and treatment championed by juvenile justice philosophy; to the contrary, they are integral to such protection. Juveniles do require protection from others and their own inexperience, but they must also be afforded protection from the coercive, punitive potential of the juvenile court. Failure to establish an atmosphere of fairness and consistency will destroy any treatment potential of the juvenile system.

Court founders believed that scientific social work would provide the knowledge and techniques necessary for accurate diagnosis and treatment of juvenile problems. Present-day court personnel must acknowledge that such faith has not been rewarded: the lack of proven treatment methods is striking. As Frederic Faust (1974) has so forcefully argued, many of the court's treatment orders are experimental and quasi-scientific at best. There must be strict guidelines directing the exercise of discretion and delimiting the court's attempts to treat juveniles. If the court's actions are to transcend mere coercion as well as maximize protective treatment, procedural safeguards must be meticulously constructed and consistently observed.

The implementation of procedural rights is a prerequisite to affording protection and treatment for adolescents. Equally important, the court must evidence renewed sensitivity to other, more-encompassing rights and needs of juveniles. In a system committed to treatment of adolescents, needs and rights become intertwined and indistinguishable. These paramount needs/rights include: 1) the need/right to understand the judicial process in which one is involved; 2) the need/right to meaningfully participate in that process; and 3) the need/right to effective legal representation. Court personnel must recognize and respond to these needs if juveniles are to be granted truly meaningful protection and guidance.

THE RIGHT TO UNDERSTAND THE PROCESS

Participation in the judicial process is often a bewildering experience for adults and adolescents alike. The formal atmosphere, legal jargon, and authority relationships are intimidating and discomforting for many juveniles. They need and have a right to comprehend the judicial process in which they are involved. Unfortunately, the clarity with which procedures and alternatives are stated varies with the orientation and organization of each court, as well as with the professional and personal ideologies of judges, lawyers and social workers.

Numerous studies suggest that juveniles often have extremely vague and confused images of what is happening to them. Grisso and Manoogian (1978) recently studied the ability of juvenile offenders to understand the *Miranda* rights warnings, using various tests of comprehension, including the juveniles' ability to define critical words in the warnings and the ability to paraphrase the warnings. They found that "except for older juveniles in the average I.Q. range, understanding of the *Miranda* warnings for juveniles as a group is at best a 50-50 proposition."

Juveniles are equally unaware of possible future developments and consequences of court procedures (Lefstein et al., 1969; Fester and Courtless, 1971; Emerson, 1969).

> ... typically the child will not testify ... He will understand little of the fast-moving colloquy between the prosecution, the defense, and the court, and his lawyer will not have time to explain much to him. Even after the court has announced its findings, in many cases the child will not know what decision has been reached until defense counsel explains the rest to him. (Hufnagel and Davidson, 1974)

Court personnel often recognize this lack of effective communication with juveniles. The following was a probation officer's response to the inquiry "Do juveniles understand what's happening to them?"

> I don't think so. I think very few understand. Most of them—I watch the kid when the hearing officer (referee) is making the statement after the disposition's been made. I watch the kids and you can tell they don't know what's going on. They're going, "Yeah. Sure. Alright. I'll sign the paper. What am I signing?" They don't know what they're signing. They're waiving their right to what? They don't know ... When I explain it to them I simplify it a great deal and say the court's going to have something to say in your life now.

Another probation officer assessed blame for juveniles' confusion on lawyers, as well as court personnel.

> When lawyers get into the courtroom a kid doesn't know what in the hell's going on ... When people start reading the petition: "Allegations of the petition are true." Heck. I didn't know what that was when I was fifteen years old. What in the world's an allegation? So, no, they don't know. People don't talk to them in plain, straight language. People don't talk to parents in plain, straight language. And most of the time, maybe, okay, alright, I just talked myself into it. Most of the time they don't know what's going on. You get out of a court hearing and the worker (probation officer) has to explain what they've been doing for 45 minutes in a hearing ... Part of it might be the jargon, the language. People getting too impressed with themselves—lawyers. I hate lawyers. They've just got their own thing ... Most of the time they've just got their head up their ass ... and our lawyers at the court are no exception. It's true.

Clear, complete explanations must be given to adolescents regarding the judicial experience in which they are immersed. They need and have a right to know what adjudication and disposition imply, what alternatives are available and what the consequences will be for each. They need to have their legal rights carefully explained and to be given the opportunity to make their decisions in a pressure-free situation.

The manner in which juveniles are informed of their legal rights is crucial. Many juveniles learn of their options through a rapid, mechanistic barrage of words: "You have the right to remain silent. You have the right to counsel. If you cannot afford counsel, one will be appointed by the court. You have the right to . . ." At the conclusion of this verbal attack follows the inquiry: "Do you have any questions?" Not surprisingly, the vast majority of juveniles, sufficiently intimidated and confused, are effectively silenced and "have no questions."

Rather than mesmerizing juveniles with a quick volley of unexplicated statements resembling assault more than instruction, court personnel must assume the responsibility of clearly interpreting these precious rights—painstakingly so, if necessary. Juveniles need to understand that they have a right to have an attorney and that their lawyer will present their case in the best light possible. They need to understand they will not be punished if they choose not to discuss anything and that the court must demonstrate their involvement beyond a reasonable doubt. Equally important, they must know that these rights are not contingent upon guilt or innocence, but rather, they are inherent in the juvenile judicial process.

Equally important, juveniles must be permitted to exercise or waive these rights in an unhurried, pressure-free situation. There is often parental pressure for juveniles to continue without counsel, for if an appointment of counsel is requested it may necessitate another trip to court for the family, perhaps creating transportation problems or additional time away from their jobs. The embarrassment experienced by parents due to their child's appearance in court also makes them desirous of settling the matter as expediently as possible. Parents may also feel financial pressure to continue without counsel, fearing they must bear the brunt of attorney fees. Thus, for various reasons, parents urge juveniles to "just tell the social worker or judge what happened." Court personnel may also exert verbal or unspoken pressure for juveniles to unthinkingly waive rights, wishing to avoid the complications and inconvenience of elaborate explanations and the inconvenience of rescheduling proceedings.

Expediency and convenience to parents or themselves must not be the foremost concern of court personnel. Their major priority should be to thoroughly inform juveniles regarding the court's workings and to encourage them to make a contribution to the process. All too frequently juveniles are asked to blindly trust in the benevolence and wisdom of the court. Social workers, lawyers and judges must take the initiative to eliminate the need for blind trust and replace it with thorough understanding.

THE RIGHT TO MEANINGFUL PARTICIPATION

Most of them (juveniles) are so used to not being part to decisions about themselves that they don't get upset about it.

Public Defender

It is a flat rule, not open to rebuttal, that officials know better than the youngster.

(Fox, 1974)

Once adolescents understand the judicial process in which they are involved and have been effectively informed of their rights they will be more able to play an active, decisive role in that process. Often juveniles become silent participants, the objects of adult decision-making. Their inexperience, lack of understanding regarding the legal process, and inability to articulate their views often place them at a great disadvantage. If the juvenile court envisioned itself as primarily punitive in orientation this inattention to juvenile thoughts and desires would be, perhaps, more understandable, but in a system espousing treatment ideals, the current situation is inexcusable.

As has been suggested, juveniles often do not comprehend the situation in which they find themselves. If this is alleviated, meaningful input from adolescents will be greatly facilitated. But it is also crucial for judges, attorneys, and social workers to sincerely solicit and respect the opinions of those they seek to help. Juveniles often have the experience of sitting silently abandoned while parents, social workers, attorneys and judges decide what is "in the best interest of the child."

It is not uncommon for parents and social workers to verbalize what they consider to be the opinions and feelings of juveniles. Some even answer questions which have been directed to juveniles. Much of this springs from genuine concern and the belief that juveniles cannot articulate well, but much is also the result of an unwillingness to respect and consider adolescent opinions. Equally disastrous, court personnel frequently express unquestioned faith in the opinions of adults—any adult. Whenever a conflict in opinion arises, be it between parent and child, police and child, social worker and child, the undeniable tendency is to denigrate or ignore the opinion of juveniles.

Although extremely reticient to admit it, most adults, even the well-intentioned, are not truly in touch with juvenile lives and needs. One reason this lack of knowledge and understanding persists is that adults do not seek or attend to the views of adolescents. When they do, it is often in a solicitous or perfunctory manner—the superficiality and insincerity of which are all too quickly comprehended by adolescents.

To assert that court personnel must listen to, and seriously consider, the feelings and opinions of juveniles is not to suggest that juveniles invariably know better than adult advisers. Admittedly, poor judgment, indiscretion and inexperience often bring adolescents before the court. Likewise, extremely young children are frequently at a disadvantage, lacking understanding of their actions or possible consequences of such behavior. The court must deal with these children, as well as those whose learning abilities and social skills are impaired or underdeveloped.

Nevertheless, many juveniles—regardless of age or educational prowess—have valuable insight into their familial and personal situations. Court personnel must sincerely solicit and painstakingly facilitate the expression of these insights. Presently, exceptional juveniles do participate in the process—those who are more articulate, more personable and more accustomed to the values or worldviews of court personnel.

Many juveniles are confused, angry, and unwilling to interact with adults, especially within the context of an authority relationship. Anxiety, resentfulness, and mistrust all decrease the communicative capabilities of juveniles. Nevertheless, juveniles should not have to be articulate or assertive or personable to participate in juvenile court proceedings. All juveniles have the right and need to be active participants: the court must recognize their reluctance and difficulties and allocate time and resources to deal with these problems.

Many of the children before the court have endured continuous negative evaluations of their behavior, their abilities and their selves. Many have never been encouraged or permitted to participate in their own futures, to express their views with the knowledge they will be listened to and respected. If guidance and protection are truly goals of the juvenile court, the most effective way of providing guidance is not through arbitrary dictates to juveniles: the maturity the court sees as so lacking in juveniles cannot be coerced or demanded, but must be created through development of the abilities and potential of each child.

To many adolescents the juvenile court is but another in an endless series of experiences of being acted upon by forces beyond their control. The court would more fully realize its goals of protection and treatment if court personnel would commit themselves to providing at least one experience—perhaps the first—in which adolescents meaningfully participate in the determination of their own fate.

THE RIGHT TO EFFECTIVE LEGAL REPRESENTATION

The role of the defense counsel greatly influences juveniles' experience within the court system, but presently the role is ambiguous and ill-defined. Juvenile court personnel may not be accustomed to the presence of a defense counsel; likewise, attorneys may be uncertain regarding their function within the juvenile court. Attorneys are confronted with numerous problems and dilemmas, none of which have been resolved conclusively. They often experience contradictory expectations and desires from court personnel, parents, and juveniles, and must balance these competing interests in their relationships and interactions with these three parties.

Private attorneys as well as public defenders are often unfamiliar with juvenile law and procedures, and they infrequently practice in that setting. Although some court personnel welcome and support the participation of a defense counsel, attorneys may encounter hostility and suspicion. They often receive the subtle or direct message that they will not be encouraged to pursue the strict advocacy role to which they are accustomed. Likewise, the treatment orientation of the court implies that resisting adjudication or treatment (disposition) would hinder efforts to help the child and attempting to "get juveniles off" through "technicalities" is not the responsible, adult course of action (Hufnagel and Davidson, 1974; Emerson, 1969).

In addition to the danger of court personnel attempting to limit the effectiveness of defense counsel, there is an equally important possibility that the defense counsel will voluntarily curtail her or his own effectiveness. Although there is increasing participation by private attorneys, the bulk of juvenile cases are represented by members of the public defender's office. Public defenders who are assigned to a juvenile court on a regular basis have the distinct advantage of experience within the juvenile court and a familiarity with court personnel. In such situations the defense counsel is in a better position to establish rapport with decision-makers, bargain more effectively for juvenile desires and perhaps gain occasional concessions for their clients because of her or his personal or working relationships with court personnel.

But, when public defenders are regularly assigned to a court, or perhaps employed by the court, there is great risk that the role of in-house counsel may limit the effectiveness of the legal representation for juveniles. Defense counsellors may become so well integrated into the court system that they adopt the philosophy and orientation of the court, becoming more an appendage of the court than representative for the child (Platt, 1977; Duffee and Siegel, 1971). Similarities between defense attorneys and court personnel in social background, education, and lifestyles create the possibility that the defense counsel's relationship with court personnel takes precedence over that with the juvenile.

In addition to potential difficulties in working with social workers, court attorneys and judges, defense attorneys must be prepared to deal with parents. In doing so they often find themselves in the awkward position of being caught between conflicting parental and juvenile desires. Those attorneys retained by parents to represent their child may experience extreme confusion regarding which party is the client. When conflicts arise, attorneys often pursue the course of action favored by parents. Even when the attorney is appointed by the court and financed by the state there is a strong tendency to support parental wishes over those of juveniles. This is an untenable position, one which attorneys must anticipate and avoid. Parents do, indeed, have the right to assert their opinions and desires, but if they are contrary to the juvenile's, they should retain separate counsel to advance those opinions. Juveniles have a right to the undivided allegiance of their legal representative.

Like other adults, attorneys often experience role disjuncture when their clients are adolescents. They are faced with the dilemma of whether to act as a strict advocate of juvenile desires or to act as a guardian making decisions regarding "the best interests of the child"—irrespective of juvenile wishes. Many choose the guardian role advanced by court personnel; some become interpreters of court proceedings and orders; and others attempt to be both a guardian and advocate and often find it a difficult or impossible task. A minority of attorneys interpret their role as the traditional adversary, arguing for juvenile desires regardless of their own opinions.

Too often the defense counsel merely joins the cadre of adult decision-makers attempting to determine what would be most therapeutic and helpful for the adolescent. Like other adults, attorneys frequently view juveniles as incapable of meaningful participation in the judicial process. They, too, distrust juvenile opinion and judgment, relegating them to an inconsequential, irrelevant position.

If legal representation for juveniles is to be meaningful, defense attorneys must establish a consistent and effective role. Juveniles are inundated with guardians-parents, social workers, psychological personnel, court attorneys, referees and judges all view themselves primarily as guardians of the child. The guardian forces are ample within the juvenile court. Adolescents need and must have at least one adult voice acting solely as their advocate, articulating their opinions and desires. Defense attorneys who act primarily as guardians are not defense attorneys; they are appendages of the juvenile court. Their presence does little to engender an atmosphere of fairness or a sense of justice within juveniles.

Juveniles do need guardians, but the fact that many court personnel see themselves in that role does not negate the prosecutorial dimensions of their actions. Court personnel often present evidence against juveniles and frequently recommend action contrary to juvenile desires. It is not sufficient to suggest that, with age, juveniles may recognize the wisdom of court action. Adolescents must know *now* that they have ample opportunity to express their opinions and that they will be aided in this expression by legal counsel unequivocally committed to their clients.

To suggest that the defense counsel play a strict advocacy role does not imply that all juvenile cases will result in full-scale adversary proceedings. It is merely to suggest that if juveniles favor this type of proceeding they will be afforded the opportunity and legal assistance to engage in it. Nor does the strict advocacy role imply that defense attorneys need relinquish their responsibility and opportunity to provide juveniles with experienced, adult counsel regarding the appropriate course of action. Attorneys need not ignore their experience or restrain from questioning the wishes of their adolescent clients. Such is certainly not the relationship between attorneys and their adult clients.

In confidential attorney-client conferences the counsellor is free, to candidly give juveniles experienced and mature advice. This is the attorney's responsibility to any client, and indeed, juveniles greatly need that advice. But once juveniles have received the benefit of such counsel they must have the right to determine a course of action and be assured that defense counsel will pursue it adamantly.

SUMMARY

What many view as the present crisis in the juvenile court also represents its greatest opportunity. But to realize the full potential of the juvenile justice system, lawyers, social workers, psychological personnel and judges must reevaluate court policies, acknowledge their limitations, and explore new alternatives. In order to do this they must become attuned to the multifaceted needs of today's adolescents. They must seek and attend to the opinions and desires of their clients as well as restructure relationships and procedures to afford juveniles meaningful participation. Only then will the juvenile court be able to successfully meet the challenge of protecting and guiding juveniles.

REFERENCES

Aries, P. (1962), *Centuries of Childhood: A Social History of Family Life.* New York: Vintage Books, Alfred A. Knopf, Inc.

Blumberg, A. (1970), *Criminal Justice.* Chicago: Quadrangle Books.

Duffee, D. and Siegel, L. (1971), The Organization Man: Legal Counsel in Juvenile Court. *Crim. Law Bull.,* 7:544-553.

Ellis, B.J. (1976), Juvenile Court: The Legal Process as a Rehabilitative Tool. *Wash. Law Rev.* 51:697-732.

Emerson, R. (1969), *Judging Delinquents: Context and Process in Juvenile Court.* Chicago: Aldine Publishing Company.

Faust, F. (1974), A Perspective on the Dilemma of Free Will and Determinism in Juvenile Justice. *Juvenile Justice,* 25:54-60.

Fester, E. and Courtless, T. (1972), Pre-dispositional Data, Role of Counsel and Delinquency in Juvenile Court. *Law Soc. Rev.,* 7:195-222.

Flicker, B. (1977), *Standards for Juvenile Justice: A Summary and Analysis.* Cambridge, Mass.: Ballinger Publishing.

Fox, S. (1974), The reform of juvenile justice: The right to punishment. *Juvenile Justice* 25:2-9.

In Re Gault (1967), 387 U.S. 1.

Grisso, J. T. and Manoogian, S. (1978), Juveniles' Comprehension of Miranda Warnings. In Lipsitt, P.D. and Sales, B.D. (Eds.), *New Directions in Psycholegal Research.* New York: Van Nostrand Reinhold.

Hufnagel, L. and Davidson, J. (1974), Children in need: Observations of practices of the Denver Juvenile Court. *Denver Law J.,* 51:337-415.

Kent v. United States (1966), 383 U.S. 541

Lefstein, N., Stapleton, V, and Teitelbaum, L. (1969), In search of juvenile justice: Gault and its implementations. *Law Soc. Rev.,* 3:491-562.

Mack, J. (1909), The Juvenile Court. *Harvard Law Rev.,* 23:104-122.

Martin, J. (1970), *Toward a Political Definition of Delinquency.* Washington, D.C.: U.S. Government Printing Office.

Paulsen, M. (1957), Fairness to the juvenile offender. *Minnesota Law Rev.,* 41:547-576.

Platt, A. (1977), *The Child Savers: The Invention of Delinquency.* 2nd edition. Chicago: University of Chicago Press.

Schullenberger, J. and Murphy, P. (1973), Crisis in Juvenile Court—is bifurcation an answer? *Chicago Bar Record,* 55:117-128.

Schur, E. (1973), *Radical Nonintervention: Rethinking the Delinquency Problem.* Englewood Cliffs, N.J.: Prentice-Hall.

Simpson, A. (1976), Rehabilitation as the justification of a separate juvenile justice system. *Calif. Law Rev.,* 64:984-1017.

Stekette, J. (1973), Community and behavioral approaches to delinquency: The Court's perspective. *Juvenile Justice,* 24:19-24.

Tappan, P. (1946), Treatment without trial. *Social Forces* 24:306-320.

Waite, E. (1921), How far can court procedure be socialized without impairing individual rights? *J. Amer. Inst. Crim. Law and Criminol.* 12:339-347.

Winship (1970), 397 U.S. 358.

PART IV
Health

8

Mental Health Care for the One-in-Seven

MICHAEL G. KALOGERAKIS

According to recently updated estimates (Report of the President's Commission on Mental Health, Vol. I, 1978), 15% of the population of the United States has sufficient emotional disturbance to require services. The latest census figures indicate that there are a total of 65 million under the age of 18 of whom 30 million are between the ages of twelve and seventeen (U.S. Census Report, 1970). Fifteen percent of this last figure, namely 4,500,000, are adolescents who should be receiving mental health care of some kind. No one knows for sure how many are actually getting such care. In 1975 approximately 50,000 children and youth under 18 were in state and county mental hospitals while some 600,000 were admitted to the mental health system in our country and perhaps another one hundred to two hundred thousand were seen in private practice by psychiatrists and psychologists.[1] Perhaps of those needing services only about a third will have been in some form of mental health care by the time they reach their 21st birthday.

The history of mental health services for adolescents is comparatively short. Although psychiatric treatment of some kind has been available for centuries (and was described in antiquity), adolescence as an age group worthy of special attention seems not to have entered public consciousness until the latter part of the nineteenth century. The word adolescence was used for the first time in the fifteenth century (Muuss, 1962) and the first psychology of adolescence did not make its appearance until 1904 (Hall,

1904). Actual programs addressing the mental health needs of the age group are of far more recent vintage.

The first inpatient psychiatric hospital unit devoted exclusively to adolescents was established at Bellevue Hospital (Curran, 1939) in 1939. However, mental health efforts with a teenage population had already been initiated under nonmedical auspices as part of the child guidance movement and in relationship to delinquent youth. The Institute for Juvenile Research in Chicago, which opened in 1909 (Beiser, 1966), the Judge Baker Clinic in Boston, which opened in 1917 (Gardner, 1953), and Pioneer House, which opened in 1946 (Redl and Wineman, 1951) are examples of mental health settings which addressed an adolescent population in which delinquency was a common finding. The past 30 years have seen a proliferation in the number and kinds of services for adolescents, which today are provided by a variety of public and private agencies. The increase in services has proceeded haphazardly, evolving more in relationship to emerging crises and political pressures than as part of a logical plan. More recently, of course, some order has crept into the picture as communities, agencies, and planning groups have sought to fill the gaps in services and funding sources have demanded cost-effective programs, accountability and elimination of wasteful overlap.

This chapter will examine current thinking on services for emotionally disturbed adolescents and describe some parameters of the way they are organized. Particular attention will be given to the role of government in funding, fostering, developing and organizing services.

THE NEEDS

Adolescent disturbances run the gamut of psychopathology including much that is seen at other ages. In addition, there are disorders which are characteristic of the age period. Acute and chronic conditions, behavior disorders and adjustment reactions, severe psychoses, intrapsychic and interpersonal conflicts occur. The psychoses—manic-depressive and schizophrenia—are first in large numbers seen during adolescence, as is much delinquency and crime. Educational and vocational handicaps become entrenched, suicide first makes its appearance in larger numbers (it is now the second leading cause of death in the age group) (see Sugar, Chapter 10), and unwanted (or unplanned) teenage pregnancy has become a major social problem (see Sugar, Chapter 13). Data on child abuse indicate that teenage parents are at high risk for becoming abusive.

The runaway is invariably an adolescent. So too is the beginning drinker (there are over 1 million problem drinkers 12-17 years of age), and drug abuser. The National Institute of Drug Abuse (Hersh, 1977) reports the following estimates for 12- to 17-year-olds: 3.8 million users of marijuana, 1.1 million users of hashish, 500,000 users of LSD and other hallucinogens, 530,000 users of cocaine, 580,000 users of tranquilizers.

Some psychosomatic disturbances, notably anorexia nervosa and obesity, are typically adolescent but may continue and evolve into adult forms of illness.

Those who work with adolescents know that the mental health needs of these youths are but one part of the overall human services that must be delivered. Education, employment, welfare, health, recreation, and general support to the youngster and his family may be equally or more important depending on the particular case. Often, there is overlap among those responsible for delivering specific services. It is obvious, for example, that a child in a private child care institution (a social service agency) may have mental health needs that must be met. Similarly, all adolescents in our mental health system require an education program geared to their specific needs. The resulting complexity in delivery of services is awesome and poses serious problems for government agencies charged with the responsibility of funding and overseeing the development of adequate services.

THE SERVICE-DELIVERY SYSTEM

Contemporary approaches to delivering mental health services are characterized by a number of features:

1. A comprehensive network of services from the least to the most restrictive in accordance with the needs of the patient.
2. The shortest possible stay in a hospital and, in general, strong preference for utilization of nonresidential approaches.
3. Voluntary participation of the adolescent and his family.
4. Multidisciplinary evaluation and treatment teams.
5. Interagency coordination aimed at avoiding duplication and eliminating gaps.
6. Use of a wide array of treatment modalities (though prevailing biases may lead to differences in emphasis among treatment centers).

The early emphasis on hospital and other forms of residential (24-hour) care has given way to a new generation of approaches typified by the day hospital and the group home. Both have sprung up in the past two decades and have attained wide use. Today, comprehensive mental health care for children and adolescents requires at least the following components: [2]

1. Consultation and education
2. Screening and evaluation
3. Emergency services
4. Outpatient services
5. Partial hospitalization (day treatment)
6. Residential treatment (including inpatient care)
7. Transitional services (including group homes)
8. Follow-up
9. Drop-in centers, runaway centers, etc.

Which of the listed services is appropriate to a given patient depends on the nature and severity of the illness, the point in its course, the presence or absence of dangerousness, the family situation, and the availability of other supports. Other factors such as the ability of the adolescent and his family to cooperate with the treatment plan play a role. Only some of the services in such a comprehensive network may be needed in a particular case. For example, some youths never require more than the support provided by a drop-in center; others, who are initially very ill, may move from emergency, to inpatient, to day treatment, to follow-up services. Criteria for admission to each type of care, and for deciding on the length of time that that service is necessary should be developed by every mental health delivery system. This is in keeping with the requirements of the Accreditation Council on Psychiatric Facilities (AC/PF) of the Joint Commission on Accreditation of Hospitals (JCAH); (Joint Commission on Accreditation of Hospitals, 1974).

Kinds of Services

The following represent some uses of the various kinds of services:

Consultation and Education

These are aimed at the community and at agencies that work with adolescents. They are likely to be most useful to schools, juvenile courts and juvenile facilities. Helping non-mental health personnel to understand the mental health needs of adolescents and to make use of basic principles of treatment may avert more serious problems and more extensive intervention.

Screening and Evaluation

These assist public and private agencies which care for adolescents to assess changes in behavior which may call for a change in the treatment plan. Determination of mental competence, assessment of dangerousness, diagnosis, and dispositional recommendations are important services provided to the court. Occasionally, a refined diagnostic evaluation may be needed by a child caring institution lacking the expertise to differentiate among various possibilities suggested by a changing clinical picture. A good example of such a need is depression or withdrawal developing in an unstable adolescent raising the possibility of a suicide attempt.

Emergency Services

Numerous emergency situations occur in the lives of adolescents, including acute psychotic episodes, suicide attempts, serious family crises and assaultive or other violent behavior (Kalogerakis, 1976). Severe anxiety and agitation, drug-related episodes and psychological reactions to physical illness are also seen. Many emergencies may be handled in the community by quick effective action; others clearly require admission to a hospital. Coordination of emergency services with other services, especially follow-up care, is essential to assure continuity of care and prevention of future crises. Round-the-clock availability, a hot-line and other features of the crisis center are necessary to deal with the variety of adolescent emergencies.

Outpatient Services

The adolescent who is emotionally troubled but is not placing himself or others in serious jeopardy, is able to function in school and manage reasonably at home, may be treated in an outpatient setting. Since this interferes least with his normal life, it is the setting of choice. At a time when deinstitutionalization has become equated with all that is good in psychiatric treatment, we must be careful not to place intolerable stress on a youngster whose ego resources are not adequate to cope with the strain of living in the community. As has been pointed out by several writers (Kalogerakis, 1973; Rinsley, 1974), adolescents are peculiarly vulnerable in this regard, cannot always make use of support networks in the community and need the greater structure provided by either day hospital treatment or inpatient care.

Partial Hospitalization

The severely disturbed adolescent who presents no risk when at liberty in the community may be placed in a day treatment program which provides more intensive treatment than does outpatient care, at the same time that it occupies many more hours of the youth's day. Partial hospitalization can either be chosen as an alternative to hospitalization or as the next logical step after a patient has been in the hospital. In the latter case, it would be recommended when the patient is not considered ready for full return to community living. In contrast to 24-hour residential care, which should be as brief as possible, day treatment for an adolescent may extend for up to a year or more. It is generally not an appropriate service for youths with problems in impulse control, especially if antisocial, since the temptation of being at liberty in the community is too great.

Residential Treatment and Hospitalization

This is used for the most severely disturbed, at the most acute phases of their illness. Though a hospital stay should optimally be brief—perhaps no more than three months—a residential treatment center in a non-hospital setting is equipped to keep a child for several years. Suicidal and assaultive patients require the additional structure and security of the hospital, often on a locked ward. This is mandatory for an inveterate runaway who may harm himself or another. Residential treatment centers, while providing 24-hour care, are invariably open settings, with a lower staff-patient ratio, and a more social service-type of care; the medical model is often eschewed. Ideally, these two components should be closely integrated, the one serving as back-up for the other, the second as a needed resource when hospitalization is no longer necessary.

Transitional Services

This includes all community-based services which provide a living arrangement other than the natural home such as halfway houses, group homes and foster care. Though intended as brief placements pending improvement in the home situation, they often end up being the definitive placement of the adolescent prior to his moving to independent living. Obviously, some homes are too destructive or chaotic to permit return of a youngster who has been removed. The group home or foster home offers the closest approximation to normal family living, allowing the normal process of growth and development to continue with a minimum of interference.

Follow-up

In the experience of this author, the lack of, or inadequate, follow-up of adolescents who have had a bout of serious mental illness, as well as those with lesser disturbance, is the major factor in recurrence of problems and ultimate re-hospitalization. In some instances, follow-up is a relatively simple matter involving a monthly visit and renewal of a prescription. More frequently, it is a complex, costly, and almost unfeasible undertaking which requires a host of support services to child and family in an attempt to substitute constructive activity for the usual activities that take up a youth's leisure time. It is more difficult when home and neighborhood are conducive to psychosocial deterioration. It is made easier if significant impact has been made, during earlier treatment, on the youth's ability to utilize his own ego resources to cope more successfully with stress and to resist the noxious influences of his peer group. To be effective, follow-up must be more than a token program. It must address all of the stresses likely to be encountered on re-entry, provide the support most likely to make a difference and be sustained long enough to permit substantial stabilization.

Drop-in Centers

The adolescent's often profound need to preserve his autonomy, as well as a common distrust of the adult world and officialdom, may make it difficult for him to reach out for help. This is all the more true for the ghetto youth who is additionally exposed to his culture's general distrust of the established power structure. So too, the drug-abusing adolescent avoids contact with the health system unless and until he becomes physically quite ill, as with an overdose. To go to a hospital clinic or even a community mental health center may be impossible, particularly if these are identified specifically as places for mentally or emotionally disturbed individuals. Thus, the generically conceived storefront operation, offering as it does a wide variety of services (health, legal, educational, vocational, recreation) will attract and hold youths in need who might otherwise receive no services at all. In this broader concept, it is often possible to achieve important mental health goals since they are far more acceptable to the youth (Lecker et al., 1973).

A special variety of drop-in center, which must be allied to a network of crash-pads or residences, is aimed at the runaway. Having more reason than most to steer clear of authorities, the runaway youth must often be approached with a "no questions asked" offer to help (Gordon, 1978). The center must be located in the areas of the city usually frequented by those who have left home. The adolescent prostitute, of both sexes, is a runaway who poses particular problems and requires exceptionally skillful and sensitive handling (Ritter, 1978).

Once a youth is engaged, referral for more specific mental health services may be possible although, even in the absence of such, a great deal can often be accomplished by such activities as peer group discussions led by a trained staff member, contact with healthy role models, etc.

All of the above services can be integrated into a community mental health center or, in part, be based in other locations and auspices, such as a hospital center. What is essential is that the full range of services be available to the youth of a given catchment area. Realities often require that some of the services be accessible in neighboring catchment areas or elsewhere in the state.

TREATMENT MODALITIES

Since most forms of psychopathology can be seen during the adolescent phase of development, most treatment modalities also have their application. Individual psychotherapy, family therapy, and group therapy are the basic treatment approaches and are likely to have the widest use. They are particularly valuable when intrapsychic and interpersonal conflict are present, and with adolescents who are intact enough to conceptualize and verbalize their problems and undergo change.

Medication, though by no means the first approach to be considered, has an important place in the therapeutic armamentarium for all patients. It is most likely to be useful for the more severely disturbed adolescent for whom psychotherapy is inappropriate. Because of concern that psychotropic drugs have been used for behavior or social control, legal forces have attempted to place sanctions on the freedom physicians traditionally exercise in prescribing medication. Not only is it important therefore to know what drug to use for what purpose—and this is an ever-changing field—but also to be familiar with the complex issues of right to treatment (and right to refuse treatment) that may apply in specific jurisdictions [3] (see Gothard, Chapter 6).

Even more than pharmocotherapy, electroconvulsive therapy (ECT) has been subjected to scrutiny and attack by civil libertarians concerned with what they perceive as the excessive power society has vested in psychiatrists. In some states, (e.g., California) the use of ECT has been severely limited by statute. In addition, the Mental Health Law Project (1978) formed at the behest of N.I.M.H. has developed model statutes governing psychiatric treatment which place great obstacles in the path of clinicians wishing to make use of ECT. The draft being circulated at this writing specifically concerned with minors in fact bars "psychosurgery, electroconvulsive therapy or other form of shock treatment, or insulin coma therapy" (New York State Office of Mental Health, 1978). As might be expected, these initiatives are being forcefully challenged by the psychiatric profession.

Fortunately, the use of ECT in adolescents is very uncommon and generally limited to catatonic states refractory to a pharmacotherapeutic approach and posing some danger to life (through refusal of food, for example).

Depression is usually reactive and should respond to psychotherapy; acute schizophrenic reactions should remit spontaneously or respond to phenothiazines. Other forms of convulsive therapy are now rarely used with adult patients, let alone minors. Psychosurgery involving minors is unknown to this author and there is no clinical syndrome for which I would recommend it.

FEDERAL LEGISLATION

Beginning with the Community Mental Health Centers Act (1963), a series of laws have been passed which impact in varying degrees on the delivery of mental health services to adolescents. In general, such legislation directs funding to specific program areas, setting standards and regulating the manner in which the funds may be used. The following is a brief summary of relevant legislation and the ways in which it pertains to delivery of mental health care to the adolescent population.

The Mental Retardation Facilities and Community Mental Health Centers Construction Act—P.L. 88-164—Expanded in 1975 from the original 5 mandated services to 12, including the addition of services to children and youth. Implementation is not occurring very quickly, however, and many states have not developed a significant network of Community Mental

Health Centers. As of October 1978, there were 647 centers in operation across the country. Many communities are unable to establish the full range of services required and some do not need them.

Among the recommendations made by the President's Commission on Mental Health was that flexibility be allowed to communities in determining what services are needed, and that priority be given in a new grant program to children, adolescents and the elderly; unserved and underserved areas; minorities; and those with chronic mental illness (Mental Health Law Project).

The Juvenile Justice and Delinquency Prevention Act (1974)—Has provided sizable funding to delinquency treatment and prevention programs, some of which has been aimed at mental health aspects. Emphasis has gradually shifted from attention to treatment of special target groups (e.g., the violent adolescent) to programs in prevention.

The Child Protective Services Act (1973)—Aimed at child abuse and neglect and geared to social services intervention, this legislation has recently been directed to mental health aspects, adolescents, and sexual abuse.

Amendments to the Social Security Act such as Title V (maternal and child health), Title X (family planning), Title XIX (Medicaid and Early Periodic Screening, Diagnosis & Treatment—EPSDT), and Title XX (Social Service Programs for Individuals and Families).

Education of the Handicapped Act—P.L. 94-142—A most important piece of legislation which directs money to the schools to foster the development of "related services," which include psychological services. This legislation has sweeping implications for both delivery of mental health services and the interface between the education system and mental health agencies. The issue of parallel systems of care which essentially duplicate one another is one that must be considered; the question of appropriate auspices for delivery of particular services is another.

Other legislation has been passed (such as the Runaway Act) which concerns adolescents in trouble in some way. In addition, there is pending activity in Washington, which will have to be taken up by the 96th Congress, that may have a significant impact on mental health services to children and adolescents. Three initiatives in particular deserve to be mentioned:

(1) *The Child Health Assessment Plan (CHAP)*—Designed to replace

Early Periodic Screening, Diagnosis and Treatment (EPSDT) of Title XIX, it will allow for periodic assessment at critical points of development, including puberty and adolescence. The psychiatric aspects of the bill are still being debated, chiefly because of costs, but it is expected that CHAP will pass in some form.

(2) *The "Most in Need" Program (MIN)*—An NIMH proposal aimed at children and youth who are severely disturbed, the MIN program seeks to spur linkages with other systems of care (health, welfare, corrections, etc.) and carries forth some of the recommendations of the President's Commission on Mental Helth.

(3) *National Health Insurance*—Though still a few years away from passage, a number of versions of this legislation are being vigorously defended. One of the major points of controversy is coverage for mental disabilities. It is thought unlikely that any but brief psychiatric care will be covered, again because it is assumed that more would be fiscally prohibitive.

THE ROLE OF THE STATES

From its beginnings, care of the mentally ill in the United States has been a responsibility of the states. The most severely disturbed (with the exception of the very rich) have invariably been cared for in state hospitals. The state has been both provider of services and the licensing, regulatory and planning authority.

Today changes are occurring in this traditional mode of care. Voluntary hospitals, no longer limited to those who can pay out-of-pocket, are taking many patients who formerly had no alternative to the state hospital. At a planning level, states are relinquishing some of their responsibilities to the localities. Some are getting out of the business of providing direct services altogether. However, for the foreseeable future, the states will continue to have prime responsibility for establishing needs, regulating and licensing mental health facilities, funneling federal and state dollars to the localities, and developing the over-all state plan. Some aspects of the role of the state mental health planning agency and the problems it faces in carrying out its mandate are considered here.

Good program development begins with an accurate assessment of population needs. Communities differ greatly in the number and type of services they need; for example, an urban population is sure to have a much higher degree of social pathology than a rural setting, as manifested by delinquency, alcoholism and the like. A reliable means of knowing exactly what such needs are would have to be based on a tracking system that begins with early identification, covers all agencies providing human services and extends throughout the lifetime of the individual. This is an impossible goal for all but the most stable societies. Even countries such as Sweden, which have a highly developed tracking system, have experienced difficulty, and highly mobile societies, such as ours, must find a compromise solution. It should be possible to achieve a fairly high degree of tracking during the school years by maintaining a central resource file on all who enter care, whether in the social service, corrections, physical or mental health areas. If statewide, such a system could maintain tracking on all but those families which move to other states or roam free in the shadows of our urban waste-lands in a quasinomadic fashion. Once an individual becomes part of the work force, tracking would be more difficult. Even a modest improvement on current performance in this area would help. It would permit a much more accurate determination of the kinds of services needed and reduce empty hospital beds, insufficient community residences and under-utilized out-patient services. It would make it possible to shift our energies to the assurance of quality care in all areas.

A state mental health agency must compete for state dollars with other state agencies. In tight fiscal times, the success it has will determine to a large extent whether programs it wishes to promulgate are funded. In this regard, the establishment of a strong constituency—an advocacy group composed of consumers and community representatives—is critical. Mental health agencies, in comparison to mental retardation, for example, have always experienced difficulty in establishing such a voice, probably because the families of emotionally disturbed children and adolescents are more likely to be disorganized and overwhelmed than the families of children with developmental or physical disabilities. This often results in a flow of dollars into other areas.

In other ways, the state mental health agency can play an important role in deciding how the available moneys are to be spent. A strong, centralized office for children and adolescents is an important way of assuring this. A separate budget will help make such an office a more effective force. Ideally, it should be headed by a high-level person from one of the relevant disciplines (if possible a psychiatrist or psychologist) to give it additional visibility, power, and status, and to enhance a creative approach to planning and development. Such a person should be able to call upon the expertise available in the community, spur advocacy activity, work well with other agencies and deal effectively with legislators.

Returning to the issue of quality care, the goal of all human services agencies, it is perhaps primarily dependent on attracting the best personnel to the field and training them thoroughly for their particular jobs. Competitive salaries, careful screening to include only those who have a genuine interest and aptitude for working with youth, and skillful teaching are essential. Attractive working conditions help us hold on to qualified staff: realistic staff-patient ratios, creative programs and effective supervision are needed.

An increasingly troublesome area for many facilities in the public sector attempting to establish good care is the degree to which personnel can be moved or fired when they are inadequate. In this connection, it is sad to see that employee unions, understandably advocating for their members, have too often become barriers to the provision of the best care for patients. This problem has affected inpatient care in particular, becoming one of the more powerful factors fostering deinstitutionalization.

Unable to get rid of undesirable employees without endless, time-consuming hearings, public institutions, have preferred to close than continue to provide poor care. Clearly, the civil service dilemma, just recently addressed by the federal government, will have to be resolved also at the state level.

THE FUTURE

Many of the directions for the years ahead have already been charted. We know that mental health services for adolescents must be part and parcel of a holistic approach to meeting their needs (as this volume amply testifies); we know that the services must, wherever possible, be provided in the community; we know, too, that they must be made increasingly cost-effective for we are living in a time of shrinking tax dollars for human services.

What we shall have to develop—to date there has been mostly verbiage—is a solid program of prevention and early intervention. Prevention can and must be primary, secondary and tertiary; intervention can and must address all age groups depending on the particular problem being tackled. Although research in genetics and obstetrical counselling may be the proper approach for autism and other developmental disabilities, peer group discussion among young adolescents may be the most effective way of intervening early with some of the major problems of adolescence. For each problem area there is a best time to intervene, and a choice of methods most likely to be effective.

To make such programs palatable to those who must dispense the funds, they must be grounded solidly in research that demonstrates their feasibility and value. The evaluation component of new programs is consequently of crucial importance.

Much of the psychopathology of adolescence is clearly preventable. It will be a major test for society and those who govern to create healthy circumstances in the environment at large, to assist families struggling with forces we know to be pathogenic within the family unit, and to intervene effectively when these efforts do not suffice. It is not a mandate we can ignore. Adolescents have a way of reminding us of our failings and the cost to society is immeasurable.

NOTES

1. All figures courtesy of the National Institute of Mental Health (Hersh, 1977).
2. The first five were those services mandated by the Community Mental Health Centers Act. Numerous descriptions of the remaining services can be found in the literature. The one used here is adapted from useful guidelines recently developed by and available from the New England Children's Mental Health Task Force, Suite 300, 25 Huntington Avenue, Boston, Mass. 02116. (July 1978)
3. Both clinical and legal aspects of this issue are discussed in guidelines recently issued by the New York State Office of Mental Health (1978). They are obtainable by writing the author at Bureau of Children & Youth Services, New York State Office of Mental Health, 44 Holland Avenue, Albany, N.Y. 12229.

REFERENCES

Beiser, H.R. (1966), Fifty-seven Years of Child Guidance: The Experience of the Institute for Juvenile Research. Proceedings of the Fourth World Congress of Psychiatry. Excerpta Medica-International Congress Series No. 150, Madrid.

Curran, F.J. (1939), Organization of a ward for adolescents in Bellevue Psychiatric Hospital. *Amer. J. Psychiat.* 95:1365.

Gardner, G. (1953), American child psychiatric clinics. *Annals Amer. Acad. Polit. Soc. Sci.* 286:126.

Gordon, J.S. (1978), The Runaway Center as Community Mental Health Center. *Amer. J. Psychiat.* 135: 932-935.

Gothard, S. (1979) The Expanding Right to Treatment for Minors. In M. Sugar (Ed.), *Responding to Adolescent Needs.* New York: Spectrum Pbl.

Hall, G.S. (1904), *Adolescence.* New York: Appleton.

Hersh, S.P. (1977), In Proceedings of Symposium "Critical Issues in Adolescent Mental Health" presented at the American Society for Adolescent Psychiatry Meeting Nov. 20, Washington, D.C.

Joint Commission on Accreditation of Hospitals (1974), Accreditation Manual for Psychiatric Facilities Serving Children and Adolescents.

Kalogerakis, M.G. (1973), Institutionalization: An Editorial. *Newsletter,* American Society for Adolescent Psychiatry, August.

——— (1976), Adolescents in Crisis. In Psychiatric Emergencies, Glick, Meyerson, Robbins and Talbot (Eds.), New York: Grune and Stratton.

Lecker, S., Hendricks, L., and Touransky, J. (1973), New Dimensions in Adolescent Psychotherapy: A Therapeutic System Approach *Pediatric Clinics of North America* 20: 4,
Symposium on Adolescent Medicine.

Mental Health Law Project (1978), Legal Issues in State Mental Health Care: Proposals for
Change—Mental Health Treatment for Minors, *Mental Disabil. Law Rep.* 2:4 (Jan.-
Feb.).

Muuss, R.E. (1962), *Theories of Adolescence.* New York: Random House.

New England Children's Mental Health Task Force (1978), *Guidelines, Comprehensive Community Mental Health Services for Children,* July.

New York State Office of Mental Health (1978), *Pharmacotherapy for Institutionalized Adolescents,* M.G. Kalogerakis (Ed).

Redl, F. and Wineman, D. (1951), *Children Who Hate.* Glencoe, Illinois: Free Press.

Report of the President's Commission on Mental Health (1978), Vol. I, Washington, D.C.,
United States Government Printing Office.

Rinsley, D.B. (1974), Residential Treatment of Adolescents. In S. Arieti (Ed.), *American Handbook of Psychiatry* Vol. II, New York: Basic Books.

Ritter, B. (1978), "Problems of Adolescent Prostitutes: A Growing Phenomenon in America,"
presented at Annual Meeting, American Society for Adolescent Psychiatry, May.

Sugar, M. (1979), Family problems in adolescent suicide. In M. Sugar (Ed.), *Responding to
Adolescent Needs.* New York: Spectrum Pbl.

———— (1979), The epidemic of adolescent motherhood. In M. Sugar (Ed.), *Responding to
Adolescent Needs.* New York; Spectrum Pbl.

U.S. Census Report. U.S. Government Printing Office. 1970.

9

The Psychiatric Response
to Delinquency

RICHARD C. MAROHN

It is now over 20 years since Sondheim (1957), in his lyrics for Officer Krupke in "West Side Story," described the disagreement, confusion, and competition among the helping professions as they confront the problem of juvenile delinquency in the United States. The disagreements center around not only causes and cures, but also the severity of the problem. The confusion shows itself in what statistics mean to whom, and in who is responsible for what. The competition is, unfortunately, not always between various modalities of intervention fighting to prove their efficacy, but between various agencies and resources attempting to pass the buck. Despite society's increasing preoccupation with serious and violent crimes, not much has changed in these 20 years.

Psychiatrists have neglected this field, either by seeking more promising and greener therapeutic pastures, or by posing as community and political experts who seek to reorganize society and neighborhoods. The primary focus of psychiatry—the psychological, psychopathology, and individual psychodynamics—is clouded and confused when we assess how psychiatrists respond to the problem of juvenile delinquency. That problem is serious and extensive.

THE PROBLEM

In 1974, there were over 6,100,000 arrests in the United States for serious crimes such as criminal homicide, forcible rape, robbery, aggravated assault, and arson; of these, 1,700,000 or just over 27% were committed by persons under 18 years of age (Rand Corp. 1976). Juveniles commit 10% of all the murders, 19 of all the forcible rapes, 32% of all the robberies, 17% of all the aggravated assaults, and 58% of all the arsons. When burglary, larceny, and motor vehicle thefts are added to this list, more than half of all the serious crimes in the United States are found to be committed by youths from 10 to 17 *(Time, 1977)*.

An exhaustive survey of youth in Illinois conducted by the Institute for Juvenile Research in 1972 demonstrated that from 25% to 95% of Illinois youth were involved in violent acts, varying with gender, race, age, socioeconomic status, and community size.

In the Offer study of modal teenage boys (1969), chosen for their satisfactory adjustment and being viewed by themselves and others as "average," some 25% of the subjects, white middle-class suburban, were involved in significant delinquency.

In Cook County, Illinois, alone, which comprises most of the Metropolitan Chicago area, 13,494 delinquent petitions and counts were filed in the juvenile court in 1976. Eight percent were committed by females, and 92% by males. Interestingly enough, this total was some 15% smaller than the 1975 figures.

The problem is serious. If, indeed, there has been a decrease in Chicago, what made it happen? People tell us there is an apparent increase in the seriousness of crime committed by female teenagers. Is this, indeed, so? Is it related to the feminist movement? Or to changing practices of child-rearing? Or is it due to differential ways of treating and cataloguing juvenile female offenders?

A serious deficiency in this data is the fact that much suburban delinquency, as well as urban, goes undetected and unreported, yet is serious. Many affluent teenagers are handled, not by the juvenile justice system but are either treated by the mental health system or, because they are affluent, not attended to at all. Many psychiatrists see these young people in their offices and they are called "behavioral disorders." True to the biases of our society, if these teenagers are ever brought to the attention of the juvenile justice system, people are surprised because they come from such "good homes" and "good neighborhoods."

SOCIETY'S PREOCCUPATION

This is consistent with society's preoccupation with teenage unemployment, racism, poor schools, and poverty as the factors primarily responsible for juvenile delinquency. Similarly, high-level debate about deinstitutionalization and institutionalization is based not on research, or even on theoretical bias, but rather determined primarily by political winds and the condition of the state treasury.

The 1967 *"Task Force Report,"* Juvenile Delinquency and Youth Crime, presented to the President's Commission on Law Enforcement and the Administration of Justice, contains 20 appendices, none of which was written by a psychiatrist, and none of which focused on issues of individual psychopathology and psychotherapy. Of course, the Task Force, itself, contained not a single psychiatrist. The Task Force made 38 recommendations, most of which had to do with improving the quality of life and communities, schools, employment, and the juvenile justice system. Three relate to treatment. The Task Force recommended that private and public efforts should be intensified to "make counseling and therapy easily obtainable." The Task Force acknowledged that despite the best of community circumstances, some families need help. "Counseling and therapy provide one promising method of dealing with complex emotional and psychological relationships within the family, and should be made easily available" (p. 47). The immediate next sentences said that "credit unions," "homemaker helpers," and help with "marketing and other household skills" are also promising. But, nothing was said about individual psychology and psychopathology.

A second recommendation was to intensify public and private efforts to "provide community residential centers. . . . Small residential centers have proved successful in a number of communities in steering youth away from incipient trouble by providing more supervision than they get at home, yet in an atmosphere that is not institutional or coercive" (p. 48). Perhaps residential treatment should not be provided in an atmosphere of firmness and limit-setting! The efficacy of residential treatment seems to derive from providing "more supervision," not from a more psychodynamically-oriented understanding of the problem.

The final treatment oriented recommendation of the Task Force with particular reference to the "slum child," was that private and public efforts should be expended to "deal better with behavior problems." Unfortunately, this appears to be an issue outside of the slum as well. The Task Force explained that "it is also important that schools learn to understand and control the child who arrives at school accustomed to autonomy, and averse to assertions of authority. New methods of dealing with behavior problems are needed that avoid labeling the child a trouble-maker, excluding him from his group, and from legitimate activities, and reinforcing misbehavior patterns" (p. 53). One wonders how the Task Force defined *autonomy*. Our own work suggests that most of our delinquents exhibit pseudoautonomy and counterdependency; this is not limited to the poor or the slum dweller.

We also hear a good deal about housing and recreation, family planning and religion, inner city life and job placement, new job opportunities and the training of police, but nothing in essence uniquely psychiatric. Have we psychiatrists been ignored, or have we let this happen?

In 1975, the Director of the United States Bureau of Prisons announced the end of the medical model in criminology and its replacement by "realism" (Carlson, 1975). For too long "we were trying to treat people for crime as if crime were some sort of disease. . . . We cannot diagnose criminality as if it were a physical and mental disease, and we certainly cannot prescribe a precise treatment or guarantee to cure the offender committed to our custody." Psychiatrists are now to treat "the small minority of offenders who are genuinely suffering from a diagnosable mental illness." It is, indeed, realistic to recognize that the criminal is characteristically resistant to change. Similarly, it is prudent to recognize that coercive treatment may not only be unethical, but may be less successful than voluntary treatment. It is naive to hope that psychiatry can change each and every individual, and when one talks about a return to "realism," one displays disappointment and disillusionment after an overidealized view of psychiatry has failed to cure. Psychiatry involves a commitment to understanding the resistance, difficulties, and long-term nature of treatment. A medical model is not simply employing medical terminology, but involves a wholehearted commitment to a program of assessment, diagnosis, planning and prescribing treatment, implementing a therapeutic plan and assessing efficacy in outcome. Psychiatry has taught us that adolescents express their emotional problems through behavioral symptoms and not always in a "diagnosable psychiatric illness." It is in the nature of the adolescent to externalize, to act. An intelligent assessment of the teenage criminal must account for this propensity.

The 1976 *Rand Report,* "Intervening with Convicted Serious Juvenile Offenders," was quite thoughful, and focused on a multiplicity of viewpoints and approaches, although in too cursory a manner; yet, it pointed up the significant need for solid research and the development of programs for the serious offender.

In July 1977, *Time* magazine featured youth crime in its cover story.

There seemed to be no significant psychiatric input in composing the article. The article highlighted the seriousness of youth crime, but tended to focus on gang rather than individual delinquency, emphasized communities as causal, especially ghettos, noted the deficient court system and problems in families, but tended to ignore suburban delinquency. The text said little about individual psychological motivation or psychopathology, and, in fact, implied that a Freudian orientation to treatment encourages or permits delinquents to blame others for their behavior.

Again, a psychiatric orientation has been ignored and degraded. Or have psychiatrists defaulted? We hear of broken homes, the ghetto, permissiveness, a loss of religious values, mass media and television violence, the lack of morality at the highest levels, urbanization, racism, unemployment, the breakdown of family ties, learning disabilities, minimal brain dysfunction, drug abuse, the slowness of the juvenile justice system, firearms, poverty, and a culture of violence. But we do not hear of the psychodynamic and psychological causes. If we program at all, we spend a great deal of money, hoping to build a "Great Society," free of poverty; or we lock "them" up and punish "them," and we try to do that as cheaply as possible; or we move "them" out of institutions and work with "them" in the community, again as cheaply as possible. We are told that violence is normal in the ghetto, and our attempts to understand the violent teenager psychodynamically are a part of our white middle-class bias. This subtle brand of racism and class discrimination deprives the inner city delinquent of the therapy available to the more affluent teenager. We hear of television and the media causing violence in our society, or the easy availability of handguns, but society consistently ignores the internal psychological development of the teenager and those psychodynamic distortions responsible for delinquent behavior. Television, poverty, neighborhoods, and statistics on handguns are seductive, because they are so tangible, and they support the resistances in all of us. They help us to avoid looking inside the delinquent by using them to deny and rationalize his irrational behavior.

If one has accepted the existence of a disordered psychological world, one is persuaded to try to do something about it. By then new resistances arise. The treatment situation includes a certain amount of helplessness, passivity, and dependency; the patient must accept such experiences in his role of patient, and the therapist must be able to tolerate these tendencies in those he helps. But many people are made uncomfortable by helplessness, passivity, and dependency and try to deny them or eliminate them. Public policy reflects our citizens' reactions of denial of dependency wishes, against being helped or being needy in the anger of many public pronouncements against those who need help.

THE PSYCHIATRIC PERSPECTIVE

Indeed, there are many contributing factors to the final common pathway of delinquent behavior. And there are a variety of cultural expressions of psychopathology, but psychopathology cannot be ignored. All behavior has psychological meaning, and the delinquent act can be understood psychodynamically.

Following Freud's (1905) finding that certain character disorders and perversions are the reverse of the psychoneuroses, a number of investigators have attempted to formulate juvenile delinquency and adolescent behavior disorders from a psychodynamic point of view. Aichorn (1925) utilized the classical transference situation in an attempt to get to and modify the delinquent's neurotic conflict. But with a certain kind of delinquent he had to first establish a relationship and then work with the narcissistic transference. Alexander (1956) observed that certain criminals acted out of a sense of guilt which they hoped to expiate by being caught and punished. In this tradition, Friedlander (1960) postulated that it was important to convert delinquent character disorders to neurotics by blocking the avenues for acting out discharge and creating an internalized conflict which could then be worked with psychotherapeutically. In a similar vein, Anna Freud (1965) viewed delinquency as a failure of the socialization process, but also (1958) noted that some delinquency develops because of the chance availability of delinquent peer groups onto whom the adolescent separating from his parents displaces his investments. The focus here is on delinquent value systems, which were also emphasized in the work of Johnson and Szurek (1952). They described children responding to the unconsciously transmitted delinquent urges of their seemingly upright parents. Glover (1950) distinguished two kinds of delinquents: the structural, who gives evidence before and after adolescence of significant psychopathology, and the functional, whose delinquent behavior is a result of the temporary psychic imbalances of the adolescent maturation process. Blos (1966, 1967, 1971) has offered a variety of psychodynamic explanations including separation struggles, precocious ego development, the propensity for action language, and delinquency as a symbolic communication. Redl's emphasis (1966) bas been on the vicissitudes of ego development and ego functioning, and he underlined the importance of a psychodynamic understanding of the delinquency in an attempt to engage the child therapeutically.

Work at the Illinois State Psychiatric Institute in Chicago has demonstrated that some delinquents act out violently when they are overstimulated, not by angry or hostile feelings, but by strong affectionate longings and emotions (Marohn, 1974); that contagion or riot in a group has many causes and results from the participation of many systems, the psychological and intrapsychic systems among them (Marohn et al., 1973); that violence escalates from verbal violence and threats, to damage to property, to personal assault (Offer et al., 1975); that newer ideas on narcissism and the self can enrich our understanding of delinquent behavior (Marohn, 1977); that we can predict the likelihood of violent behavior from psychological test data (Ostrov et al., 1976); and that we can identify four statistically and psychologically meaningful subtypes or formulations of delinquency, excluding the psychotic and brain-damaged (Marohn et al., 1977; Offer et al., 1979). We have developed ways of working with delinquent adolescents in a tightly controlled, highly structured, long-term hospital treatment program involving one to two years of hospitalization, integrating individual psychotherapy and milieu therapy, and attempting to achieve internal psychological change and character restructuring (Marohn et al., 1980).

Long-term treatment units for adolescents are faring badly; many have already closed, eliminating not only one kind of treatment alternative, but also opportunities for in-depth investigation. Pressures from state legislatures and third-party payers threaten to eliminate intensive, long-term hospital treatment of many adolescents, and of all behaviorally disordered adolescents.

THE PSYCHIATRIC RESPONSE

To treat a delinquent adolescent adequately, one must understand the nature of the transference he will develop and the kinds of countertransference problems he will stimulate. He needs to be provided with external objects and external controls, and the staff and the therapist need the option of providing treatment for as long as is necessary and not be forced into a short-term revolving door model. Truly, many adolescents can be treated in time-limited or short-term therapy, but then such a decision should be based on an understanding of their dynamics and their psychological structure, and not on some prescribed time limit set by criteria of cost and efficiency.

In Illinois, a diversion program for serious delinquents is called the Unified Delinquency Intervention Services (UDIS). A recent evaluation study of the effects of UDIS vs. Illinois Department of Corrections intervention in the life of a juvenile offender found that both correctional intervention and UDIS significantly reduced subsequent delinquent activity. A comparison of post-UDIS or post-DOC police records vs. the youth's record during the year preceding intervention found that arrests were reduced 67.8%, court appearances dropped 64.4%, violence related offences were reduced 73.7% and aggregate "seriousness" costs of the crimes of the community were reduced 65.2% (Murray et al., 1978).

An assessment of the effectiveness of UDIS intervention alone was also made, comparing the three different levels of involvement and confinement ranging from serving the youth while he remained in his home, to residential services (group and foster homes) within the youth's community, to restrictive residential programs away from the youth's community, such as the UDIS-Intensive Care Unit at the Illinois State Psychiatric Institute (ICU). The study found that the most drastic intervention, such as UDIS-ICU was most effective in reducing recidivism in terms of the number and seriousness of subsequent crimes committed. These findings are particularly impressive given that the youths placed in these restrictive residential placements were judged least likely to reform and most likely to continue their delinquent activity if left on the street.

Other investigations have also demonstrated a need to understand delinquents psychologically. Warren et al. (1977) acknowledged that a significant number of delinquents "act out internal conflicts, identity struggles or family crises." They have developed ways of classifying youth psychodynamically which point to specific treatment goals, treatment strategies, and treatment modalities. They have demonstrated that matching the counselor or therapist with specific kinds of delinquents results in more favorable prognoses, and they seriously question the idea that a good therapist has a full range of "talents, sensitivities, and interests" which enable him to deal effectively with whatever type of client comes his way. Yet even these sophisticated studies are challenged by Martinson (1974) who raises questions about the "normality" of criminality in our society, and points up the serious problems in doing competent efficacy research.

Lewis and Balla (1976) noted that the juvenile justice system is a "repository for large numbers of seriously impaired children" with central nervous system dysfunction and psychotic symptoms.

Psychiatry does not have the final answer, but it provides a segment of the answer. The psychiatrist can be helpful in understanding the juvenile delinquent psychodynamically, and in developing a treatment program that provides a milieu externally supportive to the psychotherapy process. Wilson (1977) stressed the "frightful expense" of intensive milieu therapy, yet such experience is justified because from it we can learn much, develop less expensive forms of treatment, and confront the issue that there is no ready or easy solution to our problem. It is facile to say that broken homes cause delinquency, yet it is only through studying intact families in which delinquency occurs that we may understand those kinds of family constellations and communications that might promote or precipitate delinquency. It may very well be that the same factors that cause the home to break up may also be responsible for the delinquency. This is not to depreciate sociological research, but rather to underline the importance of psychological and psychiatric research. An outstanding example of how psychoanalytic and sociological data can be integrated, correlated, and enrich each other, rather than compete or negate each other, is contained in the studies of a Chicago gang described by Baittle and Kobrin (1964).

It is important that psychiatry address itself to the issue of violence among delinquent adolescents. A far reaching study on Violent Delinquents has been conducted at the Vera Institute of Justice (Strasburg, 1978). Beginning with the knowledge that about 25-30% of all adolescents engage in significant delinquency, the study attempted to demonstrate that intact families are less likely to produce violent delinquents than disrupted families. On the other hand, it may very well be that the psychopathological factors that cause the family to become disrupted are also responsible for delinquency and violent delinquency in the children. This book, unlike previous studies, emphasizes a psychiatric perspective. Unfortunately, there is a tendency to equate violent delinquency with disturbed delinquents. We have seen quite clearly that the frequency or the seriousness of delinquent acts cannot be correlated with the seriousness of psychopathology. It is interesting to note that one psychiatric study (Kozol et al., 1972) described the lack of feeling that violent delinquents experience for others. This is quite comparable to the findings by Miller and Looney (1975) of adolescent murderers. Unfortunately, neither study addressed these potentialities or behaviors in terms of narcissistic pathology as described by Kohut (1971 and 1977; Marohn, 1977). The appreciation of the other as a part of the self to be manipulated and used for one's own needs, and the rage that results when the other is not functioning satisfactorily as a self-object, account for a number of instances of narcissistic rage. In fact, delinquency can frequently be understood as an expression of narcissistic pathology (Marohn, 1977).

There is a tendency in the Strasburg report (1978) to minimize the seriousness of psychopathology in the violent delinquent because Strasburg equates a psychiatric perspective with a clearly demonstrable mental disorder, as in the psychoses. As a result, therefore, "the great majority of violent delinquents are not psychotic or otherwise seriously disturbed emotionally . . ." (p. 79).

Nonetheless, *Violent Delinquents* (Strasburg, 1978) emphasized how unresponsive public institutions are to the needs of these disturbed delinquents by providing virtually nothing in terms of psychiatric or psychological treatment (pp. 118-119). Violent and seriously disturbed delinquents "are frequently denied access to effective help. They are subjected to long delays in processing and multiple rejections by voluntary treatment programs as well as public mental health facilities" (p. 126).

The belief that delinquents can be understood psychodynamically is viewed as a "positivist philosophy of correctional treatment" which is now being attacked because it is seen as an interference in the private lives of offenders, because its efficacy has not been demonstrated, and because criminal behavior is not a disease. Strasburg viewed the only appropriate treatment by psychiatrists as strictly in line with a medical model which includes medical interventions such as psychopharmacology and accurate psychiatric diagnosis. A psychiatrist's view of the delinquent should not be limited by psychopharmacology, or to the psychoses or by the inherent limitations of a conflict model in psychoanalytic theory. Greater understanding and efficacy is to be expected from a theory of self-psychology. This reformulation of our work can address the empathic realization of Strasburg (1978) that "the most important reason not to abandon treatment is that, particularly with regard to violent juveniles, it is unacceptable public policy to do nothing" (p. 163).

This, of course, is not idle speculation or theorizing, but becomes a crucial and vital issue when one realizes that the best predictor of adult violence is juvenile violence (Strasburg, 1978, p. 179).

There must be longitudinal studies of treated and untreated delinquents. Short-term and long-term modalities must be compared, as must family therapy and individual therapy, as must institutional programs and de-institutional programs. Perhaps then we can decide which treatment works best for whom. We must determine whether delinquency, particularly violent delinquency, is increasing or decreasing. And we must learn whether there are more female delinquents and in what ways then girls are different.

Working with adolescents and delinquents must become part of the core training of every psychiatrist, and we psychiatrists must take the lead not only in developing model diagnostic and treatment programs for delinquent teenagers, but also spearhead the training of other professionals in a psychodynamic appreciation of the delinquent.

We need to learn more about the idealizing transference and the role of deidealization in the therapy of the delinquent. We must understand more about the negative transference, and not confuse it with the absence of a working or therapeutic relationship or alliance. As psychiatrists, we must be willing to hospitalize character disorders or behavioral disorders, and we must insist that third party payers and insurance companies support such treatment. And we must revise our commitment laws so that disordered development and the need for hospitalization become the criteria for commitment to a psychiatric program designed specifically for ,teenagers, not proven or demonstrable violence. Therapy of the delinquent and the behaviorally disordered adolescent is a clinical, not a legal, issue.

Countertransference, frustration, and resistance will, of course, express themselves in new and modern disguises. We are tempted to explain away or deny psychopathology as economic problems, or organicity, or political unrest. Or we might return to theories of moral degeneracy, as cloaked in the sophisticated verbiage of a university professor:

> Since the days of the crime commission we have learned a great deal, more than we are prepared to admit. Perhaps we fear to admit it because of a new-found modesty about the foundations of our knowledge, but perhaps also because the implications of that knowledge suggest an unflattering view of man. Intellectuals, although they often dislike the common person as an individual, do not wish to be caught saying uncomplimentary things about mankind. Nevertheless, some persons will shun crime even if we do nothing to deter them, while others will seek it out even if we do everything to reform them. Wicked people exist. Nothing avails except to set them apart from innocent people. And many people, neither wicked nor innocent, but watchful, dissembling, and calculating of their opportunities, ponder our reaction to wickedness as a cue to what they might profitably do. We have trifled with the wicked, made sport of the innocent, and encouraged the calculators. Justice suffers, and so do we all (Wilson, 1977).

The problem is vast, but not hopeless. As Winnicott (1958, 1972) taught us years ago, the delinquent is continually reaching out for his lost object, the mother once possessed but later lost, whom the delinquent hopes to recapture through his behavior. We know that the delinquent is still searching, has not given up, and may, indeed, include the therapist in his search.

SUMMARY

Delinquency is a serious and extensive problem. This is a statement, easy to make, but difficult to understand. We do not understand, for example, apparent increases or decreases in the seriousness of certain crimes committed by certain people. All too often, society's preoccupation with unemployment, racism, and poverty are emphasized as causal, thereby overlooking serious psychological and personality deficits.

In many situations, psychiatry has either been ignored or has defaulted in attempts to formulate and plan for amelioration or eradication of juvenile delinquency.

There are many contributing factors to the final common pathway of delinquent behavior. Basic to all of these is the realization that all behavior has psychological meaning and the delinquent act can be understood psychodynamically. From this must flow an attempt to work with delinquent adolescents psychologically, and not minimize or deflect the impact of their psychological problems.

Though such an approach may appear costly, it is rewarding in its discoveries and accomplishments.

REFERENCES

Aichorn, A. (1960), *Wayward Youth* (1925). New York: Meridian Books.

Alexander, F. and Staub, H. (1956), *The Criminal, the Judge and the Public.* New York: Collier Books.

Baittle, B., and Kobrin, S. (1964), On the Relationship of a Characterological Type of Delinquent to the Milieu. *Psychiat.* 27: 6-16.

Blos, P. (1966), *A Developmental Approach to Problems of Acting Out.* New York: International Universities Press, pp. 69-71 and 118-136.

——— (1967), The Second Individuation Process of Adolescence. *Psychoanal. Study Child,* 22: 162-185.

——— (1971), Adolescent Concretization: A Contribution to the Theory of Delinquency. In *Currents in Psychoanalysis,* Ed. I. Marcus. New York: International Universities Press, pp. 66-88.

Carlson, N. (1975), Director, U.S. Bureau of Prisons, as quoted in *Psychiatric News,* December 17, pp. 3, 22, 23.

Circuit Court of Cook County (1975, 1976), *Annual Report.* Juvenile Division, Chicago, Illinois.

Freud, A. (1958), Adolescence. *Psychoanal. Study Child,* 13:255-278.

——— (1965), Dissociality, Delinquency, Criminality . . . In *Normality and Pathology in Childhood: Assessments of Development.* New York: International Universities Press, pp. 164-184.

Freud, S. (1905), Three Essays on Sexuality. *Standard Edition,* 8:123-243, London: Hogarth Press.

Friedlander, K. (1960), *The Psychoanalytic Approach to Juvenile Delinquency.* New York: International Universities Press.

Glover, E. (1950), On the Desirability of Isolating a "Functional" (Psychosomatic) Group Delinquent Disorder. *British J. Delinq.* 1: 104-112, and *On the Early Development of the Mind.* New York: International Universities Press, pp. 379-389, 1970.

Johnson, A., and Szurek, S.A. (1952), The Genesis of Antisocial Acting Out in Children and Adults. *Psychoanal. Quart.* 21: 323-343.

Kohut, H. (1971), *The Analysis of the Self.* New York: International Universities Press.

——— (1971), *The Restoration of the Self.* New York: International Universities Press.

Kozol, H.S., Boucher, R.J., and Garafalo, R. (1972), The Diagnosis and Treatment of Dangerousness. *Crime Delinq. Lit.,* 18: No. 4, October.

Lewis, D.O., and Balla, D.A. (1976), *Delinquency and Psychopathology*. New York: Grune and Stratton.

Marohn, R.C., Dalle-Molle, D., Offer, D., and Ostrov, E. (1973), A Hospital Riot: Its Determinants and Implications for Treatment. *Amer. J. Psychiat.* 130: 631-636.

Marohn, R.C. (1974), Trauma and the Delinquent. *Adol. Psychiat.*, 3: 354-361.

——— (1977), The "Juvenile Imposter": Some Thoughts on Narcissism and the Delinquent. *Adol. Psychiat.* 5:186-212.

———, Offer, D., and Ostrov, E. (1977), Four Psychodynamic Types of Hospitalized Juvenile Delinquents. Presented at the Annual Meeting of the American Psychiatric Association, Toronto, Canada.

———, Dalle-Molle, D., McCarter, E., and Linn, D. (1980), *Hospital Treatment of the Juvenile Delinquent*, to be published.

Martinson, R. (1974), What Works?—Questions and Answers about Prison Reform. *Public Interest* 35: 22-54, Spring.

Miller, D. and Looney, J.G. (1975), Determinants of Homicide in Adolescents. *Adol. Psychiat.* 4: 231-254.

Murray, C.A., Thomson, D., and Israel, C.B. (1978), Deinstitutionalizing the Chronic Juvenile Offender. American Institutes for Research, Washington, D.C.

Offer, D. (1969), *Psychological World of the Teenager:* A Study of Normal Adolescent Boys. New York: Basic Books, Inc.

———, Marohn, R.C. and Ostrov, E. (1975), Violence Among Hospitalized Delinquents. *Arch. Gen. Psychiat.* 32: 1180-1186.

———, ———, ———(1979), *Psychological World of the Juvenile Delinquent*. New York: Basic Books.

Ostrov, E., Offer, D., and Marohn, R.C. (1976), Hostility and Impulsivity in Normal and Delinquent Rorschach Responses. *Mental Health in Children*, 2: 479-492.

Rand Corporation (1976), Intervening with Convicted Serious Juvenile Offenders, prepared under the supervision of Dale Mann; Santa Monica, California.

Redl, F. (1966), Ego Disturbances and Ego Support and the Phenomena of Contagion and "Shock Effect." In *When We Deal with Children*. New York: The Free Press, pp. 125-146, 197-213.

Schwartz, G. and Puntil, J.E. (1972), *Summary and Policy Implications of the Youth and Society in Illinois*. Institute for Juvenile Research, Chicago, unpublished manuscript.

Sondheim, S. (1957), "Officer Krupke." Lyrics in *West Side Story*. New York: G. Schirmer.

Strasburg, P.S. (1978), *Violent Delinquents*. New York: Sovereign Books.

Task Force on Juvenile Delinquency, the President's Commission on Law Enforcement and Administration and Justice (1967), *Task Force Report: Juvenile Delinquency and Youth Crime*, Washington, D.C.: U.S. Govt. Printing Office.

Time (1977), The Youth Crime Plague. pp. 18-28, July 11.

Warren, M.W. (1977), Measuring the Impact of Specific Therapist-Patient Matches in Work with Juvenile Delinquents. Paper presented to to the Society for Psychotherapy Research, Madison, Wisconsin.

Wilson, J.Q. (1977), *Thinking About Crime*. New York: Vintage Books.

Winnicott, D.W. (1958), The Antisocial Tendency. In *Collected Papers: Through Pediatrics to Psychoanalysis*. New York: Basic Books. pp. 306-315.

——— (1972), Delinquency as a sign of hope. *Adol. Psychiat.* 2: 363-371.

10

Family Problems in Adolescent Suicide

MAX SUGAR

Adolescent suicide rates are increasing and despite increased awareness and data (Teicher, 1973; Hendin, 1970; Stevenson et al., 1972; Woodruff, 1972; Rauenhorst, 1972), there has been no improvement in the preventative or therapeutic measures for the suicidal adolescent.

Crisis lines or suicide prevention centers (McGee, 1971) seemed the long-sought panacea for suicide prevention a dozen years ago, but their promise has not been fulfilled. In the same period adolescent suicides have moved up from fifth (Stevenson et al., 1972) to fourth as a cause of mortality for ages 15-19 in the United States (Schuyler, 1973).

This chapter will review some aspects of adolescent suicide with a special focus on family problems.

STATISTICS ON ADOLESCENT SUICIDE

During 1869-1899 in Prussia there were 16,000 adolescent suicides. From 1908 to 1909 in Moscow, 4.5% of all suicides were in ages 8-14, and 38% of all suicides were aged 15-21. Lourie (1967) indicated a variable past rate of adolescent suicides; e.g., 1700 suicides in children in Berlin from 1900-1903, then a decline until 1930 and a continued upward trend since then (for which he offered no explanation). In traditional China before 1949, the female and male rates were equal, but after exposure to the West, female

149

rates became similar to those in the West with a higher number of attempts by young females than males. In India the suicide rate for ages 15-24 years equals the rate of those over 45 years, and the rate is not related to race or sex (Leonard, 1967). Lourie (1967) noted that three times more male than female adolescents, and ten times more whites than non-whites commit suicide.

Bagley and Greer (1972) criticized Hendin (1970) for his conclusion that suicide among blacks in New York was increasing since they felt that in almost all age groups white suicide is higher than black suicides. Their study of 25 "black" suicide attempts in London included West Indians, East Indians, Cypriots, Africans and Pakistanis. Grouped in this manner, their cultural and family heritages were obliterated, and they were presented as the oppressed equivalent of the blacks in New York, in contrast to whites, the oppressors. They stated, "Suicide in adolescents is a rare phenomenon, and it is of interest that the two completed suicides in our series were a girl of 14 and a boy of 15, and were both black." Using their questionable methods, their figures would lead to the conclusion that black adolescent suicides are not rare, but on the contrary, alarmingly high.

For youths under age 20, United States suicide studies (Stevenson et al., 1972) show a marked increase in attempts ranging from 8% during 1927-1958 to about 21% since 1960. For ages 15-25 in 1971 (U.S. Department of Health, Education and Welfare, 1974) suicide was the third leading cause of death for all ethnic groups, and second only to accidents in whites.

Schneer and associates (1975), using a chart study from a Brooklyn hospital, compared its adolescent suicide population of 1969-70 with their earlier study from 1957. They found that the total number and percentage of adolescent suicide attempts had doubled over the decade, although the adolescent population of Brooklyn had increased only 20%. The rate for black adolescent females jumped from 11% to 49%, and there were marked increases for all adolescent groups (black male, Puerto Rican male and female, white male) except the white female.

Stevenson et al. (1972) stated that adolescent suicides are rare, but they noted that in 1964 in the United States there were 744 suicides among those under 20 years.

In 1975 Hendin wrote that:

Suicide among young people and college students in particular has been steadily and alarmingly rising during the past twenty years. Over 4,000 persons of the 25,000 who commit suicide in the country each year are now in the fifteen to twenty-four age group. The suicide rate has increased over 250 percent in this period going from 4.2 in 1954 to 10.6 in 1973.

The survey by Hatten et al. (1977) in Los Angeles disclosed an increase in the suicide rate for 15-19 year-olds, particularly in black adolescent suicides, which reversed the previous state of a higher rate for white adolescents.

Most of the reported adolescent suicide attempters came from the lowest socioeconomic status and from state or city hospitals (Toolan, 1975—Bellevue Hospital; Schneer and Kay, 1961; Schneer et al., 1975—Kings County Hospital). Few studies detail the socioeconomic status of the adolescent subjects (Winn, 1969).

Tsuang (1977) stressed that there may be a greater risk factor where the diagnosis is manic-depressive, schizophrenia or alcoholism.

In general, statistics about adolescent suicide are not very reliable because of underdiagnosis, shielding because of social class, denial, religion, insurance, family status, race and other reasons reflecting bias.

CULTURAL ISSUES

In seven states in the United States, suicide is a crime, as it was until recently in England for about 100 years. In Israel, it is not a crime. In Japan in connection with the Sammurai ideals, before V.J. Day it was a venerated act in certain situations, and is now the leading cause of death in females age 15-29 and is second for males age 15-29 (Iga and Tatai, 1975). In the defense at Masada 70 A.D., it was a noble act of heroic status. The Talmud absolves children of sinfulness for suicide and they are buried in the cemetery because the youngster is considered psychotic. The Catholic Church denies the last rites to a suicide unless declared psychotic (Frederick, 1971; Lourie, 1967). The culture therefore appears to be a significant variable in comprehending the meaning and frequency of suicide attempts.

Webb and Willard (1975) have given some attention to the statistical distortion and exaggeration found in suicide reports on the American Indians (all ages), which discuss the Indians as if they were all from the same tribe with a similar culture, and as if the statistics could be easily universalized from one group or tribe to all North American Indians. In fact, there are only 600,000 Indians in all of the United States at present, made up of many different tribes and cultures, and therefore the suicide rates, patterns and meanings differ from tribe to tribe. They specified that often the reports vary depending on the government agency and its need to manipulate, to dramatize the need for mental health services and inaugurate them quickly.

Webb and Willard (1975) clarified that if one small tribe has a suicide, the figures can't be extrapolated to all Indians because other tribes may be functioning quite differently. For instance, the Shoshone tribe has a high rate of suicides (100 per 100,000, or 10 times the national average) because of the high level of family disorganization, while the Navajo's rate is 8 per 100,000. In the Cheyenne and Dakota tribes the suicide attempter does and says everything in reverse and invites death by placing himself in risky positions, e.g. walking backward, walking into moving vehicles or provoking mortal combat. In those tribes this is known beforehand by his wearing the sash of the "Crazy-Dog-Wishing-To-Die."

Most psychiatrists do not involve themselves with suicide prevention centers, which are managed mostly by nonprofessional volunteers. Many psychiatrists prefer not to treat suicidal patients since they are considered unsuitable for various types of therapy (Frederick, 1971).

THE CONCEPT OF DEATH

By age 3 or 4 years children are aware of death, but they erect defenses against the awareness. Up to age 5 or 6 denial is used, and death is equated with separation, departure or sleep. Between ages 5 and 9, death is conceived of as a distinct person who travels by night and is not understood as inevitable, but rather as violence (murder, retribution and retaliation), animistic, and not universal. By age 9 or 10 years death has a causal, logical explanation, coming as a result of natural processes, and is considered final and universal. Until that age the child views death as reversible, temporary or a nice place to go (Nagy, 1948; Rochlin, 1965).

MENTAL STATUS AND MECHANISMS

It is generally unappreciated that formal operations are not firmly attained by age 15, nor do all adolescents develop them, and they are subject to regression with emotional illness and stress. Levinson and Neuringer (1971, 1972) found that hospitalized suicidal adolescents had less problem-solving capacity, but no significant differences on certain TAT cards for environmental pressures than groups of normal adolescents, or psychiatrically hospitalized non-suicidal adolescents. But these conclusions do not consider the state of mind at the time of the attempt, nor the effects of in-patient psychiatric therapy on that state after a period of time.

Suicide is usually associated with depression in adults (Freud, 1917; Abraham, 1927), and a large literature has accrued on this. From this, the mechanisms of dependent ambivalence, guilt, oral incorporation, and turning of the hostility against the self are thought of as operating similarly with adolescents. Zilboorg (1936) stressed that depressive dynamics were not the only determining factors, that loss might be a significant factor and that suicide might occur with any syndrome.

Schneer and Kay (1961) considered adolescent suicide as regressive infantile behavior used in coping with an explosive oedipal conflict involving loss. They felt the parents had engendered a sadomasochistic attitude in the individual, who experienced a profound sense of rejection (through death, absence through illness, separation, etc.). Whether the rejection was provoked by the adolescent (in a bid for independence) or initiated by the parents, it constituted too severe a narcissistic mortification for the emerging adolescent ego to manage and the suicide was a route to promote "sleep" and rest.

Toolan (1975) emphasized depression as pivotal to adolescent suicide attempts and noted that object loss, helplessness of the ego, loss of a previous state of well-being, and the normal separation by adolescents from parents are involved.

Friedman et al. (1972) felt their adolescent suicide attempters had been unable to give up their tie to their parents, and instead of having a mourning-like process, the patients reacted with a state akin to melancholia. They felt that precisely those features which seem to have been established through narcissistic identification with their mother were the ones so harshly and constantly attacked by their superegos. This led them to the view that the suicide attempts were experienced as an attack, not on the adolescent, but on his body, which the youngster felt belonged to the internalized object, which was invariably the mother.

Rochlin (1965) explained that when object loss occurs the self is in the greatest danger from its own attacks, which are often expressed as suicidal wishes and impulses since destructive wishes toward a meaningful object cannot be endured. In the presence of such wishes the self must take the abuses even though its recourse is to project the source of hostility onto the other person, since the object must be spared. This is similar to some of the notions about the dangers of object loss expressed by Friedman et al. (1972) that in destroying his body, which the adolescent feels belongs to the mother, he gives expression to the wish to kill the mother.

Teicher (1973) described a three-stage progression to social isolation in adolescent attempted suicide, consisting of long-standing problems, a period of escalation associated with achieving adolescence, and a final chain reaction in the weeks preceding the attempt when his few remaining associations are dissolved. In the escalation period the issues revolve around parents' efforts to deal with a new and, to them, an unfamiliar stage of development, i.e. adolescence. It seems that by inference he felt the suicidal adolescent may be normal but living in a pathological setting.

Dizmang et al. (1974) reported on the very high frequency of Shoshone Indian suicides under age 25. They felt that all the Shoshone Indians had undergone family and tribal chaos but the distinguishing feature of the suicide group was that:

> ... [they] were frequently cared for by more than one individual in their developing years, while control subjects were almost always cared for by a single individual. The primary caretakers of the suicide group has significantly more arrests during the time they were caretakers of the subjects. The suicide group also experienced many more losses by desertion or divorce than did the control group

Thus, the dynamics ascribed to adolescent suicide attempts are not convergent, and also involve the family and culture.

PSYCHIATRIC DIAGNOSIS AND SUICIDE

Friedman et al. (1972) felt their suicidal patients were psychotic. Balser and Masterson (1959) found 4 out of 5 of their out-patient, and 19 of 32 in-patient attempters were schizophrenic, among whom 40% were hallucinating. In the records observed by Schneer and Kay (1961) less than one-fourth had psychosis in 1957, but in 1969 in this same hospital (Schneer et al., 1975) 50% had psychosis. Bakwin (1957) noted that only 10% of their adolescent suicidal attempters had mental illness. Leonard (1967) thought of the suicidal adolescent as symbiotic or schizophrenic. In Winn's (1969) group 40% of the adolescents had suicidal hallucinations just before the attempt; also, 83% had experienced hallucinations in the year prior to admission. Rauenhorst's (1972) study of suicidal women age 16-30 concluded: there was little difference in adjustment between the attempters and controls; the more serious suicide attempters were not more seriously maladjusted than the controls at follow-up; and that suicide attempts can best be viewed as a reaction to a short-lived crisis which is subsequently resolved. The rate and risk of suicide increase in manic depressives (Tsuang, 1977). Again, there is a wide divergence of opinion about suicide as an illness. But if we recall Zilboorg's (1936) remarks, it is apparent that a suicide attempt may arise from a variety of dynamics and be part of different diagnostic categories.

PRECIPITATING EVENTS

The precipitating event for patients of Friedman et al. (1972) was an experience which was felt by the adolescent to be an abandonment and which seemed to confirm the reality of the omnipotence of his death wishes to the mother, such as her injury or illness. Morrison and Collier (1969) found that in 76% of cases the precipitating event was an important loss, or separation, or its anniversary, e.g., hospitalization, household move, death, illness, marital separation of the parent or parent-surrogate. Leonard (1967) felt that adolescent suicidal attempts were due to a break in their symbiosis leading to a crisis of identity, and the suicide attempt was a cry for help to deal with this. Teicher (1973) asserted that when the adolescent's relationship with his parents deteriorated to being nonexistent, and there seemed no way left to solve his chronic problems, he attempted suicide.

FAMILY FACTORS

A number of authors (Teicher and Jacobs, 1966; Schrut, 1964; Vogel and Bell, 1960; Sabbath, 1969; Gould, 1965; Leonard, 1967; Haven, 1969) have stressed the concept of the expendable or scapegoat youth who attempts suicide. He is somehow no longer useful in fulfilling parental needs, thus he becomes a threat to the parents' homeostasis and then accepts the parental message for him to die.

Teicher and Jacobs (1966) emphasized that for 88% of the 68 adolescents in their group the suicide attempt occurred in the home, often with the parents in the next room. On the subject of the family problems and suicide, there seems to be more agreement in recent years than on other concepts.

Though we know there are often fantasies and projections, not all accounts of family behavior are fantasies. Many youngsters have been raped, battered, abused, neglected, tortured, killed and eaten by family members. Child abuse and battering are forms of discharge of homicidal impulses which occur, at a minimum, to almost 2 million children annually in the United States. Wife-beating is another similar event and the figures for this are just beginning to be counted.

Case Illustrations

These cases briefly highlight some of the family dynamics and problems about having therapy instituted or continued.

Case I

A 13-year-old girl was involved in daily alcohol inebriation, several episodes of wrist-cutting and drug overdosage. She complained that she felt unwelcome in the family since menarche and hated by her mother. Her request for psychiatric treatment was dismissed initially by the parents as mere dramatics, and responded to only after she was suspended for imbibing alcohol in school. After several years of therapy, during some sessions which involved the mother and daughter, the mother admitted her extreme hostile jealousy, competitiveness, ambivalence and patterns of derogation of the daughter, whom she experienced as a real threat to herself and her marriage, beginning with the girl's adolescence. Here, the youngster was crying for help and not receiving any until the external authorities focused it and forced the parents to help.

Case II

The parents of a 16-year-old boy, with a impulse control disorder and epilepsy, allowed loaded guns in the house and permitted the boy to hunt and ride a motorcycle. When asked about their difficulty in setting limits for him, they responded that they were afraid of his angry response should they disallow these activities. In an argument with his older brother he grabbed one of the loaded guns, threatened to shoot him, then ordered him out of the room, closed the door and killed himself. The parents were involved in passive child abuse and neglect, unheeding his need for protection from his own poorly controlled impulses.

Case III

A 13-year-old boy who had regularly threatened to kill the parents (most often the mother) was allowed to buy his own .22 rifle. After several years of continued threats they became alarmed about the homicidal possibility, but he refused to turn the rifle over to them. They still allowed him to hunt and kept the usual other guns in the house. The mother's hostility and wish to get rid of the load of children, especially the adolescents, led the boy to refuse to continue therapy. The father's unresolved hostility to the mother led him to be the puppeteer engineering the boy's defiance and threats to her, while denying the threat to himself.

THERAPY PROBLEMS

Before preventative measures can be initiated for the suicidal adolescent, resistances have to be understood. The marked variance in views about suicide, and especially the attitude that all suicidal attempts are similar, is a formidable barrier which seems to be a form of prejudice related to anxiety.

Friedman et al. (1972) theorized that at the time of the suicide experience, the body is hated for causing fantasies and sexual acts and for belonging to the mother, and not to the youngster, so that to him, dying means killing the body but not necessarily the mind. In suicide, it is the whole body that is attacked as the source of the sexual urges. In self-mutilation, the unconscious fantasy is of destroying the genitals which are seen as the source of the urges, and through displacement, whichever part of the body is attacked then represents the genitals. In a suicide attempt there is a calm state before the attempt. In self-mutilation there is a calm state after the act. This calm state is confusing to the bystanders and frequently leads to them having angry, derogatory outbursts or premature interpretations ["you did (are doing) it for attention"]. From clinical observations I agree with the suggestion by Friedman et al. (1972) that the calm state after self-mutilation might be understood as a relief that despite the injury the genitals are safe, as well as an act of self-punishment which pacifies the superego.

The physician's narcissism and omnipotence may also be threatened by the suicide attempter since he is a direct threat to the physician's mission to save lives. These factors seem to be involved in the hostile or derogatory remarks sometimes (clothed as interpretations, tho' quite premature) addressed in the emergency room to the attempted suicide.

But physicians' negative responses to the suicidal patient (Teicher, 1973) may have an additional and more significant component. Suicide by definition is murder, but of the self, and in the presence of murderous impulses bystanders have tremendous anxiety and may become frozen into immobility, angry reactions, or denial. In the face of the patient's regression at such a time the anxious phsician may deny it and expect logical thinking and behavior, or project his own exicted responses.

I submit that one of the reasons for the communication of adolescent suicidal intent going unheralded, in spite of its increasing frequency in the period immediately preceding the attempt (Stevenson et al., 1972; Teicher, 1973), is that the people (family, friends, physicians, etc.) to whom they communicate this intent respond with intense anxiety and deny the communication.

Although these murderous wishes are (or are about to be) acted upon, it is angering and confusing to most people when the attempt is accompanied by preparations for rescue. These (such as a note or an attempt within someone's sensory range) are frequently viewed, even by professionals, as mere historics or manipulativenss, instead of ambivalence and a cry for help. Subtle or overt rejection of the patient may accompany this attitude.

The presence of ambivalence in such situations is often overlooked, even by psychiatrists. Certainly there may be secondary gain and rescue fantasies involved, but these are secondary to the threat to survival. Of course, the therapist's anger may be related to countertransference problems whereby he reacts like a parent to child who has done something risky and the parent responds angrily due to the anxiety the situation provokes.

Considering the facts of the regression and loss of integration that occur in suicide attempts, it is hard to conceive of reports attributing motives of a rational nature to the adolescent suicide attempter, unless these are viewed as reflecting anxious responses of the observers. If we agree that the child's concept of death is unrealistic until around age 9 or 10, and that prior to that age there is a notion of reversibility, or revengefulness equated with the effects of running away, it is commensurable to grant that in the regression accompanying a suicide attempt the adolescent uses magic ideas of death with attendant qualities of temporariness and reversibility. Simultaneously, his abilities to solve problems and delay gratification are diminished.

The tendency to deny the murderous wishes (Haven, 1969) is the chief difficulty in assessing the strength of hostile wishes. This would apply equally to the family of the suicidal adolescent and the treating physician, including the psychiatrist.

RECOMMENDATIONS FOR IMPROVED MANAGEMENT

If we accept that there are murderous wishes in the family to the expendable adolescent, we need to consider that they are unconscious, or mostly so, and in the face of the youngster's murderous wishes the family may deny his intentions or actions as well as continue repression of their own. Thus, it is untherapeutic for the psychiatrist to note the presence of such family wishes, then deny or withdraw since this is experienced by the adolescent as another abandonment which adds to his isolation and sense of hopelessness.

One of the barriers to therapy which follows object loss, is the increasing sense of isolation and the withdrawal from, and by, support systems when the adolescent feels abandoned. If a social support system is provided, such as in a psychiatric hospital, this may militate against the withdrawal process. Another possible support system is network therapy which mobilizes active peer support in these cases. It has had the salubrious effect of keeping the peers involved and reducing the youngster's isolation, while working in therapy on his murderous feelings (Sugar, 1975).

In network therapy when a youngster reveals a suicidal attempt, the peers' shocked, angry response seems to serve the important functions of informing the youngster that he matters, that someone cares, and that he is not rejected. More suitable interpretations and even angry, but helpful, remarks have been made by peers in network therapy than issue sometimes from caregivers in the emergency room.

By the term "family problems" in adolescent suicide I include not just the kin, but anyone involved in care-giving to the adolescent, and that any, and all of them may have biases or problems related to a suicide attempt. Perhaps the divergent notions about suicidal youngsters are based on anxious reactions, denial and amibivalence about the combined murderous intentions of the family and the youngster. This distorts the receptivity and response to their cry for help.

The suicidal patient should be considered as being in a regressed state, with disintegration, magic thinking, and impaired reality-testing, whether temporary or chronic. But a careful evaluation of dynamics leading to a diagnosis is needed. Cultural, socio-economic and family factors should be included in the assessment.

Treatment of suicidal patients is often anxiety-provoking or depressing, and it may require a particular type of fortitude and optimism by the therapist to continue in this endeavor. Perhaps in the course of training and becoming aware of one's own feelings and talents the therapist could decide whether he feels sufficiently empathic to work with suicidal adolescents.

Just as the surgeon doing abdominal exploratory surgery is prepared to do an abdomino-perineal resection, the psychiatrist should then be prepared to continue with treatment and do what is necessary for an adolescent suicide attempter.

Residents might be allowed to continue treatment of the suicidal patient throughout their residency years. This would help train them for long-term treatment of such a patient and avoid having the patient experience the rejection from a turnover to another resident every 3 or 6 months, according to the service rotation.

If the therapist is aware of his own anxious feelings about a suicidal patient, he might be better able to recognize and assess the risk involved. Then, if he accepts the patient for therapy, he might be better able to continue with treatment.

Even if the therapist is aware of his anxiety in response to the suicidal patient's murderous feelings, it is a difficult situation. Perhaps it might be useful to say that it makes one nervous trying to talk with someone who has murder on his mind. But otherwise a most circumspect attitude about making early interpretations would be a caution by which to abide.

If a patient suicides, the family involvement in therapy usually ends; and similarly with an attempter, once the danger is over the family's interest in therapy often recedes. To learn more, to hopefully be able to better understand and treat the particular adolescent patient who is, or has been, a suicidal risk, family therapy should continue after the episode is over, as should the individual therapy when possible. Eventually, the exposure and understanding of hostile feelings in therapy may lead to better living arrangements for the adolescent with more suitable defenses to handle the hostile or murderous feelings.

SUMMARY

Further studies with improved research designs are needed on adolescent suicide. A suicide threat or attempt is a serious symptom, a cry for help and a sign of emotional illness. It often also indicates that somebody in the family, besides the adolescent, has an unconscious or conscious wish to have the adolescent removed somehow from the home.

The threat of murder or suicide provokes extreme anxiety in caregivers as well as others and often interferes in the assessment and treatment of suicidal risk due to denial or inhibition. This interferes with optimal responses to the youngster's cry for help. Measures to promote prevention and therapy for the suicidal adolescent should involve all his caretakers. Perhaps this awareness will lead physicians and others to improve the present preventive measures and therapy. Hopefully some of this human suffering and wastage could be prevented and decrease the alarming, upward spiralling suicide rate in adolescents.

REFERENCES

Abraham, K. (1927), Notes on the psychoanalytic investigation and treatment of manic depressive insanity and allied conditions. *Selected Papers*. London: Hogarth Press.

Bagley, C. and Greer, B. (1972), Black suicide: a report of 25 English cases and controls. *J. Social Psychol.* 86:175-179.

Bakwin, H. (1957), Suicide in children and adolescents. *Am. J. Pediat.* 50:749-769.

Balser, B. H. and Masterson, J. F. (1959), Suicide in adolescents. *Am. J. Psychiat.* 116:400-404.

Dizmang, L. H., Watson, J., May, P.A., and Bopp, J. (1974), Adolescent suicide at an Indian reservation. *Am. J. Orthopsychiat.* 44: 43-49.

Frederick, C. J. (1971), The present suicide taboo in the United States. *Ment. Hygiene* 55:178-183.

Friedman, M., Glasser, M., Laufer, E., Laufer, M., and Wohl, M. (1972), Attempted suicide and self-mutilation in adolescence: some observations from a psychoanalytic research project. *Int. J. Psychoanal.* 53:179-183.

Freud, S. (1917), Mourning and melancholia. *Standard Edition,* 14: 243-258. London: Hogarth Press, 1957.

Gould, R. E. (1965), Suicide problems in children and adolescents. *Am. J. Psychother.* 19:228-246.

Hatten, C. L., Valenti, S. M. and Rink, A. (1977), *Suicide: Assessment and Intervention.* New York: Appleton-Century-Crofts.

Haven, L. (1969), Discussion of "The Suicidal Adolescent" by J. C. Sabbath. *J. Am. Acad. Child Psychiat.* 8:286-289.

Hendin, H. (1970), *Black Suicide.* London: Allen Lane, Penguin Press.

———. (1975), Growing up dead: student suicide. *Am. J. Psychother.* 29:327-338.

Iga, M. and Tatai, K. (1975), Characteristics of suicide and attitudes toward suicide in Japan. In N. L. Farberow (Ed.), *Suicide in Different Cultures.* Baltimore: University Park Press.

Leonard, C. V. (1967), *Understanding and Preventing Suicide.* Springfield: Charles Thomas.

Levinson, M. and Neuringer, C. (1971), Problem solving behavior in suicidal adolescents. *J. Consult. and Clin. Psychol.* 37:433-436.

———. and Neuringer, C. (1972), Phenomenal environmental oppressiveness in suicidal adolescents. *J. Genetic Psychol.* 120:253-256.

Lourie, R. (1967), Suicide and attempted suicide in children and adolescents. In L. Yochelson (Ed.), *Symposium on Suicide.* Washington: George Washington University School of Medicine.

McGee, R. K. (1971), Suicide prevention programs and mental health associations. *Ment. Hygiene* 55:60-67.

Morrison, G. and Collier, J. G. (1969), Family treatment approaches to suicidal children and adolescents. *J. Am. Acad. Child Psychiat.* 8:140-153.

Nagy, M. (1948), The child's view of death. *J. Genet. Psychol.* 73: 3-27.

Rauenhorst, J. M. (1972), Young women who attempt suicide. *Dis. Nerv. Syst.* 33:792-797.

Rochlin, G. (1965), *Griefs and Discontents: The Forces of Change.* Boston: Little, Brown and Co.

Sabbath, J. (1969), The suicidal adolescent—the expendable child. *J. Am. Acad. Child Psychiat.* 8:272-289.

Schneer, H. I. and Kay, P. (1961), The suicidal adolescent. In S. Lorand and H. I. Schneer (Eds.), *Adolescents: Psychoanalytic Approach to Problems and Therapy.* New York: Paul B. Hoeber.

Schneer, H. I., Perlstein, A. and Brozovsky, M. (1975), Hospitalized suicidal adolescents: two generations. *J. Am. Acad. Child Psychiat.* 14:268-280.

Schrut, A. (1964), Suicidal adolescents and children. *J. A. M. A.* 188:1103-1107.

Schuyler, D. (1973), When was the last time you took a suicidal child to lunch? *J. School Health* 43:504-506.

Stevenson, E. K., Hudgens, R. W., Held, C. P., Meredith, C. H., Hendrix, M. E., and Carr, D. L. (1972), Suicidal communication by adolescents. *Dis. Nerv. Syst.* 33:112-122.

Sugar, M. (1975), Office network therapy with adolescents. In M. Sugar (ed.), *The Adolescent in Group and Family Therapy.* New York: Brunner/Mazel.

Teicher, J. D. (1973), A solution to the chronic problems of living: adolescent attempted suicide. In J. C. Schoolar (Ed.), *Current Issues in Adolescent Psychiatry.* New York: Brunner/Mazel

——— and Jacobs, J. (1966), Adolescents who attempt suicide. *Am. J. Psychiat.* 122:1248-1257.

Toolan, J. M. (1975), Suicide in children and adolescents. *Am. J. Psychother.* 29:339-344.

Tsuang, M. I. T. (1977), Genetic factors in suicide. *Dis. Nerv. Syst.* 38:498-501.

U. S. Department of Health, Education and Welfare (1974), Public Health Service National Center for Health Statistics of the United States, 1971. H.R.A. 75-1102, Rockville, Maryland, Vol. 2.

Vogel, E. F. and Bell, N. W. (1960), The emotionally disturbed child as the family scapegoat. In N. W. Bell and E. F. Vogel (Eds.), *A Modern Introduction to the Family.* Glencoe, Ill.: Free Press, pp. 382-397.

Webb, J. P. and Willard, W. (1975), American Indian patterns of suicide. In N. L. Farberow (Ed.), *Suicide in Different Cultures.* Baltimore: University Park Press.

Winn, D. A. (1969), Adolescent suicidal behavior and hallucinations. In H. Caplan and S. Lebovici (Eds.), *Adolescence: Psychosocial Perspectives.* New York: Basic Books.

Woodruff, R. A. (1972), Suicide attempts and psychiatric disorders. *Dis. Nerv. Syst.* 33:617-621.

Zilboorg, G. (1936), Differential diagnostic types of suicide. *Arch. Neurol. and Psychiat.* 35:270-291.

11

Health and Medical Care of Adolescents

WILLIAM A. DANIEL, JR.
ROBERT T. BROWN

Of all age groups in the United States, people from 10-21 years of age have had the least attention paid to their health needs. Less teaching and research have been directed toward these approximately 65 million adolescents than to children and adults. However, this situation is no longer static. Several social changes after World War II have altered our society's view of adolescents and we believe the next decade will see a tremendous upsurge of interest in their health problems and of research related to their growth and development. One of the changes bringing about increased awareness of adolescents has been the relative prosperity of young people which has commanded attention from the business sector. The explosive use and abuse of drugs during the 1960s, the increased number of runaways, the rapid rise in the number of teenage pregnancies, and increasing incidence of sexually transmitted disease, have caused greater concern by adults. In addition, significant court rulings concerning the rights of minors and the concept of the mature or emancipated minor, discussed elsewhere in this volume (Gothard—Chapter 6), have made possible increasing health care without parental consent. Nevertheless many myths about adolescents continue to influence the attitudes of many adults, including physicians.

One of these myths is that all adolescents are healthy. Although accidents, suicides, maligancies, and homicides are the chief causes of death during adolescence, the number of deaths is not large when compared to the entire adolescent population. But there are scanty data available concerning the effects of chronic illness and handicaps, the frequency of serious non-fatal illnesses, or difficulties in psychosocial growth. From our experience, adolescents have a host of complex illnesses and/or handicaps that affect their maturation and adjustments as adults. Many conditions appear during adolescence, others are exacerbated in this period of growth, and a few begin at puberty, although they appear more frequently in adulthood. A survey of the members of the American Academy of Pediatrics has confirmed the need for greater emphasis in health problems of adolescents during medical school and resident training. Also, the Bureau of Community Health Services in the Department of Health, Education and Welfare has recognized the need for more education about adolescent health problems for individuals working in the various health care disciplines and has established several centers for advanced training in adolescent health care. Therefore, we must consider how adolescents fit into the health care system, who cares for them, and the effects of chronic illness or handicaps on their physical, cognitive and psychosocial growth.

HEALTH NEEDS OF ADOLESCENTS

It is likely that the majority of adolescents in the United States receive adequate, if not optimal, health care. However, there are several million teenagers who receive very little health care except in catastrophic situations. There is a great need for all adolescents to have what may be called a medical home, i.e., a particular site with a physician or group of persons providing health care. This should be regarded by each adolescent as his/her source of health care. Such a medical home must provide for continuity of care, assume responsibility for providing access to more comprehensive health care, and have a professional person who can be a confidante and counselor. It should be interested in and associated with the patients' growth and development in addition to caring for their illnesses or handicaps.

Adolescents in general believe they are invincible, that the bad things will not happen to them, and that they will not be permanently disabled by illness or injury. Because of these erroneous assumptions and a level of thinking based primarily on the past and on the present, they cannot realistically evaluate the future. This developmental level of thinking is expressed chiefly by adolescents' seeking of episodic health care and by their limited appreciation of the concept of preventive health care. We provide very little health education in our schools and not much more in clinics and physicians' offices. Health education and the value of preventive health measures are not imparted by many parents to their children and physicians frequently give insufficient time to health education for adolescents. Accidents, particularly those associated with the use of motor vehicles, are the leading cause of death in adolescence, pointing up the need for greater education in this area. Suicides in the adolescent age group have increased dramatically during the past several decades indicating that frequently we are unaware of the emotional difficulties of adolescents (see Sugar—Chapter 10). Gonorrheal infection has been epidemic in the adolescent age group and, although satisfactory treatment is generally available, adolescents rarely use means to prevent sexually transmitted diseases. Another national problem is pregnancy during the teenage years and, although this too is a preventable condition, the incidence has increased in spite of many educational efforts. Based on existing data it is evident that preventive health needs of adolescents are not being met or, if the means of prevention are available, they are not being utilized.

The health status of any population group cannot be isolated from education, training, and other social factors. Educational needs of adolescents are not being met sufficiently to prepare them for jobs, and, in many instances adolescents cannot speak English. In other areas, teenagers are prevented from working because of legal age restrictions. Unemployment among teenagers, particularly those who are black, is extremely high in the United States. Few of these unemployed adolescents can fit into a technological society where skill is a requisite for a job. If an adolescent has a health problem or a handicap, his vocational and, often, educational choices may be greatly limited. Employment may be dependent upon correcting health deficits.

In summary, the majority of adolescents are receiving adequate medical care though there are a great many boys and girls who are not in the system; medical care is not synonomous with health care because the former is related more to illness or disability and the latter considers the whole person and his environment. We are failing the adolescents who do not receive adequate medical care, we are not providing high quality health care to many adolescents, and we give very little preventive health care or health education. We are also not meeting the needs of present day adolescents because professionals in many disciplines concerned with health care have been and are poorly educated in the broad needs of adolescents. Further research is also needed in all of these areas.

ADOLESCENTS AND THE HEALTH CARE SYSTEM

The majority of adolescents live with their parents although many of them have but one parent. Others have run away and seek help from many persons and agencies, and some are in the juvenile justice system or in foster homes. This diversity is further evidence that adolescents are not a homogenous group and that they cannot be stereotyped. Like adults, they should be accorded the consideration of being regarded as individuals. Those who provide care for these young people can also differ from those who are concerned with health requirements of small children.

Physicians

Undoubtedly family physicians care for the medical needs of the majority of adolescents in the United States. Physicians who treat all age groups of patients usually are accepted by early adolescents without feeling like small children if these physicians treat teenage patients as persons and respect their confidentiality. In the past, pediatricians stopped caring for children whey they reached early or mid-adolescence, but this practice has become less frequent. Even so, many young adolescents regard the pediatrician as a baby doctor unless there is evidence that he views them as being different from children. Internists care for some adolescents but they have been accused of not feeling comfortable with adolescents and tending to think more about geriatric problems than of the characteristics of emerging adults. Family physicians and pediatricians are often regarded as parental figures because they have cared for the teenaged patients since infancy. Therefore adolescents may be reluctant to confide in them, may fear their parents will be told of illnesses or indiscretions, and are uncertain how to relate to a very familiar person in a more mature manner. An adult recalled the embarrassment at age 14 when he visited his otherwise idealized family doctor complaining of groin and leg pains. These were abruptly responded to with "O.K., drop your pants," instead of an inquiry into activities and reassurance before this command.

Many physicians, regardless of classification, do not feel at ease interviewing or counselling adolescents, and are disturbed by their ambivalence and frequent noncompliance. They also may worry about payment for services if parents are not informed. Experience and a nonjudgmental approach are required before physicians or other professionals can easily relate to adolescents thereby allowing mutual trust and respect to develop. When this occurs, adolescents are found to be excellent patients. Physicians who care for patients from infancy or early childhood should gradually encourage greater responsibility for the older child or early adolescent and consider him as the central figure, shifting the mother's responsibility to the periphery.

Clinics

In most urban areas and a few rural communities, health care for large numbers of adolescents is obtained at clinics or agencies. Most often the clinic is a general one related to all age groups of patients or is considered a pediatric clinic primarily concerned with small children. All clinics have eligibility requirements, and many times adolescents cannot obtain care. This is because they are not financially eligible, they do not have a particular illness, they are not in a specific age group, or they cannot give consent for treatment. Legal rights of adolescents is extremely important and is discussed elsewhere in this volume, but often the question of consent is a major barrier to health care for an adolescent.

Eligibility can be complicated and differ from clinic to clinic or agency to agency thus making comprehensive health care almost impossible to obtain. For example, an adolescent may receive a screening examination at an ambulatory care center, be referred for specialized care to another agency but not qualify for examination and treatment at that agency. Too often geographic separation of clinics and agencies, each with its own protocol, meeting times, and staffs, makes accessibility of care extremely difficult. For example, if a parent must accompany a 16-year-old adolescent from clinic to clinic, to agencies, to hospitals, the parent may lose needed salary from loss of time at work.

Another difficulty is the fragmentation of records and services. It is not unusual for the same laboratory tests to be done several times by different facilities, thus increasing the discomfort of the patient and the expense to the parent or the taxpayer. These examples point up the greater concern: the lack of a medical home that assumes the responsibility for the adolescent patient and for correlating diagnostic information or treatment. If responsibility is not assumed, that patient too often is a medical wanderer, never knowing what is being done, what should be done, or how to cope successfully with an illness or a handicap.

We believe that an interdisciplinary health team working with adolescents is an excellent model for providing health care. In such an organization, services of physicians, psychologists, nutritionists, social workers, nurses and other health professionals are available. Ideal staffing is often unachievable but each adolescent does not require services from all disciplines. A competent physician can provide the majority of care required by adolescents, but often he has insufficient time. Other health care providers, such as skilled nurse practitioners, can render excellent care, relieve the physician in many ways, and can provide some things that he cannot. In the private practice of medicine or in rural areas limited in numbers of physicians, specific needs of adolescents may be provided by referring them to other professionals or agencies but the physician should assume the responsibility of coordinating care and of reviewing what has and has not been done. This format can be very effective and cheaper, though perhaps less convenient, than an interdisciplinary clinic.

Free Clinics

In the 1960s so-called "free clinics" appeared and gave widely varying qualities of health care for adolescents. The "flower children" and adolescents who had run away or who were abusing drugs sought care at free clinics that eliminated many of the traditional aspects of health care and did not require records of patients or their names and addresses. In general, this care was episodic, limited in scope, often of poor quality and always affected by financial difficulties. A few such clinics were, and remain, of excellent quality and have provided a wide-range of services including medical and psychiatric care, legal aid, job employment services, help in obtaining housing, etc. Currently, with less social unrest, even these clinics have gradually become more traditional so far as records, evaluation of services, and means of support are concerned. These facilities deserve credit for providing health care, even though often of less than optimal quality. Adolescents and young adults needed care at that time and could not have obtained it any other way. One disadvantage of many clinics, whether traditional or free, is that health personnel are often temporary, thus making continuity of care difficult, especially with chronic illnesses or handicapping conditions.

EFFECTS OF ILLNESSES AND HANDICAPS

Every human being is affected by genetic inheritance, influences of the environment, and by social-cultural conditions and change. A child entering puberty carries his past with him which affects growth and development significantly during adolescence. Although childhood may have been marred by difficulties that are exacerbated by adolescence, so may adolescence be a period in which corrections can be made. The biologic changes of puberty are enormous with increase in overall size, alteration of physical features, rapid growth of sexual organs and change in appearance of secondary sexual characteristics. Physicians and others should become acquainted with sex maturity ratings (Tanner, 1973) because these indicators of pubertal growth correlate closely with biochemical values of the blood, osseous changes, and increase in muscular size and strength. They suggest times for counselling adolescents on matters such as menstruation, sexually transmitted disease, contraception, and pregnancy.

Cognitive growth also brings about major changes occurring at about the time of pubescence. Although the development of thought processes is rarely completed before adulthood, there is significant change during puberty. Adolescents begin to think differently, relinquish thought patterns based only on past experience and a limited future, and come to develop the ability to think abstractly, to hypothesize, and to consider and to plan for their futures. Too often adults, including those providing health care, tend to relate to an adolescent based on the physical size of the patient rather than his/her stage of cognitive development. For example, it is not unusual for adults to treat a 13-year-old boy more as an adult if he is 6 feet tall than they do a very small 15-year-old boy. Too many adolescents feel they are addressed condescendingly by adults and that they are still regarded as small children. This impression can prevent the development of trust and hinder compliance with a physician's recommendations. Patients should, of course, be involved in decision-making to the degree they are capable, for if this is done, the treatment or recommendations are more a joint venture and are more acceptable. Teenagers comply most often because they like the physician or nurse and want to please this person, not because they evaluate the future effects of illness or because carrying out the instructions seems wise.

Psychosocial growth is extremely important and is associated with, and affected by, both biologic and cognitive change. For example, an adolescent begins to develop an idealized body image, a mental picture of what he would like to be and how he hopes to look when he is adult. There must come a time when this idealized body image is replaced by a realistic body image with which the adolescent feels comfortable. Then, normal psychological development may continue toward the formation of an identity with a realistic ego.

Although there are a great many major and minor tasks to be accomplished, it is useful to consider four broad areas of development. Separation from the family, at least emotionally, and some assumption of self-responsibility is the first. The increase hormonal influences which bring about adult sexual appearance and awareness of new and powerful desires and drives must be dealt with by adolescents. They must cope with sexual restrictions of society, they must develop a personal moral code, and it is necessary for them to establish a comfortable feeling of maleness or femaleness. A third major task is the awareness of the necessity to have a vocation, to think about possible means of livelihood as an adult, and eventually to prepare for a job or profession. The development of a mature ego identity is the fourth major task.

The first three major areas of psychosocial growth differ in their significance and meaning during early, middle and late adolescence. For example, early adolescents are body-oriented, wonder what they will look like as adults; their thoughts are directed inward and sexual desires are usually covert. Mid-adolescents are more comfortable with themselves, usually have a realistic body image, think about a dating partner and seek part-time jobs. Late adolescents are most often heterosexual, have established significant and satisfying relationships with others, are less affected by peers, are more concerned about vocational opportunities and preparation, and have become relatively confident that they can "make it" after they leave home. If indeed the young person has succeeded in these tasks of adolescence and has become an individual, has confidence and self-esteem, and commits himself to achieving his aims, he has, or almost has obtained the fourth step in maturing, ego identity.

The three large changes in growth (biologic, cognitive, and psychosocial) rarely progress at the same rate and often there are temporary pauses, deviances, or periods of disequilibrium. It should be remembered that each area of development can affect the other(s), and, in providing health care, it is imperative that we keep this in mind. Most professionals working with adolescents feel that awareness of needs in these areas, particularly those other than physical, are too often ignored, the assumption being that cognitive and psychosocial growth will take place without help or concern. The emotional health of adolescents should receive more attention than it does. These needs are not being met at the present time. Schools, for example, usually do not try to present material at suitable cognitive levels of development, but instead present for attained age level. Athletic programs are related to grades in school, ages of students, or weights and are not related to the levels of maturity of the participants. We do not meet needs in these areas, and this should be a goal for the future.

CHRONIC ILLNESSES AND HANDICAPS

Chronic illnesses and handicaps can be major or minor and the effects on adolescent development great or little. Some conditions, such as orthopedic abnormalities and injuries, have attracted attention and response from the medical profession for many years; crippled children's clinics have been available nationwide. Care of the deformity or injury has usually been excellent, and various professionals working with children and adolescents in these clinics have been concerned about their overall growth and development. But historically, care has focused attention more on the chronic illness or disability than the holistic concept of growth and development. Even today the effects of the disorder on the psychosocial growth of the child or adolescent do not generally receive the attention they should. The manifestations of illness and handicapping conditions are not static but differ according to the level of development and the age of the patient. In trying to give anticipatory guidance and in trying to help adolescents plan for the future, consideration must be given to effects at later stages of life.

How a chronic illness or handicap affects an adolescent depends on many factors. The onset of a condition—congenital or acquired—provides tremendous differences in how the adolescent copes with life. For example, a congenitally deaf child may have greater difficulty in developing psychosocial skills as an adolescent than does a counterpart who became deaf after learning language. Differences can also be present in psychosocial growth if an illness or handicap develops suddenly or over a long period of time, for the latter case may have permitted adaptation to the condition or allowed growth to take place before the full handicapping effects developed. The age of onset can be crucial in affecting maturation. For example, brain injury from an accident that occurred during puberty may affect growth more than the same injury at a later age. Injuries to the central nervous system in childhood and adolescence are not necessarily subtracted from a mature nervous system because complete growth may not yet have occurred. The attitude of parents, siblings and peers exerts an influence on the adolescent; if he is accepted and supported by people around him, coping with his problems and adapting to them can be easier. All of these factors and many others play a part in growth and change during adolescence and are often unrecognized by those providing health care.

Too often attention is not given to psychosocial problems unless behavior is unacceptable. Some illnesses or handicaps cause only minor concern or are temporary and not serious. For example, unequal length of the legs may be of little importance to a small child but because it affects participation in sports during adolescence and can prevent success in this area, status with peers may be affected. This handicap may also limit vocational choices and dating and require a far longer time for the development of a realistic body image with subsequent normal psychologic growth.

Mention has been made that one area of growth can often affect another. For example, a 14-year-old adolescent may be precocious in cognitive growth but retarded in physical growth because of ulcerative colitis. This adolescent may be concerned about his retarded physical size but can be more worried because he is retarded in sexual development when compared with his peers. Obviously health care should be directed toward treatment of the bowel disease but health providers should not ignore his concerns about his body and should provide aid and counselling to help him cope with his worries. An obese teenager may be cognitively average but extremely depressed because of the lack of social skills and acceptance by peers. Another adolescent may be physically well developed but has great difficulty psychosocially because of mild mental retardation. Many times a handicap or a chronic illness will, of itself, be a primary concern to the physician but a psychosocial area is more important to the young patient. It is tragic, for example, that there are many adolescents who are physically attractive, are socially well prepared, but are severely handicapped by true perceptual-motor difficulty. The boy who cannot read usually gets only the poorest jobs even though he may have high intelligence, and this affects his life in ways that are often difficult to evaluate or appreciate.

In caring for adolescents with chronic illnesses or handicaps it is necessary to consider a host of factors that affect physical, cognitive, and psychosocial growth and development. Reactions and responses to illnesses and handicaps do not remain the same and most adolescents require a long period of time to stabilize their feelings, accept or adapt to the condition, and concentrate on functioning in the world of adults. As providers of health care we must be alert to the possible effect on the feelings of the patients, and we must consider the person who has an illness or handicap in an holistic manner. In general, we are not consistently meeting these needs.

SPECIAL PROBLEMS OF ADOLESCENTS

In the last 100 years adolescents have become physically larger and matured earlier. At present the average age of menarche is 12 years 3 months. Although there has been little change during the last 20 years, this earlier physical maturity, at least sexually, has been a major factor in some of the problems occurring today. In addition, relative prosperity has made more money available for adolescents to spend on themselves, there is greater mobility of family and of individual travel, there has been a great increase of one-parent families, and rapid technological changes have occurred that require longer periods of education or training. The vast majority of adolescents resemble those of the past several decades, but there is greater sexual freedom today. Adolescents have greater expectations of rewards and many of them seem to be unwilling to commit themselves for long periods of education. A common finding is that today's adolescents believe they should always be happy and that happiness is the purpose of life. There are several areas of health care which demand greater attention, particularly in preventive medicine, if the needs of adolescents are to be met.

Sexually Transmitted Diseases

There is no doubt that gonococcal infections have reached epidemic numbers and are involving adolescents at younger ages each year. Early sexual maturation and a sexually oriented environment have tended to increase sexual experimentation with the result that gonorrhea has increased in the adolescent population. Adolescent boys usually seek treatment for gonorrhea fairly early after the onset of infection because of discomfort and the appearance of a discharge. Early adolescents are often reluctant to go to a physician and hope the infection will disappear; but they usually fear more that something will happen to the genitalia or that the symptoms will worsen, and they seek attention. These youngsters are often embarrassed to talk to the physician but this is perhaps the best time to discuss preventive measures because they are more acutely aware of their needs. Mid-adolescents and late-adolescents tend to underestimate the seriousness of gonococcal infection because of the rapid cure with appropriate antibiotics. In adolescent girls, the disease is often asymptomatic, and many of them are surprised when told that they have gonorrhea. Because there is usually no visible evidence of the infection and the girl may not have symptoms, the disease is also regarded as insignificant. Attempts to prevent the spread of gonorrhea and to decrease the number of infections have not been very successful, and new methods of teaching prevention need to be developed.

Pregnancy

At the present time there is an increase in the number of infants born to adolescent girls. This trend has been increasing and, although there may be some leveling off, the problem is still one of great magnitude. Contraceptive means exist but are infrequently used by adolescent girls until after they have had one child. It is commonly known that very few young adolescents are thinking about contraceptives when planning to have their first few sexual experiences. Thoughts about the use of contraceptive devices or agents most often come after there is a mutual trust and a regularity of sexual intercourse. It would seem that early adolescents and a great many mid-adolescents do not consider or cannot appreciate the results of inter-course or the difficulties produced in the future if the girl becomes preg-nant. Thinking is related to immediacy and desire, to what might happen in attempting to have intercourse rather than the effects thereof. Many mid- and late-adolescents feel that use of contraceptive devices alters the rela-tionship and tends to make it less desirable because the spontaneity of the act is gone. One of the tasks of adolescence is to develop self-responsibility and to attain sufficient maturity of abstract thought to ponder future effects. It may be unrealistic of adults to expect boys and girls who have not reached this stage of thinking to act as though they have. If this supposition is correct, health education and instructions designed to prevent either ve-nereal disease or conception will have to be revised to relate more closely to the developmental level of cognition (See chapter 13).

In many states minors of any age may obtain oral contraceptive agents or other means of preventing pregnancy or venereal disease. Some states have an age limit, frequently unrealistic, and it is important to know the law where the physician resides. Some physicians are reluctant to prescribe contraceptive agents because they fear they will be sued, because this is an endorsement of the boy's or girl's action, or because it is against their own moral principles. These physicians need to think very carefully and se-riously about their views and, if they still do not wish to provide this aspect of health care for an adolescent, then they should present this fact in a nonjudgmental manner and direct the patient to a different physician. It would seem that it is much better to prevent pregnancy than to have it occur in adolescence, but there are physicians whose religious or personal moral views will not allow them to prescribe contraceptive agents.

Abortion is now legal during early pregnancy. The question of abortion for adolescents is one that should involve particularly the pregnant girl and her physician. It is usually impossible to exclude the parents if the girl is an early or mid-adolescent living at home; however, according to many state laws, adolescents of certain ages have the right of consent. According to rulings from the Supreme Court it would seem that the pregnant girl can make her own decision. Adolescents differ greatly in views on abortion just as adults do. Many early adolescent girls believe in abortion for themselves but not for other girls who "are just the kind that would sleep with anyone and get pregnant." Mid-adolescent girls usually become angry when they learn that they are pregnant and tend to blame parents, the physician, the church, or other persons who "should not have let me get pregnant." These girls as well as late-adolescents tend to have rather mixed feelings about abortion. A great many of them realize that it would be difficult for them to care for a child, however, and choose abortion. Some of the girls, like adults, believe it morally wrong to have an abortion and prefer to have the child and release it for adoption. There are still families who insist upon the boy and girl marrying in order to legalize the pregnancy, but these seem to be decreasing in number. Data are not sufficient to give definitive evidence of the psychological effects of abortion, adoption or keeping the infant. Some girls later in life regret having had an abortion whereas others state they would have preferred an abortion to the worries about who adopted the baby, where it is, and whether the child is being treated kindly. Health providers are certainly aware of the myriad problems that can and do arise with pregnancy in adolescent girls, and this emphasizes the great need for prevention.

Education

Education for adolescents, discussed elsewhere in this volume, is becoming a problem for many millions of teenagers. Most of them view school as a place to develop social skills and interpersonal relationships and are only tangentially interested in achieving good grades or preparing themselves for future vocations. It would seem that late adolescence brings about a more serious regard for school, but even then there are a great many adolescents who do not feel that school meets their needs. In this country schools are not geared to adolescents and their problems, particularly those of early adolescence. An analysis of schooling patterns and administration shows tremendous variety about where 6th, 7th or 8th graders are grouped. There are some in elementary schools, middle schools, junior high schools, and senior high schools, all of which overlap. It would seem that educators still are not clear about what to do with early adolescents. Programs are not designed for cognitive levels of development, and many persons regard these years as a holding pattern until adolescents mature enough "for real education." Educational objectives for early adolescents, like those of the juvenile justice system, have often been made and seem to be well thought out but apparently have not accomplished their purposes. More study and research needs to be done in education for early adolescents. Even sports programs in schools are set up according to age, class, or occasionally

weight, and do not consider the level of physical maturity of the participants. In our society where boys tend to gain respect and self-esteem from
sports during their developmental periods, late maturing adolescents cannot compete with their early or average maturing counterparts. Therefore,
it would seem that, at least in sports programs, competition could be related
to developmental groupings rather than age or grade level.

INTERVIEWING AND COUNSELLING

One of the curses of modern medicine is lack of time. Practitioners are
usually very busy, clinics are frequently understaffed, and many health
workers have multiple duties with limited time. If we approach care of
adolescents with the belief that change and growth are important, particularly in physical illness and handicaps, it will be necessary to establish
confidence and trust between the patient and the provider of care. With a
few exceptions the age of the physician or other professional does not seem
to be a hindrance provided there is evidence of interest in and concern for
the adolescent patient. Most adolescents are extremely perceptive and de-
tect false concern and condescension very quickly. If adults working with
adolescents have their own problems solved and are genuinely interested in
these young patients, most interviewing proceeds well unless the boy or girl
has been forced to come unwillingly. Frequently adolescents state they have
no problems and that only their parents are in difficulty; but usually such
statements provide entree to the interview in that the parents can be discussed first.

Interviewing may be easy or difficult. Most often adolescents come to the
physician because of real or imagined physical illness or injury and are
eager to tell about it, be examined and receive treatment. An initial interview or history has two objectives: to obtain a careful account concerning
the reason for the visit to the physician and to determine if there are areas
or findings that should be explored in greater depth. For example, an adolescent may have come to a physician or clinic because of an upper respira-
tory infection but, in taking the history, it was learned that the patient was
two grades behind in school. Such a finding brings up the possibility of
learning problems, mild mental retardation, and a host of other factors
affecting schooling. These should be investigated, perhaps at a later visit.
An adolescent girl may come to the physician because of a rash but really
wishes to ask about contraceptive measures. The physician and others
working with adolescents must be alert to the possibility of unstated questions and also to the need to provide opportunities for discussion.

If there are behavior problems, drug abuse, or psychologic difficulties an interview will undoubtedly take more time; however, it is often necessary to have additional visits rather than spend 2 or 3 hours at one visit. Most physicians are not skilled psychological interviewers or counsellors, and there is a need to improve these skills. Psychiatrists and psychologists have learned time-saving methods which can be adopted by other physicians and professionals working with adolescents. Many adolescents enjoy intellectualizing or "playing games" during interviews or counselling sessions, and these must be recognized and limited. Adolescents also may have directed their thoughts to the body more than to the mind or to the emotions and may be fully cognizant of the need for physical examination and treatment but unaware of the need and value of psychologic treatment. Most adolescents are restless and many times more information is obtained in a series of very short visits than in a single long session. These young patients also need time to think about what was asked, to evaluate the interviewer, and to decide how candid and open to be in the future.

Interviewing adolescents is an art, but skill can be learned. It is necessary that the interviewer feel free to discuss any subject, accept street language, and not express surprise or disapproval. There must be a statement about confidentiality and the development of trust between the patient and the counsellor. Young adolescents often do not speak fluently, are confused about words or use them in different contexts, and are uncertain in trying to express themselves. They often convey more information by body language than by verbal communication. Anxiety is frequent and is shown by how the teenager acts, shifting positions, clenching and stretching hands and fingers, looking away from the interviewer, and moving the body. Changes in voice, the appearance of tears, and difficulty in talking are all indicators of stress, and the subject usually should be changed to allow regaining of composure. Sensitive and anxiety-provoking areas can be approached differently or at a later time, but they indicate to the examiner that further exploration is needed.

Even though training of physicians and many other professionals working with adolescents has been inadequate, most of them can provide some counselling for adolescents if it is considered a priority and if their skill is constantly upgraded. There must be an awareness of personal limitations and recognition of the need to refer some adolescents to other persons more skilled in counselling. Many psychosocial maladjustments can be cared for by interested, empathetic family physicians. A cardinal principle is to establish quickly the levels of biologic, cognitive and psychosocial growth and to determine if one of these areas is exerting a significant effect on the others. Counselling of an early adolescent who has not developed abstract thinking must not be directed along lines that require deductive analysis or construction of hypotheses about the future. Adolescents who have below normal intelligence must be counselled in simplistic terms whereas the very bright teenager who loves to spend a visit intellectualizing about unimportant minutiae must be brought around to central issues.

Adolescents also tend to assume many things that are untrue. Frequently they interpret lack of comment as an endorsement of their statements or views, or they believe that the physician will solve the problem and are extremely critical when no change occurs. If the counsellor expresses an opinion or advises an adolescent, it should be done in specific terms, clearly stated and understandable. It is of value to work out the course of action jointly with the adolescent who then feels he has participated in the process and is more likely to pursue short-term objectives. Some adolescents delight in having a counsellor advise them and then blame the counsellor for future difficulties. Involving the young patient in coming to a decision or plan of action may prevent future accusations and disappointments.

It is evident that current training in providing health care for adolescents is deficient in the art of interviewing and counselling. There is a great need for this and it is to be hoped that changes will be implemented as soon as possible. Adolescents are uncertain about themselves, what they will be, even who they are, and yet they want to be loved, admired and respected by others. It is very difficult to love someone who does not even know who he or she is and yet, if we are to care for these boys and girls, we must be aware of their difficulties and needs and aid them in becoming well-adjusted adults. Most primary care physicians can provide counselling if they are interested and obtain training.

CONCLUSION

The majority of adolescents in the United States receive adequate medical care, but large numbers have few contacts with health professionals except under catastrophic circumstances. We consider medical care to be an important part of health care, and there is less health care for adolescents than medical care. Health education, anticipatory guidance, help for behavioral adjustment and emotional problems, diagnosis and treatment of learning difficulties, and holistic management of handicapping conditions or chronic illnesses are large areas of unmet needs.

The adolescent usually fits into the health care system with difficulty. Many early adolescents are reluctant to continue with pediatricians unless these physicians and their staffs regard them appropriately. Internists care for few adolescents and are often uncertain in relating to them or unsure in thinking about their problems that so often differ from those of adults. Family practitioners provide much care for adolescents but are handicapped by lack of time and, as with other categories of physicians, by lack of training in adolescent health problems. Clinics are available in many areas but care is often limited, fragmented or prevented by legal or eligibility requirements. Our goal should be availability of health care for all adolescents, probably in a pluralistic health care system, in which each adolescent has a medical home.

Preventive health care and management of the effects of handicapping conditions or chronic illness are presently inadequate. Research to discover effective means of health education, to increase and motivate adolescents' acceptance of preventive measures, and to relate this information to levels of adolescent growth and development are badly needed. Education of physicians and other professional health workers is inadequate and must be improved.

Recognition and treatment of perceptual-motor difficulties, family stress, and behavioral and emotional problems must become part of the training of physicians and other professionals. Cognitive and psychosocial growth in adolescence largely have been ignored in medical schools and this deficit must be corrected. The physician can provide counselling for the majority of adolescent difficulties, but, to be effective, he must have the knowledge, that is, information and training, to do so.

Changes are taking place but there remain unmet needs in the health care of adolescents, and these are related to other areas discussed in this book.

REFERENCES

Gothard. S. (1979). The Expanding Right to Treatment for Adolescents—The Legal Implications for the Enabling Adults and Disciplines. In Sugar. M. (Ed.). *Responding to Adolescent Needs*, New York: Spectrum Publications. Inc.

Sugar. M. (1979). Family Problems in Adolescent Suicide. In Sugar. M. (Ed.). *Responding to Adolescent Needs*, New York: Spectrum Publications. Inc.

———. (1979). The Epidemic of Adolescent Mothering. In Sugar, M. (Ed.), *Responding to Adolescent Needs*, New York: Spectrum Publications, Inc.

Tanner, J. M. (1973), *Growth and Adolescence*, Oxford: Blackwell Scientific Publications.

SUGGESTED READING

Alan Guttmacher Institute (1976) *11 Million Teenagers,* New York: Planned Parenthood Federation of America.

Daniel, W. A., Jr. (1977), *Adolescents in Health and Disease,* St. Louis: The C. V. Mosby Co.

————. (1978), *Issue on Adolescence* (Guest Editor), New York: *Pediatric Annals.*

Emans, S. J. and Goldstein, D. (1977), *Pediatric and Adolescent Gynecology,* Boston: Little, Brown and Co.

Gordon, S. (1973), *The Sexual Adolescent,* Boston: Duxbury Press.

Hoffman, A. and Hoffman, F.: (1975), *A Handbook on Drug and Alcohol Abuse,* London: Oxford University Press.

Jacobs, J. (1971), *Adolescent Suicide,* New York: Wiley and Interscience.

Lipsitz, J. (1971), *Growing up Forgotten—A Review of Research and Programs Concerning Early Adolescence,* Boston: Lexington Books.

Moriarity, A. and Toussieng, P. (1976), *Adolescent Coping,* New York: Grune & Stratton.

Muus, R. (1975), *Theories of Adolescence,* New York: Random House.

Rice, F. (1975), *The Adolescent: Development Relationships and Culture,* Boston: Allyn and Bacon, Inc.

PART V
Sex

12

Criminal Laws Setting Boundaries on Sexual Exploitation

RALPH SLOVENKO

When we are theorizing about human behavior, there is a tendency to envision categories—for example, children, adolescents, middle-age, and elderly—and to think in terms of those categories. To some extent, the categories are meaningful and helpful, lest it not be forgotten that there are certain human desires and needs that transcend the categories, and which, in social scripting, may be frustrated, exploited, or perverted in their expression (Sheehy, 1976). Differentiating children and adolescents from other age groups may be justified in that they are in a developmental, and more vulnerable, stage of life.

Of all the experiences of the preadolescent, it would appear that sex-role or gender-role learning is dominant in the determination of later psychosexual development. With the onset of adolescence, there occurs the dramatic and celebrated biological event of puberty. Sexual exploitation, while disturbing to all, is of particular concern in this period because it upsets the quiescence of the preadolescent period and exacerbates the turmoil of adolescence.

Sex has always been surrounded with a web of controls made necessary by the force of the sexual drive, and by the disparity that prevails between psychological and biological maturity. In modern society especially, there is a wide gap between the time of puberty and social responsibility. Society

181

through its laws and customs—by sanction and stigma—must react to the tumultuous sexuality manifested during the adolescent stage of life. One of the avowed aims of the law in this area is to provide control over sexual activity among adolescents, and to deter exploitation by the adult world.

Exploitation takes various forms, ranging from commercial exploitation to abuse of young people by adults who are too inept to relate with other adults. Exploitation, we may note, is manifested in certain street language referring to sexual activity with youngsters. Boy prostitutes are sometimes called "chickens," although the term more often applies to either males or females prior to puberty who are used for pornographic films or sexual activity by adults. Also significant is the street term for a pederast, "chicken-hawk."

The true task of the adult world is not to exploit but to create youngsters who are needed, who are productive, who have value, who have self-control. Not everyone can be a poet, but everyone can be educated to be a gentleman or lady. Learning control of one's urges goes hand-in-hand with a respect for the sanctity of other people. It is doubtful that there is any aspect of humanity more difficult to manage or control than one's sexuality, and that is especially true during adolescence. "I realized," Isaac Bashevis Singer (1978) recalls in his memoirs of one liaison, "that in moments of desperation people forsake all reason."

Lack of control results not in freedom as is sometimes alleged, but in trouble. Sexual restrictions may produce personality disorders, but "spontaneity" or "letting it all hang out" may produce equally severe disabling conflicts (Strozier, 1977). There is wisdom in the biblical adage that "to everything there is a season." There are times when it is right and fitting to do things, in accord with one's age, and times when certain things are decidedly inappropriate or self-destructive.

What, daresay, is the proper time? Nature seems to have tricked the human race—the elderly have the wisdom but the young have the drive. It is one of the facts of life which, when not accepted, is intrinsically tragicomic. Indeed, there are few sights more tragicomic than the individual who will not behave according to his or her age, and the responsibilities of that age. That which is out of time, like a young child wearing makeup or an elderly woman dressed like Little Bo Peep, is risible.

In the best personality development, external controls change over into inner or self-control. Good conditions in early life tend to bring about a sense of self-control (Grummon and Barclay, 1971). When self-control is a fact, then security imposed from the ouside may be viewed as an insult. Nevertheless, although the needs of individuals vary, everyone is really relieved to know that there are some external controls. In general, the conscience works best when a policeman is near. Expressed differently, the superego functions most smoothly when the environment supports it (Freud, 1926).

There is a considerable body of legislation directed at setting boundaries on the sexual behavior of, and with, the young. The statutes of some 27 states specifically contain language conferring jurisdiction upon the juvenile court over minors whose conduct, condition, environment or situation is "dangerous to life and limb," "injurious to health, morals, or welfare," etc., who are found "on premises used for illegal purposes," "in a house of prostitution," etc., or who are "vagrant," "idle," "leading an immoral life," "in danger of becoming morally depraved," etc. (five states expressly require that such conduct or condition be habitual or repeated). There are numerous statutes outlawing indecent behavior with juveniles and molestation of children: public disorder, vagrancy, contributing to the delinquency of a minor, obscenity and pornography, sexual psychopath, incest, statutory rape, as well as statutes broadly phrased to control or prohibit "indecent behavior with juveniles."

In considerable degree, the various statutory restrictions overlap. One reason for the considerable overlap rests upon jurisprudential expressions that, under our constitution, a person cannot be subject to criminal prosecution for any act unless that act has first been denounced with sufficient legislative precision that the person sought to be held accountable will know that his conduct falls within the prohibition of the statute (State v. Wrestle, 1978). Another reason for the overlap is that whenever a heinous crime occurs, especially a sexual one, the legislature feels politically impelled to enact more (though not necessarily better) legislation. While repetitive, a new enactment may be considered a directive by the legislature to law-enforcement officials to more vigorously enforce the law. Of course, in some measure, the legislation, however enforced, alleviates the anxiety of a public seeking reassurance that they and their children are being protected from the perpetrators of these offenses.

This chapter examines the sum and substance of these laws, with comment, as they relate to the exploitation of sexual behavior of, or with, minors.

OBSCENITY AND PORNOGRAPHY

The law on obscenity and pornography aims at providing a certain cultural or social atmosphere. Unlike other criminal statutes, this law has application without demonstrating injury to a particular individual. The effort, though, to separate unprotected obscenity from other sexually oriented but constitutionally protected speech has "produced a variety of views among the members of the [Supreme] Court unmatched in any other course of constitutional adjudication" (Harlan, 1968). After 15 years of grappling with the definitional approach to obscenity that he had first articulated, Justice Brennan (1973) reached the conclusion that the struggle was hopeless. He wrote:

> In short, while I cannot say that the interests of the State—apart from the question of juveniles and unconsenting adults—are trivial or nonexistent, I am compelled to conclude that these interests cannot justify the substantial damage to constitutional rights and to this Nation's judicial machinery that inevitably results from state efforts to bar the distribution even of unprotected material to consenting adults. I would hold, therefore, that at least in the absence of distribution to juveniles or obtrusive exposure to unconsenting adults, the First and Fourteenth Amendments prohibit the State and Federal governments from attempting wholly to suppress sexually oriented materials on the basis of their allegedly "obscene" contents.

Justice Brennan specifically reserved judgment on the issue of obscenity controls in cases involving juveniles or unconsenting adults.

History shows, however, that just as the air that we breathe cannot be divided between groups of people, the social atmosphere likewise cannot be divided. The "sexploitation" of adults entails the "sexploitation" of minors as well. What is "adult" entertainment has profound resonance on youth culture (and vice versa). The Court, however, has said that when the material is aimed at adults, juries may apply only the "contemporary community standards" of the adults in the community. The Court, with eight of the nine justices concurring, overturned the conviction of a Los Angeles book and film distributor because the trial judge had told the jury to consider "the community as a whole, young and old, educated and uneducated, the religious and the irreligious, men, women and children, from all walks of life." "We elect to take this occasion to make clear that children are not to be included for these purposes," Justice Burger (1978) declared. A "jury conscientiously striving to define the relevant community of persons . . . by whose standards obscenity is to be judged would reach a much lower 'average' when children are part of the equation than they would if they restricted their consideration to the effect of allegedly obscene materials on adults."

"STATUTORY RAPE" AND
"INDECENT BEHAVIOR WITH JUVENILES"

Sexual activity with juveniles, though they may be willing, is unlawful. Sexual intercourse with a young adolescent girl is called "statutory rape." As commonly conceived, "rape" is forcible intercourse; the essence of statutory rape, however, is age. The element of consent is irrelevant. Statutory rape, as a consequence, is called a "technical" rape. Forcible rape is "statutory" too, in the sense that it is included in criminal statutes, but the term "statutory" in statutory rape refers to intercourse with a juvenile. In some states "statutory rape" is now called "sexual assault in the first degree," sometimes "carnal knowledge of a juvenile." The incest statute also applies if the relationship is one of consanguinity. When coercion is involved, the traditional rape statute, of course, applies.

Statistics indicate that approximately 80% of so-called rape convictions are of the statutory rape variety. The actual frequency of statutory-rape conduct, as distinguished from conviction, is not possible to estimate; most such cases, we may assume, are never reported to the police.

The statute, "indecent behavior with juveniles," deals with behavior that falls short of sexual intercourse. The behavior prohibited under such statutes generally includes all acts of sexual misconduct with juveniles—other than coitus—including onanism, fondling, exhibitionism, voyeurism, and enticing a minor into an act of indecency, as well as "verbal sex acts" (obscene language and pornography). The most common category of behavior covered under this statute is exhibitionism; the second is hand-genital contact. In addition, under the juvenile laws, which were promulgated at the turn of the century, the juvenile court may proceed against an adult for "contributing to the delinquency of a minor," and it may hold the young male as well as the girl as a delinquent or neglected child. In some cases, a display of severe lack of self-control may warrant hospitalization. (Special protection is given children—coitus with a girl under the age of 12, with or without consent, usually constitutes the crime of "aggravated rape," and like forcible rape, is severely punishable (Burgess et al., 1977).) From a psychological point of view, some of the prohibited forms of behavior are perversions. From a societal point of view, all of them appear to be a source of considerable concern. Pick a bud before it blossoms, and, we know, it's spoiled.

French law does not speak of corruption of minors as such, but uses the word "detournement," which means diversion, deviation or turning away; "detournement de mineur" specifically means having caused a minor to leave home. Under French law, anyone who by "fraud or violence" removes a minor "from the place where he has been put by those in authority over him" can be given a sentence, its severity depending on the harm caused. Every crime or simple misdemeanor involving a minor—any act ranging from helping a runaway to sexual seduction, inciting to prostitution, or kidnapping—is judged in terms of this statute. American law requires greater specificity, and bars crimes by analogy (such as occurred in Soviet Russia following the October Revolution when, there being no crime against adultery, adulterers were punished for "hunting without a license").

Historically, rape was defined in terms of sexual intercourse accompanied by the use of force. At earliest common law, consent was a defense to rape whatever the girl's age. In 1275, however, the statute of Westminster I made it a crime "to ravish any maiden within age, either with her consent or without it." "Within age" then meant under 12 (Hale, 1847). The age of consent for sexual intercourse has moved up in most states by statutes to coincide usually with the age of consent for marriage. Current statutes in various states have raised the age limit to 14, 16 or 18, making statutory rape the act of sexual intercourse with a girl between that age and 12.

A male who has sexual intercourse with a minor may be convicted under the statute even though he believes, with every physical justification, that his partner is of the age of consent. Reliance on a birth certificate may not even be an absolute defense. Although a certain state of mind (or *mens rea)* has long been a requirement of criminal responsibility, many exceptions have been recognized, particularly in sex offenses, in which the victim's actual age is determinative despite the defendant's reasonable belief that the girl had reached the age of consent. Crimes involving juveniles, historically recognized as a special class of persons in need of protection, usually do not require knowledge of the child's age as an essential element (State v. Elias, 1978). In furtherance of this interest in protection of juveniles, the various state legislatures have chosen to expressly exclude knowledge of the juvenile's age from the essential elements of several crimes involving that class of persons. [See Louisiana Revised Statutes 14:42(3) (aggravated rape); 14:80 (carnal knowledge of a juvenile); 14:81 (indecent behavior with juveniles); 14:86 (enticing minors into prostitution); 14:92 (contributing to the delinquency of juveniles); 14:93 (cruelty to juveniles).] The young, whatever their wishes, are thus protected against themselves. The law on statutory rape theoretically applies, even though the girl is divorced, has worked or is working as a prostitute.

Some commentators, however, have called the crime of statutory rape "one of the most obsolete concepts in the law" (Abrahamsen, 1960). A number of them have urged its total abolition, while others have urged at least a modification of the law to permit defenses of prior unchastity or mistaken age. A few states now allow these as defenses to a charge of statutory rape (Pieragostini, 1970). Washington allows a defense to a charge of statutory rape that the defendant "reasonably believed the victim to be older based upon declarations of age by the victim" (Washington Pattern Jury Instructions/Criminal, 1977).

Unlike most other sex crimes, the male offender in the case of statutory rape usually has no particular pathology; the girl may be the one more in need of counselling or psychiatric care. She may actually be the seducer or aggressor; she is popularly called "jail bait." Nabokov's (1958) Lolita, of course, is the picture of the all-knowing and incredibly seductive nymphet. At common law (except in Vermont) it was not a criminal offense for an underage girl to aid and abet in the commission of sexual intercourse or to solicit and incite. The law on statutory rape is designed for the protection of the girl, hence it has been ruled that she may not be held as an accessory. With the enactment of juvenile delinquency laws, however, young girls who are promiscuous have been brought within the jurisdiction of the juvenile court.

In theory, the law on statutory or common-law rape originated to protect property, not virtue. It is a heritage of feudal times when marriage rights and wardships were valuable property rights. The feudal lord, given the *jus primae noctis* (the right of the first night), protected the girl's reputation. The absence of virginity on the wedding night could be attributed to the lord; the girl's nonvirginity or pollution as property would thus be excusable. If the lord discovered she was not a virgin, he promised to be discreet and never tell.

In a communication to the New York State Law Revision Commission, Governor Lehman (1937) said: "I do not think it is sound to predicate a crime arbitrarily and exclusively upon age." Responding to the criticism the state of New York at that time defined a new crime—misdemeanor or third degree rape, when the defendant is under 21 (New York Penal Law 2010). Actually, as a matter of law enforcement in nearly all states, the prosecutor exercising the broad discretion granted him enforces the law on statutory rape only in those cases where there is a considerable difference in age between the male and female. The law, reflecting public attitudes, is applied only to maintain a boundary between the generations. Only the middle-aged or elderly are charged with the crime or with an attempt to commit the crime. In recent codes, different punishments are provided according to the age group of the parties; the younger the girl, the greater the penalty.

The crime of statutory rape does not apply when the male is the younger party, leaving it for prosecution under a "contributing to the delinquency of a minor" or similar law. Thus far, equal protection attacks based on such discrepancies have not been successful. A number of state courts—in California, Colorado, the District of Columbia, Iowa, Missouri, Montana, Oregon and Wisconsin—have all upheld male-only statutory rape laws against charges that they violate the constitutional guarantee of equal protection (State v. Craig, 1976). The Supreme Court recently left standing a decision that New Hampshire's statutory rape law was unconstitutionally discriminatory, but because the Court's only action was to decline to review a lower court ruling, no national legal precedent was established. However, under its ruling, the ban on gender-based statutory rape charges remains the law in Massachusetts, New Hampshire, Maine, Rhode Island and Puerto Rico, which make up the First Circuit of the U.S. Court of Appeals. The district court decision in this case represented the first time the issue had been decided in the federal courts; the First Circuit's affirmance was unanimous. The State Attorney, defending the former New Hampshire law, argued unsuccessfully that the traditional exclusive application to males was proper because only females can become pregnant, female rape victims suffer more injury, males are more likely to be attracted to underage females and some young males are incapable of becoming victims and thus need less protection (Meloon v. Helgemoe, 1977). In an English case, Justice Veale (1968) said: "I cannot help feeling that [male-only statutory rape laws] are in accordance with common sense. If one were to ask any jury the plain question, without any legal niceties—if a woman has sexual intercourse with a boy of 15, both parties being very willing, and indeed eager for the act, has the woman assaulted the boy? I have no doubt the jury would say that of course she has not." Two states (North Carolina and Washington), however, provide that an adult female who seduces a young male may be found guilty of misdemeanor (North Carolina § 14-26, 1969; Washington, § 9.79.200, 1977).

INCEST

The legal and social prohibitions against incest, or "intra-family sex," are designed to prevent emotional and physical disorders, and to maintain the integrity of generational boundaries. The language in some societies which we translate as "incest" refer to blood-shame, disruption of order or behavior that is out of place. Malinowski (1927) put it thus: "Incest would mean the upsetting of age distinctions, the mixing-up of generations, the disorganization of sentiments and a violent exchange of roles at a time when the family is the most important education medium. No society could exist under such conditions." Should an offspring be born of a parent-child union, one can readily imagine the verity of Malinowski's observation.

It has been said, "There are only two or three human stories, and they go on repeating themselves as fiercely as if they had never happened before" (Cather, 1941). One of these oft-repeated tales is that of Oedipus. Freud (1912) ascribed the origins of civilization to the primal crime in which the sons banded together and killed the father, the paternal male who dominated the primal horde. This was done in order to possess the sexual resources, the mothers and sisters he had kept to himself. Afterward, stricken with guilt, they agreed not to partake in their winnings. From this derived the legislation of the incest taboo, the beginning of all human social order, and the band of brothers was the first society. In a famous inversion of St. John, Freud wrote, "In the beginning was the deed." Freud's *Totem and Taboo* (1912), while not a historical instance, covers thousands of years and is repeated thousands of times.

Incest is not only a powerful but a universal temptation. In the face of a temptation which is to be restrained, there must be an equally strong prohibition, either strong inner restraint or external control. In view of the great temptation, it is not surprising that incest, like rape, is surrounded by heavy criminal penalties. It is also a subject reserved to tragedy. Raskolnikov in Dostoyevsky's *Crime and Punishment* (1959 ed.) killed the old woman who symbolized incest. In mythology, the offender is punished even though there may not be the intent as is required in modern criminal law. Oedipus was destroyed by the gods even though he violated the taboo unknowingly (Graves, 1959). King Arthur's downfall followed his sexual involvement with Margeuse, who, unbeknownst to him, was his half-sister (White, 1958).

All 50 American states have declared incestuous fornication or incestuous intermarriage a crime. The strength of the prohibition in criminal law is in proportion to the relationship, the penalties ranging from 1 year to 50 years in prison. In the United States, however, the concept of incest as a crime is generally defined much more broadly than in other countries. Apart from the father-daughter, mother-son and brother-sister relationships, many states in the United States have enlarged the prohibited degrees of relationships to include grandparent-grandchild, uncle-niece, aunt-nephew, and first cousins. The belief in some other societies, though, is that cousins should marry, even though the inbreeding could result in physically unattractive or otherwise undesirable offspring by the emergence of recessive genetic characteristics. The Hapsburg family's physical and mental abnormalities, a notable example, have been well documented (Hodge, 1977).

Animals, including primates, do not recognize their own kin once they have matured, and in the human race, apart from the nuclear family unit of father, mother, son and daughter, other relatives today can also be strangers to each other. It is noteworthy that the legal prohibition on incest in other countries has tended to contract as the family unit diminished socially, but the law in most American states has remained unchanged, even though the contracted nuclear family is at least as prevalent, if not more so, in the United States as in other countries.

The incidence in the United States of reported incest in relation to the total number of sex offenses is approximately three percent. Father-daughter incest is the most common, brother-sister the next, with mother-son least common. There is often enough distance between a father and his daughter to allow an attraction of the same type as is found between strangers to arise, while there is at the same time sufficient closeness between them to enable them to know each other well. Mother-son incest, on the other hand, is like returning to the womb, and so it rarely occurs, law or no law (Herman and Hirschman, 1977; Margolis, 1977).

The incest law in many states, while broad, does not cover non-consanguineous sexual relationships as between adoptive or stepparents and their children. Thus, they seem to be based on the hypothesis of harmful biological effects and a consequent concern for the production of defective progeny. Also, many of the statutes were enacted prior to a time that a 50% divorce rate has made the adoptive or stepparent situation common. In a few states, though, the incest law forbids sexual intercourse between stepfather and stepdaughter (Georgia), or between stepmother and stepson (Indiana), or between brother-in-law and sister-in-law (Ohio). As a matter of actual incidence, the sex act occurs far more frequently between stepfather and stepdaughter than between natural father and child. In any case, the law on contributing to the delinquency of a minor is usually available to prosecute an exploiting stepfather.

An act constituting incest may also constitute statutory rape (or rape if the act was forcible), and the prosecutor may elect to proceed on one charge or both. Should incest itself, though, be considered a crime? Some favor its decriminalization. Incest as an indictable offense did not exist at common law, it being considered that church sanctions were sufficient. A common finding in any case of incest is that one or both partners is psychotic. In some places, incest between even close members of the family may occur due to the need for some outlet for the sexual drive, but in the majority of cases, the taboo against incest is rarely broken, although all of us act out this primal drama in symbolic terms. The taboo, based on custom and psychodynamics, would at least partially prevail irrespective of the criminal law. According to anthropologists, mother-son incest is the only taboo that is universal. The anti-incest response is instinctive based on biology, common to all human societies, but it is regarded as a moral decision.

There are some exceptions. Among the Incas and certain other preliterate societies, and at times in ancient Egypt, sibling marriage was permitted or even encouraged among royalty, and in certain bellicose tribes intercourse between brothers and sisters was and still is encouraged before battle. At different times and places in the Hellenic culture, half brothers and half sisters of the same father were allowed to marry, though never those of the same mother. Other than these exceptions, the taboo appears to hold in all societies, both past and present, it is as nearly coterminous with mankind itself as any custom every has been (Young, 1964). Among the chimpanzees, man's closest primate relative, incest is rare. Siblings, even in captivity, show no desire to copulate with each other as they approach maturity. If one animal were removed for some weeks and then reintroduced to the group, its sibling might then approach it sexually, but only if it were no longer recognized.

Anthropologists Tiger and Fox (1971) make the interesting observation that a person is limited in the number of bonds or patterns of relationship he or she may have with another person, one kind of bond seeming to preclude another. While there may be the temptation, it is difficult to maintain more than one type of major bond with another person. One good bond seems to inhibit another, they say, and this is why so much of the discourse about incest is misplaced and erroneous. To commit incest, one must disrupt an already established bond and substitute another typically antithetical one. The bond with parents is nurturant; the bond between lovers is sexual. That humans resist the effort to imperil an established bond yet remain fascinated by the possibilities of a different bond—because they are sexual, and humans are fascinated by sex—is inherent in the very nature of bonding. The mother-child nurturant bond is posited as the strongest of all bonds and the least likely to be disrupted or replaced by a sexual or courtship bond since the cost of losing the nurturant bond is too high a price to pay. On another level, it is often seen that when parents attempt to be teachers to their children, their role as parents is affected, just as when employers attempt to be lovers with their employees, their management role is affected. In terms of central tendency, most people do not commit incest, and most people who have had a long superordinate-subordinate relationship do not easily convert it to a bond of equality. As Tiger and Fox (1971) said, "Bonding is too serious for us to promiscuously transmute one tie of great intensity into its opposite, and then run both together."

More often than not, the incest offender is psychotic, and should he belong in an institution, it is a hospital, not a prison. However, when the occurrence of incest comes to the attention of the district attorney, the offender is sometimes placed in a "criminally insane unit" alleging that he is "not competent to stand trial." More often than not, however, the district attorney shuts his eyes to the criminal law and seeks, although technically beyond his jurisdiction, to have the offender civilly committed to a mental hospital. In the internal political hierarchy of a prison, the incest offender is generally considered a "patsy" and used as a sexual object as well as being exploited in other ways.

It rarely accomplishes much to only remove the offending spouse from the home, since the other spouse is involved in one way or another. There is a feedback system which involves all members of the family. The incest taboo is usually reinforced by the mother serving as a barrier to father-daughter incest, and the father serving as barrier in mother-son incest. Where incest occurs, the barrier is not only absent, but the other spouse has often actually encouraged, consciously or not, the offending spouse or child into the act. In such a situation, the spouses are equally disturbed, and the child is troubled, particularly when the child feels that she is taking part in a conspiracy with one parent against the other. Particularly when the child feels that she is engaged in surreptitious behavior with the parent, it plays a significant role in the etiology of lack of female sexual response later in life (Summit and Kryso, 1978).

A number of studies have pointed out that a considerable number of prostitutes had incest with their fathers before beginning prostitution as a lifestyle. Does this mean that incest in some sense causes prostitution? Or does it mean that a certain matrix may give rise to both incest and prostitution, without the one causing the other? James and Meyerding (1977) found:

> The pattern that emerges includes 1) a lack of parental guidance that leads to early, casual sexual intercourse to the exclusion of the more usual non-coital sociosexual experimentation; 2) the discovery that sex can be used to gain a kind of social status, coupled with the subsequent discovery that this status is perceived by others as negative, making the individual unacceptable to the majority culture; and 3) the emotionally destructive experiences of incest and rape. Because the range of acceptable sexual behaviors is much narrower for women than for men, and because women more than men are judged (by themselves and by others) on the basis of their sexual desirability and behavior, sexual experiences may be a more important factor in a woman's development of self-identity. A woman who views herself as sexually debased or whose sexuality is more than normally objectified may see prostitution as a "natural"—or as the only—alternative.

Usually, when the incest relationship is discovered, it has been of a long-standing nature, often two or three years. At times, there is only masturbation and fondling of the genital area and breasts of the daughter. At other times, there is actual sexual intercourse with penetration; and at other times, the father has his daughter perform fellatio on him. It is usually the child's delinquent behavior outside the home which brings the situation to the fore. The incestuous behavior also often comes to light when the daughter becomes angry with her father and tells the mother out of spite. Often, the anger will have developed because the father has not bought her a car or a stereo or even a box of candy. The mother will act enraged and call the police or the prosecuting attorney and demand that the father be placed in jail for the rest of his life. The father's usual reaction is one of intense anxiety and depression. The family doctor may be notified, and recognizing the seriousness and complexity of the matter, he often refers the father to a psychiatrist (Snodgrass, 1977).

The occurrence of incest, which is a sign of serious trouble for all family relations, indicates that the entire family is in need of therapeutic attention (Weinberg, 1963). In nearly all cases, there is a breakdown in the husband-wife relationship, and in many cases the wife, at least unconsciously, has encouraged her husband to seek a sexual outlet with some other person by refusing him sexual congress. At other times, the daughter becomes sexually aggressive and seductive to the father. To counter this, the father may become an ogre, acting hatefully, in order to handle incestuous feelings, and thus separate himself from his daughter.

In most of these cases, it is necessary for the family to stay together. It is considered unwise to cast out of the home the only breadwinner. But the incestuous relationship must be stopped and life must go on in a more positively harmonious fashion. In general, after the father's conduct has been revealed, he no longer continues the incestuous behavior, but the family situation becomes like a police state to keep the father from bothering the daugher again. In many instances, a divorce has been the end result.

Incestuous sex crimes, particularly when the father or mother live in the same home with the girl, pose difficult problems for law-enforcement officers and social workers. Police preventive measures are almost impossible, and after the offense has been committed, it is often necessary to remove the girl from the home to prevent violence. The mother may also be in danger, for her husband may retaliate physically if she reports him to the police. Court action rarely solves the problem, since a jail sentence serves only to remove the offending parent on a temporary basis. It does not solve the underlying problem which manifested itself in the incestuous behavior. Also, it is probably much worse for the child if she must go to court; it often takes months for the trial to come up and she has to keep repeating her story. Then, if the offender is sent to jail, nothing much has really been accomplished—all parties are injured emotionally, psychologically, and perhaps even physically. However, the threat of punishment that may actually hang over an individual may deter the offensive behavior, or may encourage counselling with positive results.

One law commentator who sees no compelling reason why sexual experiments between brothers and sisters (though hardly to be encouraged) should lead to criminal proceedings, suggests that the law of criminal incest might be abolished as such, and replaced by a law of sexual abuse of authority, which would extend not merely to parents, but also to teachers and other persons in charge of young people (Honoré, 1978). Indeed, there are already countries, such as France (French Penal Code art. 333) and Belgium (Belgium Penal Code art. 377), in which incest is not a crime but instead "abuse of authority" is punishable. If this policy were accepted, it would not necessarily lead to any change in the law, since there are already many criminal statutes governing these sexual relations, but it may shift the focus of attention.

DISCUSSION

The numerous laws on sexual behavior of and with juveniles, often overlapping, indicate great public concern. The law as it exists on the statute books, however, only superficially resembles the law as it is enforced. To be sure, there is a wide gap between principle and practice in the regulation of many aspects of human behavior, but in the area of sex one finds an unusually wide gap between the formal law and the actual operation of the law. That is because (1) the laws are not very effective, and (2) there is need for flexibility. Individuals are not only members of the human race and of various categories and subcategories but they are also individuals with unique problems and circumstances. As a rule, sex offenders (rape offenders excepted) are frightened, guilty, woefully inadequate individuals (Gagnon and Simon, 1973; Gebhard et al., 1965). It is in the area of disposition (what to do with those who are apprehended) that leaves so much to be desired. For that reason, if not for others, the focus must be on the matrix that gives rise to such behavior.

Urbanization, we well know, has brought a breakdown of family and social ties, magnifying the impact of peer pressure on young people. Family and kinship ties are well-nigh totally disintegrated in the anonymity of contemporary urban life (Morris, 1969). Divorce rates are escalating, further weakening family control. The single or two-parent family is taxed trying to meet children's emotional needs. The vacuum is often filled by peers whose influence is harmful, and by a culture that exploits sex as well as aggressive tendencies, creating an atmosphere of frenzy. The level of cultural life is generally low, some say atavistic, as a glance at the "entertainment" page of any newspaper would indicate. There is a preoccupation with violence, cruelty, and the sexually perverse, and it is made to look exciting (Bell, 1976; Hendin, 1975).

Against this massive "sexploitation," the law has drawn few boundaries. Seeking to safeguard liberty, the law protects purveyors of pornography within the protection accorded the expression of thought and opinion. Further, the expression of vulgarity has even been defended by some expert witnesses as "therapeutic"; and to turn language topsy-turvy, the word "mature" is used in labeling pornography to imply that it is for a mature audience. Honesty, we might say, would call for a label, "for the over-18 emotionally and intellectually immature." With the apparent collapse of the law, there were even cheers in some quarters when a vigilante shot Larry Flynt, a notorious purveyor of pornography (Time, 1978).

More often than not, parents feel they are without an adequate support system in raising their children. They may feel they are without a "motherland" or "fatherland," or "common-weal." Indeed, instead of providing support, they may feel that society undermines whatever influence or authority they might exercise. Assuredly, there comes a point when the best of parents are outdone. Thus, a parent could handle a salesman who might come to the home to solicit a pre-schooler directly (the parent would most likely not let him in the house), but he slips in now, bypassing the parent, by way of television. Just as a beautiful city makes it easy for a denizen to host a guest, so would a society that offers support lighten the burden on parents in raising their children: Just as junk food advertisements make it harder for parents to discipline their children on eating habits, it is also true in other areas of life.

The declining role of family and community ties has meant that there is now less ability to influence behavior by means of reputation. Today, so often, one does not even know the name of one's neighbor; indeed, one may wonder whether a neighborhood any longer exists. A mother used to caution her daughter: "Think of your reputation. You'll be ruined for life." This or any other warning no longer has any force, no more than would a charge of a traffic violation. With the decline in family and community ties, greater reliance must be placed upon the policeman to maintain social order. Yet at the same time, the law is an awkward, impersonal apparatus.

In matters of sexual behavior, focusing on social conditions that may be described as "criminogenic" is more promising than the attempts via the criminal law to deal with the wrecks of society. The parameter common in cases of "battered child," "battered wife," or "battered husband" is social isolation. But the public and, in turn, the legislature rarely act with the same enthusiasm in the support of child-care services, schools, parks, the arts, work programs, and recreational facilities as in the support of some criminal sanction. We are all against sin, especially when it calls for no immediate price tag.

Youth is a time of vibrancy, strength, and energy; yet the problems of our time have produced an age of melancholy for so many young people. For a "high," to deal with depression and social alienation, they turn to drugs and alcohol. Suicide and homicide account for a high proportion of deaths among young American males; the rate of death among young women is lower, but there is the equivalent of depression and promiscuity. The issue raised is whether society is sufficiently responsive to and responsible for youth as a vulnerable species. Is the search for faith and community—cults, communes, and cohabitation—reflective of their wish for stronger guidance and other endeavors?

SUMMARY

Only a relatively small number of individuals are involved, either as victims or offenders, under the numerous statutes covering sexual behavior of, and with, young people, but every denizen is affected by what might be called the mental or social pollution resulting from the exploitation of sex which essentially goes uncontrolled. Social pollution might be compared to environmental pollution. We bathe in our atmosphere, every one of us are affected by it. To deal with particular sex offenses, such as statutory rape or incest, is like focusing on the car and not the traffic.

All people—especially young people—have always been deeply concerned about sex, but now there is a preoccupation with physical sex to the exclusion of the more subtle and romantic aspects of sex that give meaning, purpose, and vitality to male-female relationships (Brozan, 1978; Sorenson, 1973). Sex, which is a normal part of life, is more gratifying when not overemphasized; but commercial interests, hiding under the umbrella of free speech, make a profit out of the exploitation of physical sex.

Young people have a particular need for attachment to a family and a society that will provide some structure for them, and that will provide sanctions for behavior that runs counter to a healthy and prosperous development. Without it, they form relationships in a "family" that may have a psychotic character, as in the Manson family. It gives them a feeling, albeit delusional, of being needed and valued. A young girl may attach herself to a pimp because he provides structure to her life and even his exploitation of her makes her feel more valuable in a world in which she may have felt of no value to anyone. Hence, society must provide young people with positive alternatives in an atmosphere that can lead them to a productive and constructive life. The more supportive and facilitating the environment, the fewer will be the anxiety-ridden and aimless souls haunting the streets. We reap what we sow.

REFERENCES

Abrahamsen, D. (1960), *The Psychology of Crime.* New York: Columbia University Press.
Belgium Penal Code (1965), art. 377. Bruxelles: Bruylant.
Bell, D. (1976), *The Cultural Contradictions of Capitalism.* New York: Basic Books.
Brennan, W. (1973), dissenting opinion in *Paris Adult Theatre v. Slaton,* 413 U.S. 49, 112-113.
Brozan, N. (1978), A new survey of teenage sex—With teenagers asking the questions. *New York Times,* Feb. 25, p. 18.
Burger, W. (1978), opinion in *Pinkus v. United States,* 98 S. Ct. 1808.
Burgess, A.W., Groth, A. N., Holmstrom, L. L., and Sgroi, S. M. (1977), *Sexual Assault of Children and Adolescents.* Lexington, Mass.: Lexington.
Cather, W. (1941), *Oh Pioneers.* New York: Houghton-Mifflin (p. 119).
Dostoyevsky, F. (1959 ed.). *Crime and Punishment.* New York: Modern Library.
Freud, S. (1912), *Totem and Taboo.* London: Routledge & Kegan Paul (1950).
——— (1926), *Inhibitions, Symptoms and Anxiety.* (Standard Edition) Vol. XX. London: Hogarth Press, 1959.
French Penal Code (1960). art. 333. S. Hackensack, N.J.: Rothman.
Gagnon, J. H. and Simon, W. (1973), *Sexual Conduct/The Social Sources of Human Sexuality.* Chicago: Adline.
Gebhard, P.H., Gagnon, J.H., Pomeroy, W.B., and Christenson, C.V. (1965), *Sex Offenders: An Analysis of Types.* New York: Harper & Row.
Graves, R. (1959), *The Greek Myths.* New York: Braziller, 2 vols. (vol. II, p. 9).
Grummon, D.L. and Barclay, A.M. (Eds.) (1971), *Sexuality/A Search for Perspective.* New York: van Nostrand Reinhold.
Hale. M. (1847), *The History of Pleas of the Crown.* Philadelphia: Small (Vol. 1, p. 631).
Harlan, J.M. (1968), separate opinion in *Interstate Circuit, Inc. v. Dallas,* 390 U.S. 676, at 704-705.
Hendin, H. (1975), *The Age of Sensation.* New York: Norton.
Herman, J. and Hirschman, L. (1977), Incest between fathers and daughters. *Science,* 17:4-7.
Hodge. G. P. (1977), A medical history of the Spanish Hapsburgs. *JAMA,* 238:1169-1174.
Honoré, T. (1978), *Sex Law.* London: Duckworth.
James, J. and Meyerding, J. (1977), Early sexual experience and prostitution. *Amer. J. Psychiat.,* 134:1381-1385.
Lehman, H. (1937), In *Leg. Doc. No. 65 (J) 1937 Report,* New York Law Revision Commission. p. 31.
Louisiana Revised Statutes (1950), 14:42(3), 14:80, 14:81, 14:86, 14:92, 14:93. St. Paul, Minn.: West.

Malinowski, B. (1927), *Sex and Repression in a Savage Society.* London: Routledge & Kegan Paul.

Margolis, M. (1977), A Preliminary Report of a Case of Consummated Mother-Son Incest, in Chicago Institute for Psychoanalysis, *The Annual for Psychoanal.,* 5:267-293. New York: International Univ. Press.

Meloon v. Helgemoe (1977), 564 F.2d 602 (1st Cir.), noted in *New York Times,* June 6, 1978, p. 14.

Morris, D. (1969), *The Human Zoo.* London: Jonathan Cape.

Nabokov, V. (1958), *Lolita.* New York: Putnam.

New York Penal Law (1967), § 2010. Brooklyn: McKenney.

North Carolina Criminal Statutes (1969), § 14-26. Charlottesville, Va.: Michie.

Pieragostini, D. L. (1970), Reasonable mistake as to age—A defense to statutory rape under the new Penal Code. *Conn. L. Rev.* 2:432.

Sheehy, G. (1967), *Passages/Predictable Crises of Adult Life.* New York: Dutton.

Singer, I.B. (1978), *A Young Man in Search of Love.* New York: Doubleday.

Snodgrass, R.E. (1977), "Sexual Problems and Deviations Seen in Private Psychiatric Practice" (address on March 25, 1977, at Methodist Hospital, Indianapolis, Ind.).

Sorenson, R.C. (1973), *Adolescent Sexuality in Contemporary America.* New York: World.

State v. Craig (1976), 545 P.2d 649 (Mont.).

State v. Elias (1978), 357 So.2d 275 (La.).

State v. Wrestle (1978), 360 So.2d 831 (La.).

Strozier, G. (1977), Teenage sexuality: What's going on/pressure, pleasure, pain or pregnancy? *Detroit Free Press,* Nov. 20, p. 1-F.

Summit, R. and Kryso, J. (1978), Sexual abuse of children: A clinical spectrum. *Amer. J. Orthopsychiat.* 48:237-251.

Tiger, L. and Fox, R. (1971), *The Imperial Animal.* New York: Holt, Rinehart & Winston.

Time (March 20, 1978), p. 20.

Veale, J. (1968), opinion in *R.v. Mason,* 53 Crim. App. Rep. 12.

Washington Criminal Statutes (1977), § 9.79.200. St. Paul, Minn.: West.

Washington Pattern Jury Instructions/Criminal (1977). 19.04. St. Paul, Minn.: West.

White, T.H. (1958 ed.), *The Once and Future King.* New York: Putnam.

Weinberg, S.K. (1963), *Incest Behavior.* New York: Citadel Press.

Young, W. (1964), *Eros Denied.* London: Transworld.

13

The Epidemic of Adolescent Motherhood

MAX SUGAR

In recent decades adolescent motherhood has become epidemic in the U.S.A. To better understand this it seems useful to separate the components on the path to motherhood from the beginning through the post-partal period, since each part involves a decision by the adolescent. This chapter will explore some features of the decision and program considerations, as well as helps and hinderances to these.

Currently the U.S.A. has the highest rate of adolescent pregnancies of all industrialized nations, along with one of the highest infant mortality rates. This involves rural as well as urban girls, whites and non-whites. Among the decisions involved are: engaging in sexual intercourse; the use of contraception; pregnancy; abortion; adoption; early motherhood; marriage; unwed motherhood; and further pregnancies in adolescence. These are affected by the girl's relationship to her family or origin and have effects on: the child raised by the young unwed mother; the girl's emotional development to adulthood; and the girl's socioeconomic and academic development.

SOME FACTS OF THE EPIDEMIC

In 1971, 26.3% of white teenage girls between 15 and 19 had had premarital sex and about 6% became pregnant, but in 1976, for this age, 37.2%

had intercourse and 10% became pregnant. For black girls of similar age having intercourse for the two dates the figures also increased from 54.1% to 64.3%, while the percentage of those who became pregnant remained at about 25% for both study years.

In 1976, the rate of illegitimate births among blacks was 50.3%, almost double that of 1965. This appears to be due to increased contraceptive use among married black women compared to the single ones. But the rate of illegitimacy among whites also almost doubled in the same period going from 4% to 7.7%.

Abortions among white girls age 15-19 rose from 33% in 1971 to 45% in 1976, while for black girls for the same years the figures went from 5% to 8%. The ratio of first pregnancies terminated by abortion among these girls, black and white, almost doubled from 17.7% in 1971 to 30.6% in 1976. Within a year of giving birth, 1 of 4 girls is pregnant again. About 300,000 teenagers were having abortions annually before the recent restrictive H.E.W. legislation was passed (Alan Guttmacher Institute, 1976; U.S. News & World Report, 1978).

In 1951, the teenage birth rate was 96/1000, whereas in 1974 it was 58/1000, and 80% of these births are out of wedlock. Figures for abortion rates are still not entirely accurate although more are recorded now than a generation ago. Most likely at that time, of those who did not have an abortion, most of the upper and middle class girls gave up the baby for adoption. At present this group mostly opts for an abortion, while lower or working class girls keep their babies in about 95% of cases (Fisher, 1978). This is the basis of the present epidemic surge of baby-keeping. The different maternity rates between the middle and lower class may be a reflection of the greater number of options available to those of better advantage such as abortion, schooling, or job opportunities.

From one view this results in 11.7 billion dollars spent annually in federal, state and local Aid to Families with Dependent Children (A.D.C.); women who become dependent thus in their teens cost taxpayers about 6 million dollars a year in welfare.

However these facts smart, they are impersonal and each adolescent who begins coital activity early, becomes pregnant or not, carries to term or not, keeps her baby or not, is a unique and separate individual with a specific personal history and family, dynamics, cognitive abilities, educational attainments and talents. At each stage along the road from beginning sexual activity to motherhood there are some very specific and significant decisions to be made by each individual girl.

THE DECISION ABOUT CONTRACEPTION

The decision to become sexually active is a complex one for which the onset age figures are hard to clarify. Those looking at it from only a social or economic view miss the multiple emotional tributaries and the contributions from the family, the antecedent personal development as well as the prior and current reality situations. Furstenberg (1976) noted that in the very strict families among the lower social class the girls were more likely to become sexually active earlier than in the more liberal or less rigid family. Early coital activity was also partly related inversely to the girl's educational ambitions.

Early sexual activity is rarely promiscuous and occurs most often in the context of repeated intense relationships (Kantner and Zelnick, 1972; Sorensen, 1973). Sexually active white girls had more partners than agemate black girls, but 70% of white girls had only one partner (Kantner and Zelnick, 1972).

Psychological and sociological theories are at odds in explaining the low use of contraceptives. A study of nonpregnant mentally ill teenagers for factors in non-contraception (Abernathy and Abernathy, 1974) indicated that: high-risk girls in contrast to virgins more often had a relationship with their father which excluded mother; they depended less on mother for sexual information; the virgins expressed open dislike for father. Gottschalk et al. (1964) found no evidence of any undue psychiatric disorder before pregnancy in a group of pregnant and non-pregnant white and black girls.

Education ambitions most accurately predicted the eventual successful practice of birth control by previously pregnant youngsters (Klerman and Jekel, 1973; Furstenberg, 1976, p. 120).

As is well known, the hormonal levels and the regularity of ovulation and menses are not predictable or reliable in the first few years after menarche and thus, fertility is low in these years. But this may be used as part of a pattern to deny the possibility or the effects of sexual activity. "The pattern of frequent dating over a long period is eventually accompanied by sexual activity and few adolescents are able to remain sexually active for long before pregnancy occurs" (Furstenberg, 1976, p. 42). Furstenberg (1976, p. 46) found that the mother's estimate of the incidence of sexual activity of the nonpregnant teenage daughter was so low that it suggested her having a stake in being misinformed, and releasing her from responsibility to prevent pregnancy. An example of extreme denial is the 15-year-old white middle-class girl who saw her pediatrician with her mother about general malaise. A short while later she delivered a full-term infant in his office, with the girl and her mother claiming ignorance of the pregnancy.

Kantner and Zelnick (1973) noted that 25% of 13- to 15-year-old unwed girls had used contraception. Furstenberg (1976) found that only 6% of his study group were unable to identify any method of contraception. Fisher (1978) felt that 80% of girls had knowledge about contraception but didn't apply it. Possibly much of the increased sexual activity may be a reflection of the current sexual freedom and better birth control methods. In 1976, 30% of sexually active teenagers used contraceptives, which is an increase of 12% over 1971.

A frequent finding in programs to aid the pregnant teenager is the conflict with the parents about the daughter's sexuality (Nadelson, 1974; Fisher, 1978) and the family plays a part in transmitting expectations about birth control. Parents may supply information, by which they reveal awareness of the daughter's coital activities. The adolescent is then allowed to acknowledge her own sexuality and hence may regard sex less as a spontaneous and uncontrollable act and more as an activity which is subject to planning and regulation (Furstenberg, 1976, p. 49).

Hattie Williams (1978) noted from her personal experiences as a volunteer in a Chicago black ghetto that the girls lacked simple knowledge of physiology and followed fearful superstitions about contraceptive pills. The girl was unprotected against the rapacious young men in the building and allowed herself to be used by the boy who raped her since "you have to have one boy so he'll protect you from the others, or they'll run a train on you." But most black and white pregnant girls are not living in such a milieu. Are parents negligent in this respect? Are the girl's needs to go steady also reflecting other needs such as loneliness, fears of fusion with mother, etc.?

In the Baltimore black ghetto (Furstenberg, 1976, p. 51), brief sexual encounters were often unexpected and undesired and virtually none of these women had used birth control. In contrast, among the women who were still seeing the father of the child, a majority (69%) had used contraception if discussion of birth control had occurred in the home. When parental intervention was absent only 22% had contraceptive experience prior to conceiving. To a great extent the influence of the family depends on the nature of the couple's relationship.

THE DECISION ABOUT PREGNANCY

The assessment of the adolescent mother is compounded by the fact that most studies are retrospective, without controls, and converge on, instead of separating, facets of some of the most complex and difficult emotional and developmental adaptations: adolescence, pregnancy, and parenthood with or without marriage.

Is the early onset of menarche (12.8 years; Peterson, 1979) condensing the prepubescent and latency phase so much that early onset of coital activity and pregnancy are natural sequiturs? Historically in this country and England, the average age for first pregnancy, until recent decades, was in the early twenties (Wynne and Frader, 1979).

Some view adolescent motherhood in whites as due to psychopathology and in non-whites as due to sociological factors. Kinch et al. (1969) felt that the majority of these youngsters are neither very disturbed nor promiscuous. The causes given for adolescent pregnancy vary from all to none of psychological, social, biological, and economic features. Most research on this is limited, faulty, or biased. Psychiatric studies are usually small, without controls, and deal with a patient population that is pregnant. Bonam (1963) theorized that pregnancy was an escape from conflict, especially with the mother, and the patients had narcissistic character disorders. Khlentzos and Pagliaro (1965) considered the pregnancy as a means of meeting oral dependency needs. Barglow and associates (1968) found problems of passivity, dependence, and depression. Babikian and Goldman (1971) related acting out and a weak ego to the pregnant adolescent. The girl who has a character disorder, oral dependent problems, or other neurotic problem is quite different from the schizophrenic or the manic, pregnant or not. Pauker's (1971) longitudinal study stressed that there was no one personality or motivating causality model to explain all out-of-wedlock pregnancies.

Sarrel and Davis (1966) assessed the pregnant teenager similarly to Webb et al. (1972) as having a syndrome of failure: "failure to fulfill her adolescent functions, remain in school, limit her family, establish stable values, be self-supporting and have healthy infants."

Schaffer and Pine (1972) found a regularly recurring theme of conflict in the pregnant girl about mothering and being mothered, as well as gross denial. Nadelson (1974) stressed denial as a factor in explaining the largest number of requests for late abortions coming from adolescents. She also noted that pregnancy in an adolescent may be a way to announce her adulthood; that pregnancy may be a response to a loss, often of a parent.

Sugar (1979) found that 56% of adolescents as compared to 35% of adults had serious crises in their pregnancy. A large number of these youngsters had a symbiotic tie with their own mothers and conflicts at a preoedipal and oedipal level (Sugar, 1979). "Pregnancy in an adolescent may be an unconscious effort to effect a separation; an attempt to make up for the loss of the infantile objects; a substitution and avoidance of early separation-individuation conflicts; or an accident to avoid regression" (Sugar, 1979). Cutright (1976) observed that decades of study have provided no comprehensive psychopathological theory of illegitimacy. However, it is possible that middle class girls have been observed psychiatrically in considerable detail, whereas the lower class girl has, instead, largely been studied only sociologically or in obstetrical clinics.

The sociological idea that a culture of poverty promotes premarital pregnancy has been seriously questioned by Furstenberg (1976). But his post-partal observations about feelings during the pregnancy raise issues about methodology. In addition, it has been noted that as a result of being snowbound, the pregnancy rate goes up and it would seem logical that the high unemployment rate of adolescents (especially of black adolescents) would affect teenage pregnancy rates. Shlackman (1966) believed that the association between poverty and early pregnancy was due to problems about access to contraceptives. Johnson (1974) correlated poverty as increasing the chances of adolescent pregnancy and pregnancy increasing the chances of continuing poverty.

Plionis (1975) noted that the multiple theories of causality result from a lack of clarity in defining the problem and this contributes to program design difficulties.

Vincent (1961) said that most of the data about unwed mothers "may tell us less about factors contributing to illegitimacy than about the clientele of given charity institutions, social agencies, out-patient clinics, and physicians in private practice" (p. 21).

TERMINATE OR CONTINUE THE PREGNANCY?

After discovering her pregnancy, the next level of decision-making for the girl is whether to abort or continue her pregnancy. Prior to the 1973 Supreme Court decision most therapeutic abortions were based on psychiatric indications. From then until the recent new law limiting some abortions there was a marked drop in the psychiatric need and requests made for diagnoses.

Frequently abortion has been recommended by the physician and/or family without consulting the girl. Probably a similar percentage of girls decide on and obtain an abortion on their own to avoid being told what to do.

The selection of counsellors who may aid the girl and her family to understand their situation, conflicts, possible choices and services for them is a crucial first step in a thoughtful, considered approach. The counsellor may then become the most vital and continued link in a support system helping the girl arrive at her own decision, while maintaining a neutral objective position. That the counsellor should be involved in counselling pre- and post-abortion and for specific assessment are sine qua nons of the work. These include the girl's motivation, ambivalence, ability to tolerate stress, ego strengths and pre-abortion anxiety. They also should support and provide information and education (Nadelson, 1974).

Nadelson's (1974) group found the presence of a successful maternal figure and the peer group fundamental to the program. The recidivists and the late abortion seekers were girls with special problems needing especially sensitive handling.

Recidivism in illegitimacy is usually associated with socioeconomic status and race. Among unwed mothers in Vincent's study (1961, p. 21) 62% of county hospital blacks and 23% of county hospital whites were recidivists, compared to 10% and 7% of blacks and whites, respectively, in private practice and maternity homes.

Very aggressive pressures have surfaced recently to proclaim against abortion and have a disturbing effect on many girls in their planning. Thus, a private decision has now become a matter for public forums on TV and other media adding to the strain of the decision-making.

The decision to carry through to term is often ambivalently based on hopes of a marriage, or it may be in defiance of the parents' wishes despite the best of programs. The girl in the deprived group that Barglow et al. (1968) studied appeared better adjusted in mid-term, but in most cases resentment and depression followed the infants' birth. Gabrielson et al. (1970) found that 13% of their study girls who had delivered before age 17 had attempted suicide. Furstenberg (1976) found retrospective unhappiness about having a baby in 80% of the single mothers which is similar to the findings of Barglow et al. (1968). Only 20% of his group were married one year post delivery and of these 78% were happy about the pregnancy (p. 56). Over 60% of premarital conceptions (therefore not limited to teens) in one survey resulted in marriage (Cutright, 1976). But teenage marriages are problem-filled as will be detailed further.

BE A MOTHER OR GIVE UP THE BABY?

If the girl decides to continue with the pregnancy to term, she has to plan and decide if she will keep the baby or give it up for adoption. This decision is a complex one and has many contributory channels which include: the girl's psyche and conflict with her parents; the parents; the girl's wish for further education and career; attitudes of rejection or acceptance by the culture and neighborhood; the socioeconomics and options available for support of the girl and her baby; religious convictions.

If the girl decides to give the baby up for adoption she has some of the same issues to contend with as during the pregnancy, with the added feature of feelings of loss about her own baby. This may be a factor in depression, feelings of guilt, a later search for the infant, or other restitutive measures. In one institution the young woman's task was made more difficult by the hostility of the priest-director. He made each girl attend and care for her own baby in the adjacent nursery until she left 3-5 days postpartally, as a punishment to make her not have an out-of-wedlock baby again.

To keep the baby the girl has to have a supporting environment and its absence often leads her into a move to another neighborhood or state, an impulsive marriage or other unsatisfying arrangements. If she stays with her own parents she may face continued regression and dependency, rejection, guilt, scapegoating, and perhaps the social taboos of the culture. A popular arrangement with the increased incidence of baby-keeping is for the girl to stay with her mother. This helps to magnify the conflict between them about her sexuality and dependency (Fisher, 1978; Sugar, 1979). The girl's arrested development may be reflected in her use of the infant as a transitional object, sleeping with the infant in her bed for years, disallowing the grandparents to be involved with the infant in her presence (Sugar, 1979).

Early motherhood has been related very closely with the girl's inadequate education, economic deprivation and if married, with dissolution of her marriage. Among those giving birth at or before age 15, one third of their marriages ended in separation/divorce, in contrast to a 10% dissolution rate in women who first became mothers after age 22. Marital instability is much greater among blacks than whites. Of those giving birth before 16 who were ever-married, nearly one third lived in poverty in 1967, which constrasted with one tenth of the women over 22. For blacks the probabilities were 2 to 3 times greater than those of whites in each age group. For women who gave birth before 16, nearly two thirds attained eight or less years of formal education, and only one fifth finished high school (Bacon, 1974).

Cutright (1973, p. 594) felt that for blacks and whites the long-term economic effects of being pregnant premaritally were small, Coombs and Freedman (1970) found the opposite effect in white women who conceived before marriage in that they remained disadvantaged economically for years.

Protein deficiencies were found in 50% and vitamin deficiency in 90% of the girls in the YMED program (Osofsky et al., 1973).

EDUCATIONAL PREJUDICES

Nationally, the schools that provide sex education give facts of reproduction and v.d. but don't dwell on the emotional or responsible aspects thereof (Castile, 1976; Calderone, 1966). As of the date of this book's publication, Louisiana law prohibits sex education in public schools—a distinction that it shares with no other state.

Louisiana in 1976 ranked: second in the country in infant mortality; sixth in perinatal defects; seventh for illegitimate live births for girls under 20 (the total rate of 49% was made up of a 27% rate for whites and a 75% rate for non-whites); second for syphilis in those under 14 and fourth for syphilis for ages 15-19 (V.D. Fact Sheet, 1976; V.D. Statistical Letter, 1976). In 1978 the founder of the Louisiana Family Health Planning entered federal prison for a two-year term for defrauding the federal government. That program had offered cognitive birth control help but provided no counselling. In 1978, a new program to help pregnant adolescents under Title XX in another institution in Louisiana was vetoed.

Although Louisiana is a leader among the states for the above, other states generally are not far behind and all have many educational deficiencies for pregnant adolescents as well.

Once a girl is pregnant most schools reject her. In 1967, for the 17,000 school districts in the U.S.A., there were 35 special school programs for the pregnant teenager; in 1972, the number was 225, and in 1975 there were only 350 (Hansen et al., 1976).

CASE REPORT

The following case may not be representative of most but reflects some of the problems outlined above that these girls may have.

Unmarried Ms. A

—age 15—delivered a female child;
—age 16—delivered a female child;
—age 23—delivered a male child;
—age 27—pregnant with fourth child and seeking welfare.

At age 22 she developed hypertension (and gained a large amount of weight) which fluctuated according to her diet and weight. At the same time, she was using illicit drugs and alcoholic beverages excessively. At 24, and again at 26, she was hospitalized for a schizophrenic reaction. On discharge from the hospital she gave her two youngest children to relatives to keep since she couldn't suitably look after them.

Although her use of psychotropic medication at age 27 during pregnancy resulted in remission from the schizophrenic reaction, her symptoms were: insomnia, running about the house scared on awakening from sleep; sleep was possible only when her mother stayed with her and during the daytime; fear of heights; fear of crowds, which restricted her going out to shop or socialize; inability to cook since she fell asleep over the stove, requiring that her mother cook for her; auditory hallucinations (which stopped since taking antipsychotic medication regularly); and the feeling of bugs crawling all over her. She had a seventh grade education, with limited work experiences, and tested as a borderline retardate. There were no jobs available for her with the limitations for employment that her conditions required and she needed rehabilitation training to develop emotionally and physically to enable her to work. Now, she wanted to regain custody of the two children.

Doubtless, she was not given a thorough psychiatric evaluation nor counselling when pregnant at age 15, nor special education during her school years.

INTERVENTION PROGRAMS

There have been a variety of programs designed for the pregnant adolescent but few are comprehensive enough to involve primary and secondary prevention and later support for mother and infant for the desired minimum three years postpartally.

Where programs are short-term and short in funding they get short-term results which are poor and militate against success and a sense of accomplishment. Sarrel (1967), LaBarre (1972), Osofsky et al. (1973), Klerman and Jekel (1973), Furstenberg (1976) and Fisher (1978) among others have described some of these deficiencies and positives with an indication of some drop in recidivism.

The Carter administration has recently declared itself positively for further programs to be established. What kind of programs will these be? What are the ingredients of good programs?

The programs have to be comprehensive and start with the girl who is vulnerable psychologically to risk-taking in conception, to include abortion counselling, education about contraception, physiology (especially of reproduction) and nutrition, as well as general medical, dental, dietary, obstetrical, and psychiatric services.

The girl at risk for conception may be quite different from the one at risk for early motherhood and separate specific profiles need to be delineated for them as well as for the pregnancy repeater, the abortion repeater and repeat adolescent mother. Obviously, further research with improved research design is needed and should be built into the program.

Fisher (1978) stressed that the setting should promote the girl's self-worth and self-esteem before pregnancy as well as before motherhood is decided on, if pregnant. She described seven characteristics of such a setting:

1. It must provide a peer group of similar age girls.
2. It must provide models of nurturance who help nurture the girls and show them simultaneously how to nurture their own young.
3. It must provide models of admonition, the rule-givers, who, within this setting, gently discipline them where indicated and become models of limit-seeking of the young.
4. It must provide structures to maintain and teach age- and role-appropriate skills.
5. It must provide educational and career facilities for further development of the girl.
6. It must provide adequate physical care for the pregnant girl and the baby.
7. Lastly, of great importance (though most difficult for nonprofessionals to perceive), it must continue beyond the separation-individuation phase of the child, to involve mother and child in continuous contact with the programmatic setting and the modelling persons; because it is at this time that these mothers have the most difficulty; it is at this juncture that most abuse and foster placement occur as well as new pregnancies; for this is the developmental phase that these mothers have never struggled beyond, to achieve genuine autonomy for themselves.

SUCCESS AND COUNTERTRANSFERENCE

Perhaps the programs that do not continue or succeed have deficiencies in one of these areas due to countertransference problems in the caregivers. The difficulties in offering continued suitable education and sex education to pregnant girls may be similarly based. Countertransference may be related among other things to their attitudes about the adolescent's sexuality, dependency, deviant behavior, ordinary developmental tasks of adolescence, the adults' ending of reproductivity, their envy of, hostility to or competition with, adolescents.

One of the earliest and most problematic areas is that focused on adequate funds for the sexually active teenager. This becomes involved in increasingly heated controversy the longer the program lasts, and especially so if the program calls for continuity until the infant of the young mother has progressed beyond the separation-individuation phase. At these junctures the community ire becomes strongest to these girls.

An anti-abortion ordinance in Buffalo, New York, was barred from enforcement on November 17, 1978, which would have required women seeking abortion to view photos of fetuses, be informed of all the possible consequences of an abortion—hemorrhage, sterility, psychological problems, and emotional disturbances. A similar ordinance passed in Akron, Ohio, *(New York Times,* 1978) while a parallel law in Louisiana is now being contested in court.

Another reflection of the countertransference problem is the statement that these girls get pregnant to get A.D.C. and avoid working. A regularly-occurring assumption indicating countertransference difficulty is the xenophobic remark that low-income girls become pregnant because of indifference within their cultural patterns. This has been amply disqualified (Furstenberg, 1976). The absence of psychiatric and pediatric participation in framing PL94-142 and its exclusion of pregnant teenagers and adolescent mothers from consideration as handicapped youngsters for obtaining education or vocational skills is another reflection of countertransference difficulty at a governmental level. This also implicates the legislative branch of the government for passivity and guilt in not having a national policy for children and adolescents. This is mirrored in the relative paucity of suitable schooling—sex education and education programs—especially for the pregnant and postpartal girl.

Since most children are "surprise" children, even to married adults, it is strange to expect that adolescents should have any less percentage of "surprises." The inability of the adolescent to plan ahead is often viewed as part of her psychopathology and this may well be the caregiver's and the psychiatrist's countertransference. The above outlined foci for decision-making by the adolescent are not necessarily meant to be taken as signs of pathology if she has problems making these decisions. The usual teenager spends an inordinate amount of time agonizing over what clothes to wear. With such difficulties in making decisions it should be apparent that in other matters with which she has less experience, or which are more exciting, her decision-making would be more likely anxiety-ridden and incautious. All decision-making (and especially those related to her: sexuality or continence; contraception or pregnancy; delivery or abortion; and motherhood or adoption) have highly-charged considerations and are influenced by the presence or absence of psychopathology. They are also affected by the girl's intelligence level and her ability to abstract. We need to recall that half the population has an I.Q. of less than 100. Some with a low I.Q. or those who are under-stimulated (especially the poor) may never achieve the ability for formal operations (Piaget, 1972). Without the ability to plan ahead, decisions are most difficult. These items are frequently overlooked in the research design or program variables. Are these oversights and unrealistic expectations also countertransference-based?

The congressional legislation of the autumn of 1978 providing for programs for pregnant adolescents and teenage mothers has yet to be implemented, although it is purported to be backed adequately with money. Hopefully, the programs will be properly preventative and comprehensive with continuity as outlined above and they will provide some surcease from the epidemic of adolescent motherhood.

SUMMARY

This chapter has reviewed some of the facets of the epidemic of adolescent motherhood, i.e. increased baby-keeping by adolescents. There is an extensive, needy and fecund population waiting for prevention and intervention. If suitable help is not provided, the burgeoning of baby-keeping will continue and be followed by an expanding population and generations of children raising babies.

There are multiple determinants and differences in intelligence, nutritional state, socioeconomics, emotional development, culture, dynamics and psychopathology involved in the decision to engage in coital activity, use contraception, become pregnant, abort, carry to term, give the baby up for adoption or keep it.

Problems abound in the research of this arena, e.g. separation of early from illegitimate motherhood; the lack of proper population comparisons;

insufficient controls; population groups from different cultures and socio-economic groups are insufficiently defined and separated; psychodynamics are confused with maturation or developmental arrests; sociodynamic contributions are not entirely convincing and do not explain all.

Many programs have been short-lived and often focus only on facts of reproduction and contraception but provide no counselling and comprehensive continued care.

Learning about causes and optimal solutions to problems is most difficult when observations and decisions are loaded with prejudices. Countertransference features are viewed as contributing to some of the lack of clarity in theory and inconsequential intervention programs.

REFERENCES

Abernathy, V. and Abernathy, G. (1974) Risk for unwanted pregnancy among mentally ill adolescent girls. *Am. J. Orthopsychiat.* 44:442-450.

Alan Guttmacher Institute (1976) *11 Million Teenagers.* New York: Planned Parenthood Federation of America.

Babikian, H. and Goldman, A. (1971) A study of teen-age pregnancy. *Am. J. Psychiat.* 128:755-760.

Bacon, L. (1974) Early motherhood, accelerated role transition, and social pathologies. *Soc. Forces* 52:333-341 (Spring).

Barglow, P., Bornstein, M., Exum, D., Wright, M. K., and Vistosky, H. M. (1968) Some psychiatric aspects of illegitimate pregnancy in early adolescence. *Am. J. Orthopsychiat.* 38:672-687.

Bonam, A. F. (1963) Psychoanalytic implications in treating unmarried mothers with narcissistic character structures. *Soc. Casework* 44:323-329.

Calderone, M. S. (1966) Sex and the adolescent. *Clin. Pediat.* 5:171-174.

Castile, A. S. (1976) *School Health in America.* Kent, Ohio: American Health Association.

Coombs, L. C. and Freedman, R. (1970) Premarital pregnancy, child spacing and later economic achievement. *Populat. Stu.* 25:389-412.

Cutright, P. (1973) Timing the first birth: does it matter? *J. Marriage & Fam.* 35:585-596.

———. (1976) Family planning program effects on the fertility of low income women. *Fam. Plann. Perspect.* 8:100-110.

Fisher, S. M. (1978) Teenage pregnancy: an anthropological, sociological and psychological overview. Presented at Am. Acad. Child Psychiat. Meeting, October, 1978, San Diego, California.

Furstenberg, F. (1976) *Unplanned Parenthood.* New York: The Free Press.

Gabrielson, L. W., Gabrielson, I.W., Klerman, L. W., Currie, J. A., Tyler, N. C., and Jekel, S. F. (1970). Suicide attempts in a population pregnant as teenagers. *Am. J. Public Health* 60:2289-2301.

Gottschalk, L. A., Titchener, J. L., Piker, H. N., and Stewart, S. S. (1964) Psychosocial factors associated with pregnancy in adolescent girls: a preliminary report. *J. Nerv. & Ment. Dis.* 138:524-534.

Hansen, C., Brown, M., and Trontell, M. (1976) Effects on adolescents of attending a special school. *J. Am. Dietetic Assoc.* 68:538-541.

Johnson, C. L. (1974) Attitudes toward premarital sex and family planning for single-never pregnant teenage girls. *Adol.* 9:255-259.

Kantner, J. F. and Zelnick, M. (1972) Sexual experiences of young unmarried women in the United States. *Fam. Plann. Perspect.* 4:9-18.

———. (1973) Contraception and pregnancy: experiences in young unmarried women in the United States. *Fam. Plann. Perspect.* 5:21-35.

Khlentzos, M. and Pagliaro, M. (1965) Observations from psychotherapy with unwed mothers. *Am. J. Orthopsychiat.* 35:779-786.

Kinch, R. A. H., Waring, M. P., Love, E. J., and McMahon, D. (1969) Some aspects of pediatric illegitimacy. *Am. J. Obstet. Gynecol.* 105:20-31.

Klerman, L. V. and Jekel, J. F. (1973) *School-Age Mother: Problems, Programs and Policy.* Hamden, Conn.: Lennet Books.

LaBarre, M. (1972) Emotional crises of school-age girls during pregnancy and early motherhood. *J. Am. Acad. Child Psychiat.* 11:537-557.

Nadelson, C. (1974) Abortion counselling: focus on adolescent pregnancy. *Pediat.* 54:765-769.

New York Times (1978) December 17, Section I, p. 47.

Osofsky, H. J., Osofsky, J. D., Kendall, N., and Rajan, R. (1973) Adolescents as mothers: an interdisciplinary approach to a complex problem. *J. Youth Adol.* 2:233-249.

Pauker, J. (1971) Girls pregnant out of wedlock. *J. Operat. Psychiat.* 1:15-19.

Petersen, A. C., (1979) Female Pubertal Development. In M. Sugar (Ed.), *Female Adolescent Development.* New York: Brunner/Mazel.

Piaget, J. (1972) Intellectual evolution from adolescence to adulthood. *Hum. Develop.* 15:1-12.

Plionis, B. M. (1975) Adolescent pregnancy: review of the literature. *Soc. Work* 20:302-307.

Sarrel, P. M. (1967) The university hospital and the teenage unwed mother. *Am. J. Publ. Health* 57:1308-1313.

Sarrel, P. M. and Davis, C. A. (1966) The young unwed primipara, *Am. J. Obstet. Gynecol.* 95:722-725.

Schaffer, C. and Pine, F. (1972) Pregnancy, abortion, and the developmental tasks of adolescence. *J. Am. Acad. Child Psychiat.* 11:511-536.

Schlackman, V. (1966) Unmarried parenthood: an approach to social policy. *Soc. Casework* 47:494-501.

Sorensen, R. C. (1973) *Adolescent Sexuality in Contemporary America.* New York: World Press.

Sugar, M. (1979) Developmental Issues in Adolescent Motherhood. In M. Sugar (Ed.), *Female Adolescent Development.* New York: Brunner/Mazel.

U.S. News & World Report, June 26, 1978, 59-60.

V. D. Fact Sheet (1976) Ed. 33 U. S. Dept. H.E.W. Center for Disease Control. Washington, D.C.

V.D. Statistical Letter #126 (1976) U. S. Dept. H.E.W. Washington, D. C.

Vincent, C. E. (1961) *Unmarried Mothers.* New York: Free Press.

Webb, G., Briggs, C., and Brown, R. (1972) A comprehensive adolescent maternity program in a community hospital. *Am. J. Obstet. Gynecol.* 113:511-523.

Williams H. (1978) *The Times Picayune* (New Orleans), Section 3, p. 19, Nov. 3.

Wynne, L. C. and Frader, L. (1979) Female Adolescence and the Family: An Historical View. In M. Sugar, (Ed.), *Female Adolescent Development.* New York: Brunner/Mazel.

PART VI
Work

14

Between Two Worlds: Emotional Needs of Adolescents Facing the Transition from School to Work

DAVID E. SCHARFF

"Leaving school is like being born. It's like being pushed out of your mother's womb and when you're out, you're useless."

Benjamin, age 16
London

The transition from school to work is an important step for an adolescent and his society. In a relatively brief time he must, for the first time, bring together his own accumulated resources and make a choice about the outer world which will have lasting implications. Academically able teenagers routinely delay this choice for four or more years. Paradoxically, the less able children must choose it sooner, and the least able may do so by defaulting in school at an even earlier age than sanctioned by law. Those least able to profit from an educational system and most in need leave it at the earliest moment.

The paradox is even more complex, for this abrupt school-leaving then occurs at the height of adolescent turmoil and is experienced as traumatic for the young school-leaver. He is maladjusted for work and for the society around him—unable even to hold one of the few jobs he can get. Statistically this is seen as "high juvenile labor turnover" (Carter, 1966) and contributes to high rates of youthful unemployment. This phenomenon often represents a mismatch between the needs of a growing person and the resources provided by society.

This chapter explores the emotional needs of adolescents who find themselves in this situation. It draws on research groups and interviews of students and teachers from secondary schools in London and in Washington, D.C., from 1972 to 1974. In addition, I have drawn on work with a number of 16- to 18-year-olds seen in psychotherapy just before or after leaving school.

A DEVELOPMENTAL LINE FOR CONCEPTS ABOUT WORK

J.M.M. Hill described a developmental line of approach to work in children from 7 to 18. He traced the process by which the child gradually blends his fantasy wishes and the increasing need to adapt to reality (Scharff and Hill, 1976).

At the age of 7 or 8, the child's ambitions are concrete and tied to the real world by superficial observations. For instance, an 8-year-old boy interviewed in Hill's project described the work of his father, an author:

"One gets a typewriter and one starts thinking of things to write and one has to cross them out when they are wrong. One has a lot of telephone calls ... One needs a good mind to think about what to write, strong fingers and long arms." On being asked why one needed long arms, he said, "to reach the telephone from the chair."

At this age there is a split between the children's observations and the function of the work echoing a wide separation of the child's fantasy from the realities of, function of, or reward in, actual work.

By age 11, many children give up fantasies to develop what Hill calls "an imaginative approach to reality." There is a better-rounded, more interesting description of work with a more realistic consideration of salary, training, and intangible rewards.

At approximately 14 or 15 another development occurs. As the adolescent's bodily and emotional growth push him toward autonomy and separation from childhood and parents, decisions begin to be made about what to do after high school—courses of study, what to do about after-school work, whether to plan for further education. The child who earlier developed an imaginative approach to reality should now build a further bridge to reality by developing "a strategy of approach to the world of work"—a kind of game plan about which curriculum to take, which interim jobs to seek, how to consider rewards and costs for himself and his family. The strategy should become increasingly realistic with continual testing and revision.

However, some children reach 15 without achieving this development. They retain a wide split between fantasy and reality. For example, some insist on unrealistically lofty ambitions while performing poorly in school, and maintain an air of denial that truancy or academic failure relate to poor prospects. These adolescents retain a view of the world of work characteristic of younger children. They hope someone will take care of them or maintain they can conquer the world without skills. But they also often become deeply depressed, delinquent, increasingly truant, or apathetic. In short, they exhibit behavioral signs of anxiety about difficulty in maturing and inability to use help. For many struggling adolescents, this developmental problem shows up in the many uneven aspects of their own development with regressive trends and moves under stress.

Example 1: Regressive Occupational Planning

Mike, a 16-year-old British boy participating in our investigation, had been enrolled in a special program leading to a catering career. As summer approached, he exhibited more manic denial of the losses involved in leaving school for an apprenticeship. He gave up a family and school-supported strategy and reverted to regressive occupational planning.

> Mike: I changed my mind. I'm leaving school. I'll start working in the borough of X. I haven't had an interview, but I'll definitely get in. I'll be jumping on scaffolds. In 4 years' time I'll earn anything from £50 to £100 a week . . . Did you ever see an Irish exam paper? They ask: "What time is the 9 o'clock news?" They're really thick. Reviewing for exams doesn't do anything.
> Dr. S.: I remember you didn't do any.
> Mike: I knew all the questions in my exams . . . You should get fresh air on a building site. Imagine I'm the boss in a Rolls-Royce when I'm driving the digger on a building site . . . I might still work in a restaurant. I don't know what I'm going to do really but I will try. I might take this apprenticeship course with the borough and once I'm trained, I'll leave and start my own business. I'll walk about, buy a van, ladders, pots of paint and call it "Mike & Co. Ltd." My mum would like me to be a teacher. I'll be a presser. There's good money doing that.

Dr. S.: You're not frightened by working on a building site?

Mike: I was frightened once, but I'm not scared of anything except spiders. I'm petrified of them . . . I want enough money to be rich.

Dr. S.: You look as though you're feeling pretty anxious about leaving school.

Mike: I'm enjoying myself and having a bit of fun . . . it'll be hard for me to find a job because I like doing everything.

Mike's pressured speech, his retreat into fantasy, and his flight from my confrontation of him all serve to hide his overwhelming sense of loss. To triumph over that loss, he magically makes himself the boss instead of the laborer—but Mike's images of bosses are full of sadism, greed and childishness and he fears them. Unable to see any other kind of "boss" within himself he sees bosses and their world as threatening his fantasies, and he blames them for the pain of losing school. Under the threat he regresses to fluid, fantasy-bound occupational choices, abandoning the one in catering for which he has worked. The wide split between fantasy and reality is typical of a young child.

Mike's regression emphasizes a central problem: although leaving school to go to work (or college) takes place at a defined moment, the process of bridging the gap between the worlds of school and work takes place over the whole range of the child's growth and draws on the strengths of his previous emotional and cognitive achievements. When we see adolescents only in school groups, we seldom have developmental information which would tell us whether they had earlier difficulty. Nevertheless, the trouble leaving school resembles problems many children have with previous separation crises which are its precursors: the toddler's anxiety at separation from his mother; school phobias when the child attempts to leave home for the first time; or severe homesickness at summer camp. These previous separations may have been difficult for some of these adolescents or they and their parents may have found defensive paths around them, enabling them to avoid problems until the age of about 16 when the adolescent must confront reality either by leaving school or by school performance adequate to permit him to stay.

MOURNING IN THE PSYCHOSOCIAL TRANSITION

School-leaving is a major psychosocial transition, one of those turning points in development which involve major life shifts. (Others are: entering school, marriage, childbirth, divorce, loss of a home, the coming of old age, and the approach of one's own death.) Colin Parkes (1971) noted that each such transition involves moving from a familiar, known world into a new and therefore unfamiliar one. In a relatively concentrated period, large sections of one's internal and external worlds are involved in a confrontation between social realities and individual issues of growth and development.

The transition from school to work is unique for three reasons. It is the first major decision to be made by the adolescent as he emerges from childhood. Secondly, because this transition must occur unless postponed by decision and performance, decisions about alternatives must be made actively by the adolescent or they will be made by default. For instance, if he does not keep up with at least a minimum performance in school, he will be out by default. He has to be active in school work even to postpone school-leaving. Thirdly, for the first time in his life, the adolescent has the central role in decision-making. He can no longer sit by while his parents decide and then either comply or resist. Although he may still lean heavily on his parents, teachers or friends, he is now center-stage.

In all psychosocial transitions the old familiar world must be mourned and surrendered like a loved person who has died. Simultaneously, fears and anxieties about the new, unknown world will have to be faced and tolerated. These processes constitute the emotional steps to be encountered in the transition from school to work and we can outline adolescent needs according to vicissitudes in them.

Four such areas for us to consider in exploring responses to adolescent needs in leaving school are suggested:

1) How can we facilitate loss and mourning of the old world?
2) How can we help adolescents manage anxiety about their future world?
3) Which *persons* will help the adolescent through these processes and accompany him across the gap between school (and home) and the unknown life in work?
4) Do schools and work settings currently help or hinder the transition? What is required that they could add?

LOSS AND MOURNING OF THE OLD WORLD

One London adolescent said to us:

A friend came up and talked to me and I started to feel sad and out of place because I'm leaving. I was happy at home this morning, but when I got to school, I felt bad.

It is important to be able to undergo a normal grieving process. As defined in classic studies by Lindemann (1944) and Bowlby (1973), the phases of grieving include:

1) numbness and disbelief, followed by
2) searching and increasing belief in the loss, accompanied by
3) angry protest directed against the lost person or thing, others who are held to blame, or the self;
4) sadness and despair, followed by
5) gradual detachment from the lost object and reattachment to other objects. Parts of the lost person continue as memories and as an internalized object. Energy should be freed for new relationships.

This boy was proceeding normally to give up school, however sadly, and move toward a work life which he expected to value. Pathological grief develops in a person who becomes stuck at *any* one of the intermediate stages. Teenage truancy, apathy, delinquency, alcoholism, and the more obvious signs of depression or anxiety, are possible indicators of pathological grieving. The manic response to the loss of school seen in the interview with Mike was an example of a pathological reaction to loss—a flight into disbelief that anything would be lost and an insistence on childhood omnipotence. Another example is provided by the anger of many surly and rebellious adolescents which represents the "angry protest" of the grieving process, a reaction to the death of the old life of being a child who is taken care of.

Example 2: Difficulties with Mourning

The following group of 16-year-olds are having various kinds of trouble with mourning during the last week of school at "Lake School" in London:

Nan: I don't want to leave school. Once you've gone, all right. You get into your job, you don't think about it any more, but when you're at school it's your whole life and you feel secure. You don't know about the world at all. This is the worst time. You're never going back to school again. You only go to school once, don't you?

Linda: My two years of typing has been a real waste of time. I should have done an academic course. I wish I'd thought of it sooner. If this is the way I feel now, I must have been able to do something better.

Andy: I don't want to leave school and I don't want to ever be older than 21.

Nan: When I left primary school, I didn't like it either.

Panic, regret, nostalgia, fear, and wishes to regress reign in this group. The mood of the room verged toward chaotic terror, even if tinged with ironic humour.

THE MANAGEMENT OF ANXIETY ABOUT
THE UNKNOWN WORLD

Anxiety about the future, unknown world overlaps mourning, looking forward rather than back involving untested fears about the future.

Example 3: Defenses Against Anxiety

A group of Washington, D.C. 16-year-olds chosen for potential difficulty with the transition into work gave graphic illustration of the psychological defenses against anxiety. In this February 1974 meeting while Nixon was hanging on as president and the gasoline shortage was acute, the group has been discussing going on drugs as an alternative to going to work at all:

Sam: I used to have a doctor who went into the backroom of the hospital and got high. Maybe it's a good idea to blow your money staying high instead of saving it.

Mack: If you're a junkie, it costs less to smoke pot. It's a good way to pay for it.

Sam: Yeah. It's not a bad idea. But when I get out of school I want to drive a truck and travel to see my family. They're cool, but they're all over.

Sandra: I want to be a lab tech for a doctor, but I don't want to be in the U.S.—I want to travel too.

Dr. Scharff: It sounds like everyone wants to get away.

Mack: They won't go anywhere. They'll all end up right here in D.C. You'll see.

Sam: It's not in my mind. I'm gonna travel.

Mack: They won't really go away. (Under his breath:) Doom is coming and we all gonna die in D.C. (He is sketching a picture at his desk.)

Sandra: D.C. is a bad place. You get tired of it. People might come here to visit but if you're born here, you jus' want to get away. People say you can visit the White House, but I say, "Hell, I pass it every day!"

Sam: Folks come here from the South, movin' here. But there's no happiness here either.

Dr. Scharff; It sounds like you feel Washington is a lousy place no matter what you do and the job makes no difference.

Mack: The world is coming to an end.

Sam: This country seems to have gone from being one of the best, negotiating with everybody, to being one of the weakest. It's turned against us. What does it matter what you do.

Mack: Nixon messed it all up and even if he gets caught, he won't go to jail. Even if there gets to be a good president, it will be years before it's fixed. Besides, Agnew didn't even go to jail. And you know what they would do to one of us for much less! (He shows around a picture of Nixon as an evil eagle which he has drawn.

Dr. Scharff: So how does this matter to you?

Sam: There's no gas, fewer deliveries, not as much work for trucks and no truck jobs. They're all being laid off and I won't be able to get even a summer job driving a truck.

While the group continued to talk in depressed terms about their poor prospects for jobs, Mack drew a final sketch of a crying clown. While I can only speculate on the unconscious significance of the drawing, it fits with the group's pessimism. The laughter and clowning of an earlier time in this meeting and, symbolically, of childhood meet the realities of the world represented in the discussion about Nixon and jobs—and laughter turns to tears. It's as though Mack's picture were saying: "Here we are, just a bunch of clowns crying. We'd like to think the world is fun, but it's just a vale of tears."

Two months later Mack dropped out of school for the rest of the year. Sam stayed on, keeping his anxiety within manageable bounds, and working toward a job which still felt personally rewarding. Mack was stuck with pathological grief, feeling without personal and family support, which he projected onto the punitive and arbitrary environment around him—Nixon, the country, the economy. Although he shared this in varying degrees with other members of the group, unlike them he was unable to progress. Even if dread is expressed on the scale of local, national, or international problems, it represents the adolescent's worry about whether he can personally manage impending realities based on past experience. In times of national crises the personal crises are emphasized more, but they are still fundamentally developmental crises of the individual. The sense of crisis in the group stemmed from internal disappointment and apprehension that the world would never be their oyster.

Example 4: Helping to Counter Anxiety

Models of the new world to be faced are based largely on what is known and feared about past worlds, but can be modified both by exploration of specific areas of personal anxiety and by education about reality. For instance, role-play of aspects of job choice may illustrate worries which can be addressed in rehearsal, as in the example below from the "Lake School" group in London:

> Susan, a 16-year-old junior who faced leaving school in 3 months, was discouraged about her school performance. Yet she was a class clown, frequently late and negligent in her work. Her parents were not supportive, and the school's efforts had been sabotaged by her own inability to cooperate with several people who had tried. Her anxiety that no one would be available to help in the future was a prediction based on her current experience.
>
> In this role-play which she and her classmates constructed she was ejected from school for poor performance in accord with her notion that the school would not want her back (an untrue assumption since I knew specifically the school still wished to help her). When she failed to get a job in acting, her fantasy choice, she was undaunted:

> *Susan:* I'm happy enough though the school and the acting agency don't want me because I think *somehow* I'll be able to get a job. I'll look on the bright side. I'll try an employment agency.

The employment agent, played by Sally, was tough on her and to her surprise charged a fee, but also decided she needed help. Since she felt Susan deserved a chance, Sally decided that she would offer Susan a place in the Dorchester Hotel as receptionist. Sally herself would accompany Susan to the hotel to back her up and defend her during this practice run of an apprenticeship.

> *Sally:* (acting as senior receptionist) Here are the books. We have all these people's addresses and phone numbers and you have to put them in order after I show you how to do it . . . If the phone rings, take a message. Push the button. I'll do it once, and then you do it next.

They get to chatting and Susan looks excited. Various guests come, including David Cassidy, a teen singing idol. Sally handles most of it, then gets up to leave Susan on her own.

> *Susan:* Please keep helping me.

Sally: I have to go and have lunch. If you need help, press this button and I will come. Goodbye.

Susan: Goodbye.

Dr. Scharff: How are you feeling on your own, Susan?

Susan: Excited; rather nervous in case I make a mess. Somebody may fire me.

Judy: (calls on the 'phone angrily) This is No. 3. I have not had my morning coffee. I asked for it at 9 o'clock and it is now 11 o'clock.

Susan: So sorry, madam. (to herself) Must get the kitchen. (Picks up the 'phone—Jack takes the role of cook.)

Jack: (from the kitchen, with self-righteous indignation) The coffee has already been sent up—it will go on her bill.

Susan: (now very confused picks up the 'phone to room No. 3) The chef says he sent the coffee up. Are you sure you didn't drink it?

Judy: Well! (slams down the phone).

Mrs. Jacobs (the co-leader): (waits near desk for some time and is finally noticed) Excuse me, are you the only receptionist here?

Susan: (putting down the 'phone, still confused and torn) Can I help?

Mrs. Jacobs: (indignantly) I was wanting to reserve a room, but the service is not too good around here. I ought to go somewhere else. (Susan rings bell for senior receptionist and Sally returns promptly.)

Mrs. Jacobs: (to Sally) Are you the head receptionist? I have been waiting for 10 minutes . . .

Sally: (to Susan with a knowing frown) But we do have some awkward customers!

Mrs. Jacobs: I want to reserve a room for tonight, it must be at the back and very quiet; I want good service.

Sally: Cheque or cash?

Mrs. Jacobs: Cheque.

Sally: How about room No. 13?

Mrs. Jacobs: Have you something higher up in the building?

Sally: 121?

Mrs. Jacobs: That will do. (she goes)

Sally: (to Susan) Could you tell me what happened?

Susan: You went off, Room No. 3 rang up again, you know what she's like. She said she hadn't had her coffee. I 'phoned the kitchen and the chef said he had sent it, and I rang back and explained and she got a bit rude.

Chef: (rings again) I'm sorry I didn't send the coffee up. It was my fault.

Sally: (to Susan) If anything happens again and you are on you own, say, "Would you like to take a seat, I will be busy for a couple of minutes." If the customer is too impatient to wait or they are just difficult or being rude, you say, "If you do not like the service and the way we run our hotel you just jolly well find another hotel." (group laughs)

In this role-play, the class group, and especially Sally, saw to it that Susan got several of the kinds of personal help she would need in a real situation to learn on the job. For the first time she is helped to develop a strategy of approach to work which counters her specific anxiety about abandonment and fear of repeated failure by people who support her efforts. The group has helped her to begin suspending maladaptive defenses against anxieties while testing new ways of operating.

PARENTS, TEACHERS, AND THE MEANING OF WORK

Work achieves personal meaning and sense of reward only through its connections to those people with whom the worker is involved emotionally. This was symbolized when a boy who valued communication in his own family wanted to be a telephone repairman to help other people talk. In addition the money he hoped to earn would support the people in his own future family, while personal reward would also be enhanced if he enjoyed his co-workers. Sam, the Washington boy who wanted to be a truck driver, drew his ambition from the idea that he would visit his scattered relatives, making personal links to his widely-separated family. But any of these rewarding connections to caring people in the worker's life can be interrupted.

When adolescents look to parents, teachers, and fantasy idols, they either want to be like those they like, do better than those who let them down, or be the opposite of those they dislike.

Example 5: Identification and Job Choice

One Washington boy wanted to be like one teacher and unlike another:

I'd like to be a P.E. teacher. I had one who let me play at junior high even tho I wasn't very good at basketball. A coach has to win all the time, but a P.E. teacher can stop and help kids. I've been working for the recreation department in the summer and I know I like that.

The support of parents and teachers during the loss of school is doubly important, both for help during the crisis, and for the memory of caring they instill. Mature self-reliance in adulthood stems from an initial experience of secure reliance on parents and teachers in childhood (Bowlby, 1970). Many teenagers facing most difficulty leaving school were unsupported in some major way by their parents, although not necessarily for lack of repeated attempts by the parents. The adolescents often also cut themselves off or were cut off from support by teachers and counselors.

Example 6: Lack of Parental Support

An example was given by a 16-year-old Washington girl whose ambition was to be a lab technician but who was having difficulty following through.

> I'll have arguments with my mother every day. She wants me to be a doctor or a lawyer. I get on better with my dad, but he doesn't care what I do. My brothers are doing well in college, but my sister got married and had kids. My mother says, "You're going to turn out bad, just like your sister."

This girl denied that her mother's ambitions for her had any impact, but the daily struggle drove her toward an apathetic surrender of her own more realistic ambition, pushing her either to drop everything and drop out, or to continue listlessly.

THE INTERLOCKING OF ISSUES BETWEEN THE ADOLESCENT AND HIS ADULTS

But parents and teachers have their own issues to deal with. They also undergo loss of the child and a reciprocal process of mourning. Mourning a child who has been successful is hard enough, but if the small or halting gains of the child seem insignificant then the adult's anger is apt to interfere. The adult may now defend against his own loss by withdrawing defensively from a belligerent, delinquent or poorly performing child. This withdrawal represents a failure around separation, substituting shared defenses for grief and cutting the teenager off from supporting persons just when he needs them most.

Example 7: Adult Obstructiveness as A Defense Against Loss

When Susan, the student we focused on in the "Lake School" role-play began doing well with help from her peers, suddenly I felt uncomfortable and asked my co-leader, Mrs. Jacobs, to be a "belligerent hotel guest," which she did. Later I realized that I had felt a loss myself—that as Susan and the group finally began to do well, they no longer needed me. I lost my usefulness as their "helper" and reacted in a symbolically punitive way, just as teachers or parents may if they feel no longer useful when an adolescent leaves the school or family. As a defense against loss, the adults may cling to the child, attempt to control him, or get in his way as we did in the role-play.

When adults' life development runs aground, they may also be more likely to withdraw from adolescents. For instance, a teacher's mid-life crisis involves an assessment of his or her life's work. If he feels his contribution is not valued, he may become withdrawn, bitter, or despairing. This reaction is common in inner-city schools where social conditions often weigh heavily against personal progress and against recognition for student and teacher alike.

Example 8: Teacher/Student Echoes of Despair

One 50-year-old Washington teacher said:

The families only want us to babysit. Maybe we should kick out all these kids who don't want to be here and see what happens. They slip away from us even when we try . . . Besides, these kids are not the only ones who are depressed. There are other times in your life when you're just as depressed as they are.

This depressed teacher talked of her own fear of violence in the hallways, of the hopelessness of her task, of the thanklessness of the children. Other teachers were able to remain interested and hopeful, but she felt overwhelmed by the school and by her own aging. It is particularly the adolescents of small achievement and little hope who will echo such a teacher's projected despair and empty hope.

Example 9: Parent/Child Echoes in Family Therapy

The interplay of issues between parent and child is even more important than with teachers. A boy I saw with his family at the Tavistock Clinic, London, provides a clear example.

Keith was a 16-year-old who was shakily established in the world of work, having recently left school at the normal time. He was now in a four-year apprenticeship as a draughtsman with one day a week spent at a college for further education. He had found school difficult the year before he left, and now he found the day at college threatening. An old fear of being called on to speak publicly in class had spread to a fear of using the telephone at work. He grew increasingly afraid at work that he would be unable to answer the telephone or explain himself. When he went to his family doctor to ask for help, he was alarmed to find his father also there. When the general practitioner referred Keith, we asked him to advise Keith to bring his family.

After Keith outlined the phobia in the first meeting, it emerged that his whole family had been under great strain. A psycho-social transition was upon the whole family because father had given up a job of many years' standing as a minor executive in a large printing firm to buy a dairy shop previously owned by the mother's family.

In subsequent therapy, it became apparent that mother had "borne all the burdens of the men in the family" who made her do things for them and then resented her. The father had had a checkered career while he worked his way up to supervisory position. Recently, he had realized that because he lacked a university degree, there would be no further promotions. He and his wife made the decision to invest in the family dairy shop which would be more lucrative although less "professional." His own anxiety about the move had taken him to the family doctor just when Keith had gone to him. The father also recounted having overcome a public speaking phobia of his own. Several years earlier he deliberately set out to organize religious forums in which he would be called on to speak in order to overcome a dread similar to the one now confronting Keith.

Keith's growing uncertainty about work which was expressed through the inability to use the telephone echoed the family's crisis. Father's depression, bitterness about his own career, and the general pattern within the family of "pinning everything" on mother all contributed to Keith's increasing anxiety about pursuing a new career which involved learning, promotion, and a progressive assumption of independent responsibility. Like his father, he had pursued a career which would be without academic acknowledgment. He was not aware of any of the same bitterness that his father felt, or of anxiety about his own career, but he was aware that his inhibition threatened to remove him from his job.

Our exploration of the family pattern during a dozen sessions linked Keith's trouble with father's disappointment and with the threat of the mother becoming more of a bread-winner than either her husband or Keith could tolerate. Interlocking and reinforcing family themes emerged. Keith could see that the life issues his father had found crippling did not need to be taken on; the mother was relieved of the burden generated by her husband's and son's work life; and father mourned his old ambitions successfully. When the father and Keith began to work together to relieve the shared anxiety, Keith found himself able to use the phone at work, to take on more difficult tasks, and to move toward competence at work and college.

In this case, as in many, the adolescent's anxiety often relates to strains within the family and to issues about work for several members of the family. When a parent is vulnerable about work, he is less able to support his child's transition into work.

THE ROLE OF SCHOOLS: SOCIAL DEFENSE MECHANISMS AGAINST LOSS AND ANXIETY

Social defense mechanisms are those structures and methods of operating which shield an institution and its personnel from anxieties they would otherwise have to face (Jaques, 1955). In schools, teachers and administration are shielded by defense mechanisms which aid denial of problems, and by substitute formations—for instance, awarding honors for the athletic achievement of a few while ignoring the failure of many. In Washington, a teachers' group told us that while students who slipped away had a poor prognosis, no one knew what happened to them. There was no mechanism to follow-up these students, and no way to provide counselling to them. Paradoxically, the college-bound students that by definition needed counselling less than the nonacademic early school-leavers would be more likely to get it during their continuing education.

In England, a national final examination structure operated as a social defense mechanism, forcing students and teachers to lose contact with each other the last few weeks of school during the exams—thereby decreasing the amount of support available to students during the stress created by the importance of exam results for job entry. The school structure aided the formation of a defensive mutual withdrawal. It interfered with the process of saying goodbye and mourning the loss—an ambivalently felt loss often mixed with disappointment on both sides. These ambivalent losses are most likely to be defended against and hardest to work through at both personal and social levels.

DIFFERENCES BETWEEN AMERICAN AND BRITISH SCHOOLS AND SCHOOL-LEAVERS

The differences in the American and British school systems and requirements are important in a first assessment of the transition from school to work. In Britain there is the emphasis on national examinations as barriers and requirements at the secondary school level. There is also a highly differentiated continuing education system which ranges from university and trade-specific colleges, to apprenticeships beginning at 16 which carry continuing education opportunities. The educational system in the United States is moving in this direction in some ways with the GED as a substitute for time in school and a range of training programs in the growing community and technical college systems.

In some specific ways, the American approach is more developed. There is more integration of job experience with curriculum in secondary schools. In Britain, attempts to develop this kind of program have run immediately into restrictive child labor laws, which apparently are less of a problem in the U.S. In the U.S., a higher percentage of adolescents also go on to college, delaying the day of reckoning.

Not so commonly recognized, however, is that a high percentage of the American students leave college unexpectedly in the first year, facing a sudden transition into work. One school I worked with estimated this happened to fully one third of the college-bound students! In addition, in times of high unemployment, these poorly prepared adolescents will be the first to lose their jobs (Hill 1977).

A word about the work side of the transition is in order, although not the focus of my own research. Employers often encounter young adolescents in the midst of the processes we have been exploring—seeing rebellious attitudes which mask anxiety and fear, or apathy substituting for grief. They seldom have the experience in helping adolescents to understand these processes except in large businesses with a regular large intake of recent graduates and a personnel program aimed at adolescents. This inexperience results in more confrontation, probable mutual dissatisfaction for employer and young worker, and frequent early job-changing.

PROGRAMMATIC RECOMMENDATIONS

There are four basic levels of intervention aimed at helping the student to leave school successfully, varying from broad programmatic approaches to intervention with individual adolescents.

1) The incorporation of job and outside world materials into the various classroom curricula so that students think about the process of leaving school adaptively from many vantages of their educational growth. For instance, an English curriculum may include writing job applications, as well as reading about and discussing the process of working. One excellent anthology by an English Headmaster offers literary selections about the experience of working (Marland, 1973).

2) The actual integration of work with school. For some children, actual work experience should come early and then be talked about as the primary educational experience. The non-academic adolescent *requires* an early supervised work experience to help his lagging development toward a strategic approach to the world of work. But all adolescents would probably benefit by it, as evidenced by recent experience at some highly academic college preparatory schools like the Madeira School in Washington, D.C., as well as in pilot public schools like Philadelphia's Parkway School.

3) There is a need in the United States and Britain for a bridging institution, for a counselling system which begins in school years and extends beyond school-leaving into the first work experiences. It should help the student as he becomes a young worker, and support untrained *employers* in dealing with disoriented and confused young persons.

4) Clinical intervention is important. Here I would urge teachers, counselors, and clinicians to bear in mind the developmental aspects of the transition from school to work. I believe it is especially important to be on the alert for blocked grief reactions, for masked depression and unmanagable anxiety, and for uneven growth toward a strategy of approach to work. Once these are identified, appropriate group, individual, and family therapy or counselling may be applied or curricular modifications may be created in individual schools.

SUMMARY

The adolescent's path from school to work takes him through a psychosocial transition which recalls earlier separation crises. Like these, it requires the adolescent to mourn and surrender old expectations and to tolerate anxieties about the future.

From the age of about 7 the child develops a progressive ability to meld his inner fantasies with the requirements of external realities. At best, he develops an imaginative strategy of approach to the world of work by 16 or 18. But many adolescents are unable to achieve such a blend, blocked by uneven development and incomplete mourning for home, school and childhood.

Parents, teachers and counselors may be hampered in their efforts to support young school-leavers by the defensive behavior of the adolescents, by difficulties in their own reciprocal mourning for the adolescent, by interferences stemming from their own adult life phase, and by institutional social defense mechanisms which reduce adult anxiety.

Nonacademic adolescents could be helped by the incorporation of both specific job information and material about working life into the general curriculum; by integrating an earlier work experience with school; and by enabling counselling systems to offer a continuity of support fom early adolescence through early employment.

If clinicians and teachers are alert for blocked grief reactions, disguised depression and anxiety, and unevenness in growth, they may better support the shaky adolescent in his lonely flight from the world of school to the world of work.

ACKNOWLEDGMENTS

I am indebted to my London collaborators, John M. M. Hill and Marion Jacobs of the Tavistock Institute of Human Relations, to Randy Thurman of the District of Columbia Public Schools, and to the staff and students of the schools involved. Support of the London work by the Baxi Trust from the P.S. Baxindale Settlement, and of the Washington work by Dr. Arthur Stein of Area 'B' Mental Health Center is gratefully acknowledged. My thanks to Careers Consultants, Ltd., London, for permission to draw on *Between Two Worlds: Aspects of the Transition from School to Work,* by D. E. Scharff and J. M. M. Hill.

REFERENCES

Bowlby, J. (1970), Self-reliance and some conditions that promote it. In: R. H. Gosling (Ed.), *Support, Innovation and Autonomy,* London: Tavistock, 1973.

———— (1973), *Attachment and Loss, Vol. 2: Separation.* London: Hogarth Press.

Carter. M. (1966). *Into Work.* Harmondsworth: Penguin.

Hill. J.M.M. (1977). *The Social and Psychological Impact of Unemployment.* London: Tavistock Institute of Human Relations. Doc. No. 2T 74.

Jaques, E. (1955), Social systems as a defense against persecutory and depressive anxiety. In: M. Klein, P. Heimann, R. Money-Kyrle (Ed.) *New Directions in Psycho-Analysis,* London: Tavistock; New York: Basic Books.

Lindemann. E. (1944). Symptomatology and management of acute grief. *Am. J. Psychiat.* 101:141-148.

Marland. M. (1973). *The Experience of Work: An Anthology of Prose, Verse, Drama and Picture.* Hong Kong: Longman.

Parkes. C.M. (1971). Psycho-social transitions: A field for study. *Soc. Sci. Med.* 5:101-15.

Scharff. D.E. and Hill. J.M.M. (1976). *Between Two Worlds: Aspects of the Transition from School to Work.* London: Careers Consultants, Ltd.

15

High School Preparation for Employment in a Segmented Labor Market

THOMAS W. COLLINS
GEORGE W. NOBLIT
DAVID H. CISCEL

Apparently, we have designed a difficult world for youth. Only a short century ago, those whom we now call adolescents were consumed by work and family commitments which they had made in their early teens. Adolescent women were ready for marriage, childbearing, and family life and adolescent men were ready for their careers on the farm, in shops, or in the newly burgeoning industrial revolution. Times have changed. Youth now pass these same years in passive and dependent roles where they previously created their lifestyles and were vital contributors to the economy. Nevertheless, youth have changed little. Instead of youth maturing later, they are maturing even earlier, both physiologically and intellectually. This is in direct contrast with our current set of policies that affect youth. Child labor laws, compulsory school attendence and other public policies, while having some admirable, humanistic orientations, have developed the enforced servitude that we call adolescence. They hinder youth from attaining the productive, competent roles that we, as adults, consider so vital to our identities. Phelps (1976, p. 282) wrote:

> A majority of adults consider work the most important of their obligations; therefore, the transition from school to work is a critical expe-

rience for youth. It is more difficult for the dropouts and those with official delinquency histories. The young person has not been considered useful in the labor force. Public policy emphasizes keeping youngsters in school as long as possible, and this pattern delays the entry of young workers into the labor force.

Even with the recognition of these problems, however, it does not seem that we can roll back the history of public policy concerning youth. In spite of the recognition of these issues, legislation to promote youth employment has met resistance, and when enacted usually ends up more as vocational preparation than actual employment. One could argue that this will remain the case until the demand for human labor at least equals the supply—in short, a full employment economy. But even more intriguing is the fact that these vocational preparation programs have been based upon the same economic theory that has led us to the current problems of youth—passivity, dependence and, most notably, unemployment.

More recently, however, a critique of that economic theory has been proffered that can assist us in assessing vocational preparation programs for youth. Let us develop that critique, and then using ethnographic data on a distributive education program in a southern high school demonstrate the problems with our current responses to the problem of youth unemployment.

ECONOMIC THEORY AND VOCATIONAL EDUCATION

Seemingly, the corporate system in the United States has evolved a dual economy. Parallel to the affluent sector of the society stands an economy riddled with instability, insecurity, and poverty. Unfortunately the poor segment, often called the marginal economy, is not merely a remnant of an earlier time, but is an integral part of the structure of corporate society. The affluence and power of the primary sector of the economy, made up of the participants in the management and production of large unionized corporations, are protected and cushioned by the existence of this marginal economy. The continuation of poverty and the re-creation of the poorer classes in each new generation is fundamental to the continued stability of the affluent society. It seems that the uneven development of a corporate society is a basic characteristic, not a fluke, of the postindustrial, high mass consumption economy.

The structure and functioning of the educational system parallels the structure and functioning of the economy, existing to create the dual labor force required for a dichotomized society (Katz, 1971). This study, an ethnography, will illustrate the process by which a particular group of high school students in a desegregated southern school are channeled through a job training program, i.e., distributive education, into a crowded insecure and unstable secondary labor market.

Contrast this picture to that of the conventionally understood role of vocationally directed education in the United States. Educational policy was developed during the 1960s with the direct aim of facilitating the continuity of transition from public education to employment. In general, the development of occupational or vocational programs has been heralded as an effort to counteract the high unemployment experienced by females, youth and racial minorities. The objective of the multitude of new education and training programs has been the improvement in personal productivity through public investment in "human capital." Simply, the theme has been that better education provides better workers which results in both a healthier economy and higher personal incomes. In 1973, many of these earlier programs were dismantled or modified by the Comprehensive Employment and Training Act (CETA). Moreover, CETA placed an even greater emphasis on career education and vocational training. It was believed and argued that if the individual child is motivated enough to improve his or her human capital, he or she will be able to get a "good" job. In short, public education was seen as meeting its historical tradition of being the great equalizer, providing the opportunity for social and economic mobility.

The lack of success of the several vocational programs has led to considerable criticism of the programs' management, efficiency or placement techniques. However, only recently has the human capital theme itself been challenged. Critiques of the current conception of education and vocational education emerged on two fronts.

First, studies of the labor market and of employability of minorities by economists such as Piore (1975), Gordon (1971), and Fusfield (1973) have identified the existence of a dual (or segmented) labor force. Instead of a fluid and competitive labor market where the individual advancement is limited only by individual initiative and opportunity, these studies found a market where selected social groups, e.g., women and blacks, are systematically constrained from competing with white males working in high income, unionized jobs in large corporations. Ignoring individual exceptions, most members of minority groups are channeled into work situations in the marginal sectors of the economy. Plagued by a life of economic instability, insecurity, and poverty, individual members of these groups quickly develop personal characteristics that help maintain their unacceptability to the affluent sector of the economy.

Doeringer and Piore (1971) argued that classroom education and training does not necessarily result in employment in the primary sector of the labor market which provides better pay, preferred working conditions, more chances for advancement and job security than does the secondary sector. Instead they posited that acceptance into the primary sector requires a period of "on-the-job" socialization that produces a modicum of social acceptability and reputation that cannot be bought through education and formal training. Thus the dual labor market theory simply implies that vocational education programs cannot provide access to regular employment if they do not provide the necessary socialization. In their study of the labor market in Chicago, Baron and Hymer emphasized that the dual labor market requires the existence of non-competing or separated groups.

> In more specific terms, a racially dual labor market means that there exists a primary metropolitan labor market in which firms recruit white workers and in which white workers look for jobs; side by side with the major market there exists a smaller labor sector in which Negroes look for employment. For each sector *there are separate demand and supply* forces determining the allocation of jobs to workers and workers to jobs (p. 96, emphasis added).

Thus, the work group the new workers join is largely independent of any specific vocational direction he or she has received in the public school system.

The second critical stance emerges from historical analyses of education itself. In recent years a furor has developed over the role education has played (and was meant to play) in acculturating, integrating and assimilating the poor and/or immigrants into the mainstream of economic well-being in our society. The "Great School Legend" is not completely accurate. In fact, the progress and development of public education in this country seems to imply that schools were only selectively "integrating the poor." Public education in this country was geared from its inception to train the masses of poor and illiterate peoples to produce a class of industrial workers for the newly emerging manufacturing corporations and at the same time to maintain social stratification.

As Katz (1971) showed for the 19th century origins of public schooling, and Karier, Violas and Spring (1973) demonstrated for education in the 20th century, the persistent logic of the public school movement has emphasized assimilation over intellectual development—with the often explicit goal of teaching "the norms necessary to adjust the young to the changing patterns of the economic system as well as to the society's more permanent values" (Karier, Violas and Spring 1973). Thus these critics of education imply that one of the essential motives of public education was to train the poor to be workers in, and subject to, the industrial labor market.

Both economics and the history of education, as distinct disciplines, have emerging perspectives which imply that vocational education cannot achieve its oft-stated goal of moving the poor into stable employment. Unfortunately, there is a paucity of research which provides an understanding of how public schools pre-select and categorize youth for the secondary labor market. One reason for this lack of data can be attributed to the relative scarcity of ethnographic studies of education in general. A second factor has been the prevailing assumption that vocational education is for the less capable but possibly diligent student. All too often the existing procedural and organizational mechanisms that categorize people are assumed to be legitimate because they are functional, i.e., "It works, therefore, it is right." Let us examine this more closely.

RESEARCH PROCEDURES AND SCHOOL DESCRIPTION

The data for this investigation were abstracted from a recently completed ethnographic study which documents the process of interracial education. Two ethnographers observed and interviewed in a predominantly black (71%) urban southern high school for two years. From the outset, this project has been concerned with the issue of preselection for the labor market through the process of schooling.

A number of factors determined selection of the target school. First, at the time it was chosen it had the most equal racial balance of any school in the system. As of April 19, 1975, it had 216 white students and 328 black students, or 40% and 60% respectively, of the total 544. By the completion of the study however, the school had become 71% black. Second, the student body was highly representative of the various socioeconomic groups, black and white, in the city. Children came from families of the upper middle class and the working class, as well as from the recent rural migrants to the city.

Following the usual pattern of southern cities, black neighborhoods are interspersed among white residential areas. Over the past three decades these residential patterns have remained stable without the usual "white flight" of the northern cities, and once the zoning boundaries were altered the residence patterns were such that it was necessary to bus only a few of the children to achieve a minimal racial balance. There is also a wide range of socioeconomic groups within each racial area. The housing varies from upper income family units to blue-collar family units, with one large and several small low-income public housing complexes in the black area. For the most part, these units are occupied by clusters of extended family networks with rather enduring ties to nearby rural counties.

The physical plant of the high school, located on a 37-acre tract of rolling landscaped park and playground area, was another major factor governing our choice of schools. Built in 1948 on what was then the outer limits of the expanding suburban area at a cost of 2½ million dollars, the school is well-maintained and as modern as any in the system. These conditions contrast sharply with those reported in most ethnographic studies of inner city schools (cf. Kohl, 1967; Kozol, 1967; for an exception, see Levy, 1970). Moreover, the school has maintained a reputation for high quality education. Before desegregation, it was considered a superior upper middle class school where 95% of the graduating seniors enrolled in college, and the college preparatory tract still receives major emphasis in the curriculum.

In short, the target school was unique in the sense that it had an excellent physical plant and academic program, and a wide range of socioeconomic and racial groups from which to draw students. The residential barriers are extensive, and in no sense of the word can the district be considered an integrated community, although the facility is located close enough to neighborhoods of both blacks and whites for the students to consider it "their school." The range of students reflects a respectable cross-section of the values and attitudes of the whole community in which it is located.

It is also important to place the school and the students in terms of the prevailing milieu of the community. The city has served as the commercial and distribution center in the south for most of its history. In the 1940s and 1950s, this made it a focus for the mass migration of poverty-stricken share-croppers, both black and white, who were removed from the land in the aftermath of the mechanization of agriculture (Collins, 1973). Many of these migrants over the years have been temporary, remaining in the city only long enough to gain the necessary urban skills before they moved farther north to industrial urban centers. Recently, however, the migration to the urban north has been stalled by the high unemployment prevalent in the northern industrial centers. Even with this history, the city continues to retain certain characteristics or orientations that are similar to those of the surrounding rural counties. The people are generally politically conservative and maintain the localisms, religiosity and paternalism characteristic of the rural south.

For black teenagers the history of the city's economic and social development has been particularly critical. Unemployment rates for all 16- to 19-year-old workers has been several times higher than the rates for older adult groups throughout the 1970s. Unemployment for black teenagers has been two to three times the rate for white teenagers. In early 1978 teenage unemployment (16-19) made up 21.6% (11.7% black, 9.9% white) of total city unemployment. This dismal employment picture sets the stage for ex-

amining the importance of the role of distributive education's job placement potential in the life of the high school student in need of work.

A LOCAL HISTORY OF DISTRIBUTIVE EDUCATION

The federal legislation concerning distributive education dates back to
1937 when states were encouraged to establish "D.E." programs through
the availability of federal matching funds. It took 20 years, however, for the
city to take advantage of this initiative. In 1957 a new curriculum option
was made available in the segregated white high schools which served the
white blue-collar residential areas. Thus, distributive education was geared
in the local situation to provide training so that white working class students
would be able to maintain the social class they had inherited from their
parents.

However, in 1963, the substantial urban black community escalated its
demands for an improved economic situation (Collins 1974). One of the
supposed positive responses to these demands was the expansion of D.E.
curriculums into three black high schools. Interestingly enough, this expansion was not unrelated to an expanding economy in the local area, which
suggests that at least one impetus for this positive response to the black
population came from the business community. However, distributive education has remained to this day, a program that better serves the white
working class than the black community. The jobs that were available with
major enterprises, merchandising, and chains, were and are located in the
white suburban areas of the city; yet the local economy in the 1960s was
such that even the black students were in demand and successfully placed
in jobs. A closer scrutiny of the viability of this program for minority youth
is portrayed by one informed source who noted that while black students
were easily placed, this was only possible through strict screening of the
black students by the black high school coordinators. For the black community to get jobs in business it was necessary to pull recruits from the potentially college-bound, and some of the most capable black students with
immediate economic advantages were channeled into vocational programs.
In short, employers demanded, and depended upon, the coordinators to
send them the best of the black students. This seemed to reduce the anxiety
of this new situation of white employers interviewing black applicants for
formerly white-only positions.

Of course, one would not argue that the poorest students should have
been channeled into employment. Nevertheless, the net effect of the program was to provide employment opportunities to students who had career

options via higher education while leaving the student who did not have such easy access to further education with few career options that could be actualized.

Today, there are 600 business firms involved in the city-wide program serving 1700 students. The program is still the most active and viable in the white community, and the highest rate of students enrolled and placed in cooperative employment is in the largely white, but now desegregated suburban high schools. Moreover, these same programs place their students in better, more attractive employment. The overall rate of retention in the D.E. developed job is 50% for all high schools, but drops to 25% or less in the individual programs that serve a substantial number of black students. One educator readily admitted that it becomes necessarily more difficult for high school coordinators to place students in jobs if the black ratio becomes too high. As this educator put it, "Business firms won't take 100% black applicants, they want a selection." Given this obvious bias of employers, the D.E. coordinators find themselves courting these employers to keep their program alive. As one put it, "We cannot dictate to the businessman; he knows what he wants."

The recent tightening of the economy has forced the coordinator to more readily cater to the wishes of the employers and to seek out less suitable employment for on-the-job training of students. For the most part, the 600 firms do not represent those firms or corporations which are firmly in the core sector of the economy, i.e., major corporations with regional dispersed outlets. D.E. now provides access to marginal operations in the economy. Black students are predominately placed in the jobs in fast food restaurants and food chains that are characterized by low pay, low job security, high turnover, and little chance for advancement. In the tightening economy, more and more of the primary sector jobs in merchandising are filled by trainees with some college education. It would appear that D.E. is creating secondary sector workers for the marginal economy of the city.

This vocational training curriculum seems to have evolved into a program which differentially traps black students in the secondary labor forces of marginal industries. It is interesting that while a tightening labor market, particularly for blue-collar and service employment, would argue for closer reins on the extensiveness of the program, a less selective policy for releasing students to cooperative work experiences was instituted by the predominantly white school board subsequent to desegregation of the city schools. The significance of this seems evident: the new policy was geared to facilitate more channeling of black students, who were believed to be less capable than the whites, into the secondary labor force.

"THE GOOD OLD AMERICAN WORK ETHIC"

The National Association of Distributive Education Teachers sees that D.E. coordinators have six areas of responsibility to employers:

1. Provide part-time students who will grow in ability to produce for the benefit of your business.
2. Help set up a study program beneficial to the student and valuable to you.
3. Develop individual job attitudes such as personal grooming, safety practices, punctuality, so that the student will perform his job more effectively.
4. Provide individual instruction to the student in specific job areas related to his work.
5. Evaluate the student's performance in order to determine additional instructional needs.
6. Maintain a desirable working relationship with the student's parents.

If these six responsibilities are even approached, distributive education is by design a comprehensive attempt to socialize the student to fit into the desires and needs of the business world. Note, for example, that emphasis lies in three areas of socialization: distributive education is designed to provide skills, to develop acceptable attitudes and personal characteristics, and to utilize parents as a reinforcing mechanism in the preparation of students for work. Ultimately, however, our observations showed that the program teaches values and dress codes regardless of any supposed skill emphasis.

In actuality, it was reported that employers preferred (and seemingly required in the case of blacks) students with three faculties. Obviously, merchants are sensitive to the need for some mathematical skills in the handling of money and inventory. Second, employers preferred to employ students with good verbal and written communication skills, and last, employers are sensitive to the student's tardiness and attendance records at school. In fact, employers have contacted coordinators to validate reported attendance records. Coordinators feel it is necessary to cooperate with these requests to maintain the relationship with employers even though this is not fully in accordance with the legislated confidentiality of student records. Even if not pressured however, coordinators do not seek placement for students with poor attendance records. As an informant noted, "Teachers will not put up with a kid not going to high school classes while she is working out in business." Further respect for the employers' demands is reflected in his statement, "A student must have a pleasing personality, be dependable and responsible; a good academic and attendance record are crucial." As the coordinator explained it, the single program experience reinforces the notion that the students selected for the program and those who are placed in jobs as a result of the classroom instruction must be capable and portray "the good old American work ethic."

This is reinforced by the reports of school guidance counselors who note that the program is for "good students who are not really scholarly." The program observed, with a majority black enrollment, selects out students who are capable of good academic work early in their high school career because they are believed not to be "scholarly." Further, interviews with the black students reveal that a major reason for accepting enrollment in the program is not a desire for a career in retail business, but an immediate economic need that can be satisfied by part-time employment. As will be discussed later, the black students see themselves as capable, but recognize a lack of responsiveness by the school to their academic needs.

In the D.E. classroom we observed, the socialization of black students was attained through four methodologies: direct instruction, discussion, role playing, and participation in Distributive Education Clubs of America activities. In each, however, it was almost impossible to separate the teaching of skills from the promotion of acceptable attitudes. Since on-the-job experience is a reward for the students' acceptance of the socialization program the significance of the four distinct methodologies was grossly muted by the attitudinal modification the coordinator believed he was engaged in. Regardless of which methodology was being employed, skills development was only incidental in the experience. Students reported that they knew this and begrudgingly engaged in demonstration of the skills while actively discussing values and attitudes, even as they recognized that ultimately only one set of values was to be accepted and portrayed.

For example, in one role-playing setting of a sales counter built into the classroom, two students were portraying clerk-customer interaction in barely audible tones. The class as a whole was bored and unimpressed by the role-playing situation; the students were amusing themselves by talking and daydreaming. However, when the teacher critiqued the role-playing, arguing that the clerk needs to be forceful and confident, the students transmuted the statement into an entire discussion first of customer sanctioning of clerks, then into questioning and discussing "the customer as king." The student participation is surveying the various attitudes that could exist toward the customer ceased however when the teacher phrased a question that left no doubt as to the acceptable attitude toward customers. He asked, "Why is the customer always right?"

In a second example concerning a discussion of sales technique, the teacher asked the students how they should respond to a customer who argues the cost of an item is too much. Leaving the responses open stimulated a barrage of "contrary" values. One black male wanted "to help the dude out, and give him a little cash." The teacher permitted this discussion for a couple of minutes and then indicated that the appropriate response was to agree with the customer but note that the item was of high quality. If the customer still balked at the price, the teacher argued, the clerk should discuss layaway and charge plans as a means of enabling the sale. Student participation in the discussion almost terminated as a result of the teacher's indication of the appropriate attitude and technique.

Nevertheless, it is intriguing to speculate that the elaborate socialization routine that occurs in distributive education is without any major purpose. That is, teacher emphasis on attitudinal change and student interest in free discussion of value issues ultimately have little meaning. The D.E. teacher noted that these students tend to identify with the work ethic more than others, and his selection procedures sought out students who already indicate the rudiments of the "appropriate" attitude and who have moderately good academic skills. Further, since D.E. must also be elected by the student, those who enroll tend to be seeking employment. Their attitudinal set, then, is at least minimally appropriate prior to entering the program. The socialization process of distributive education seems to have its primary meaning not in the learning of skills and values that is to take place in the classroom, but in its ability to provide access to employment. "Retail Socialization" does not actually occur; it is a process that students put up with in order to get a job. Since only those with the "correct" skills and values are admitted, no significant changes in the students can take place. Little preparation is necessary for these students to be employable. The seemingly interested participation of the students in the discussion of attitudes and values, even though the acceptable ones are known, is probably best understood as an attempt by the students to manipulate the D.E. teacher into thinking change is taking place and thus to reward the students with a job.

Further evidence for this manipulation of the socialization process in D.E. is to be found in the use of D.E., primarily by black females, as a second attempt to break into the primary job market. Inasmuch as the "good" but not "scholarly" students are counseled and recruited into the program and because it will help resolve immediate economic needs of the student, D.E. selects black students who indicate promise but are not regarded as "college bound." The black females see themselves being denied access to college and use D.E. as a vehicle to complete high school while maintaining good grades and resolving economic problems so that they can attend the local community college and later transfer to the university. Thus the process of retail socialization is manipulated by students to get a job and to get a second run at college and the primary labor market.

Unfortunately, the manipulation of the program by students does not effectively resolve the college access problem. D.E. itself represents a preselection process that denies students many of the credits and skills necessary to matriculate at a four-year college or university. Participation in D.E. yields three units of credit which substitute for academic subjects such as math, language and science. Of all the students interviewed, none have taken any of the normal college preparatory subjects other than English, and even the English courses taken are not in the college track. Not surprisingly, none of the seniors in this year's program who has taken standardized college admission tests was able to score high enough to make the minimal cut for any of the state universities or nursing schools.

"Retail" socialization, it appears, is not at all a true socialization process since little needs to be changed in the students. Rather it represents an attempt to preselect youth for the secondary labor market. The significance of the socialization lies in the students' manipulation of its process rather than assumption of appropriate knowledge, attitudes and behavior. It minimally solves short-run economic needs, but does not lead, for black students particularly, to stable employment. In short, it is used as a mechanism to try to beat the preselection process in public schools by facilitating admission to community colleges.

DISCUSSION

Following the argument of human capital development the federal government has continually placed its emphasis on education and training to eradicate poverty. Vocational education has received increasingly greater emphasis in public schools as the rational path to improve productivity, and there are numerous vocational programs available in high schools, all generally supported by matching federal funds. It is felt the result should be better employability of American youth about to enter the job market. But our study of a typical distributive education (D.E.) program in a desegregated southern school demonstrated that such programs are, for the most part, ineffective and possibly vacuous for minority youth, and through no fault of the individual can have an adverse effect on a child's educational development and the quality of future labor force participation.

In order to insure success of the program the best of the black students are selected to participate. These students are articulate, aggressive, and generally committed to school as demonstrated by attendance records. They already possess the characteristics of reliability and dependability which are most desired of workers at the job-entry level. Unfortunately, these students become less competitive in the labor market by being channeled away from the academic subjects which will prepare them for the upper tier of the primary sector of the market. Not only does this block entrance to four year colleges, but chances for internal mobility within a firm are stagnated by the vehicle of their entry into the work force. Moreover, by concentrating on the best possible black students, the program ignores a pool of students without stable school performance. It is this pool of students, according to D.E.'s own logic, who are more in need of skills and attitude change and employment.

The vocational program under study recapitulates intergenerational segmentation in the labor market. Graduates of the vocational program enter jobs which ultimately may be able to provide them with stable employment and some job security, but certainly do not enable them to pose much of a threat to their white classmates in the competition for jobs. The monopoly of the labor market held by the middle class continues.

Since these vocational programs seem to emerge from an economic theory that is of questionable validity, it is obvious that programs that would attempt to move youth directly into the primary labor market may well resolve the problems that were revealed by this study. Nevertheless, for this to occur, dramatic political and economic realignments would be necessary. Assuming, at least in the short run, that this will not occur, it seems that those who are currently in the position to serve youth need to develop strategies to overcome the consequences for youth that the human resources approach engenders.

Primarily, it seems that those who work with youth should be aware that participation in a vocational program may not be indicative of the interests, especially over the long term, of trained youth. As we found, many minority youth participate, not to enable their entry into the secondary labor market, but rather to satisfy immediate economic needs and/or to facilitate high grades so that they may take a "second run" through community colleges to the primary labor market. In all, then, many of the minority students who are recruited into the program do not see the program goals as their personal goals, and furthermore have higher aspirations than the program can satisfy. This obviously may result in frustration and demoralization of these youth, and suggests that those who work with these youth must be cognizant of, and responsive to, the incongruity of secondary labor market entry goals of the program and primary labor market entry goals of the youth. To satisfy their interests, job placement alone is insufficient. Placement should be enhanced whenever possible by efforts to promote more full socioeconomic mobility. Without that, the youth will attempt to manipulate the program to satisfy their personal goals and, if unsuccessful, will interpret the program, as one vocational-technical school student put it, "another way to keep us poor."

It is evident that families are hard put to provide many of the socialization experiences necessary to successful school and work adaptation. Note, for example, the epidemic vandalism in New York during the summer of 1977 blackout. Families simply were not able to control their children. Nevertheless, it is also evident that much of this is the result of other social institutions encroaching on the role of the family. Historically, one's family provided major access to the labor market for youth. They owned the farm or shop, passed on a trade, or could prompt preferential hiring by the concern which employed them. Today's access is much less controlled by families. Schools, training programs, and employer selection procedures now impose more universalistic criteria in employment. Families suffer from this because they have lost some power and thus ability to support their youth. Youth are consequently quite alone and at least insecure as they seek employment. Further, since schools separate youth from adults, youth have little knowledge of what it actually means to work and often difficulty making the adjustment. Unfortunately, schools do not prepare youth well for the role changes and emotional trauma that accompany entry into the labor market.

SUMMARY

In this chapter, we have analyzed one high school vocational program to attempt to better understand the effect of such programs on youth. Primarily, we found that the program is based in a rather naive economic theory but nevertheless any success it purports to have emerges not directly from program content but its initial selection procedures whereby "acceptable" youth are channeled into employment. The recently emerging critical theories in both economics and in educational history better capture the problems of vocational education programs.

Further, it seems apparent given the encroachment of social institutions on the power of families that more and more of our employment will be controlled by institutions and organizations that are outside the purview of family influence for most Americans. Obviously efforts to bolster families are and will become more important. Nevertheless, youth are increasingly dependent on schools and vocational programs to prepare them for employment. These programs at least in the short run, need to provide the support and the social mobility that families no longer can. Otherwise youth are abandoned in the labor market, disillusioned, alone, and emotionally vulnerable.

ACKNOWLEDGMENTS

The work upon which this publication is based was performed pursuant to Contract 400-76-0009 with the Field Studies in Urban Desegregated Schools Program of the National Institute of Education. It does not, however, necessarily reflect the views of that agency.

REFERENCES

Collins, T.W. (1973), Regional Migration in the South: A Case Analysis of Memphis. Paper presented to the Annual Meeting of the American Anthropological Association, New Orleans, LA.
———. (1974), An analysis of the Memphis sanitation strike. *Public Affairs Forum,* 3(6) April.
Doeringer, P., and Piore, M. (1971), *The Internal Labor Market.* Lexington: D.C. Heath.
Fusfield, D. R. (1973), *The Basic Economics of the Urban Racial Crisis.* New York: Holt, Rinehart and Winston.
Gordon, D. M. (1971), *Problems in Political Economy.* Lexington: D. C. Heath.
Karier, C., Violas, P., and Spring, J. (1973), *Roots of Crisis: American Education in the Twentieth Century.* Chicago: Rand McNally.
Katz, M. (1971), *Class, Bureaucracy and Schools.* New York: Praeger.
Kohl, H. (1967), *26 Children.* New York: New American Library.
Kozol, J. (1967), *Death at an Early Age.* New York: Bantam.
Levy, G. (1970), *Ghetto Schools.* New York: Pegasus.
Phelps, T. R. (1976), *Juvenile Delinquency: A Contemporary View.* Santa Monica, CA: Goodyear Publishing Company, Inc.
Piore, M. J. (1975), Notes for a theory of labor market stratification. In: *Labor Market Segmentation,* Ed. R. C. Edwards and associates. Lexington: D. C. Heath.

Index

HV
1421
R47

Responding to ado-
lescent needs

18909

DATE DUE

OCT 27 '83	NO 30 '95		
MAR .8 '85	5/19'98		
MAR 26 '87	MR 22 '00		
APR 27 '87			
DEC 3 '87			
NOV 6 '89			
DEC 20 '89			
DE1 4 '90			
JA 7 '93			
MR 29 '94			